LEFT
OF
BOOM

LEFT OF BOOM

HOW A
YOUNG CIA CASE OFFICER
PENETRATED THE TALIBAN
AND AL-QAEDA

DOUGLAS LAUX AND RALPH PEZZULLO

ST. MARTIN'S PRESS ✠ NEW YORK

www.stmartins.com

Designed by Omar Chapa

Photo research and editing provided by Liz Seramur of Selected Shots Photo Research, Inc.

Library of Congress Cataloging-in-Publication Data

Names: Laux, Douglas (Intelligence officer), author. | Pezzullo, Ralph, author.
Title: Left of boom : how a young CIA case officer penetrated the Taliban and al-Qaeda / Douglas Laux & Ralph Pezzullo.
Description: First edition. | New York : St. Martin's Press, 2016.
Identifiers: LCCN 2015037095| ISBN 9781250081360 (hardcover) | ISBN 9781466893214 (e-book)
Subjects: LCSH: Afghan War, 2001—Personal narratives, American. | Afghan War, 2001—Secret service—United States. | United States. Central Intelligence Agency—Officials and employees—Biography. | Qaida (Organization) | Taliban. | Smith, John (Intelligence officer) | BISAC: BIOGRAPHY & AUTOBIOGRAPHY / Military.
Classification: LCC DS371.413 .S66 2016 | DDC 958.104/78—dc23
LC record available at http://lccn.loc.gov/2015037095

Our books may be purchased in bulk for promotional, educational, or business use. Please contact your local bookseller or the Macmillan Corporate and Premium Sales Department at 1-800-221-7945, extension 5442, or by e-mail at MacmillanSpecialMarkets@macmillan.com.

First Edition: April 2016

10 9 8 7 6 5 4 3 2 1

Dedicated to my brother, the only one who truly knew until now. . . .

CONTENTS

LEFT OF BOOM

1

ATTACK ON KHOWST

We will get you CIA team. God willing, we will get you.

—Humam Khalil al-Balawi,
Jordanian suicide bomber

It was ten o'clock the morning of December 30, 2009, as I slid into a booth at the State Lake Tavern in downtown Chicago, focusing on my girlfriend Kate, who literally glowed in the overhead halogen light. She was everything I'd ever dreamed about and more—beautiful, vivacious, caring, fun to be around, sexy, and intelligent.

"You look great this morning," I said, pouring on the Midwest charm despite feeling anxious about meeting her BFFs in the afternoon, which was meant to serve as an introduction to the big blow-out celebration we'd planned for New Year's Eve.

"Thanks," she cooed back.

"I'm a damn lucky guy."

"I know." Her smile never failed to amaze me—the way it transformed her face and seemed to light up the space around her.

Part of me told me to grab her, take her up to our room, and rip her clothes off. Another part of me suggested that I order a Bloody Mary first, then consider the day ahead. I wanted Kate's friends to like me.

Kate and I had been introduced by her mother, whom I met while watching an Ohio State football game at the Rhino bar in Georgetown.

Her mom was there in her role as a lobbyist, entertaining some business associates. I was there with some of my rowdier friends cheering on the Buckeyes. She ended up buying us shots, and let drop that her daughter would soon be moving to DC. Cool lady.

A year later, Kate and I were two twenty-somethings in love. I sipped the Bloody Mary as she studied the menu. "I think I'll order eggs Benedict," she announced.

"Great," I said, while my mind searched for the word for "egg" in Pashtu.

What?

It was a natural response. For the past ten months I'd been studying the language full-time. Just last Friday I had passed my competency exam with a 3/3 ILR (Interagency Language Roundtable scale), which was pretty surprising considering that up until the attack on the World Trade Center I couldn't pick out the country of Afghanistan on a map. Nor had I left the Midwest at that point. I certainly didn't know that the Pashtuns were the most populous tribe of Afghanistan, and that there were an additional twenty-nine million Pashtu speakers in Pakistan.

Kate knew nothing about the language training, or the identity of my real employer. I had told her I was a ███████████████████████. I used the same cover with my parents and close friends.

"What are you having?" Kate asked.

"Let's see."

As I picked up the menu, I felt something vibrate in my pants pocket. Although I hate people looking at their phones while they're sitting with others in a restaurant, something told me to check it.

On the little iPhone screen I read four words that would dramatically change my life: "Dude, we got hit!"

The message was from my buddy Ben Z., who had recently deployed to ███████ Afghanistan, right in the middle of the shit. Something inside me released a burst of adrenaline, which caused my brain to spin.

I texted back, "What the hell happened? Explain," through the

Google text program (Google Voice) that transferred my message to the other side of the planet in a matter of seconds.

"Camp Chapman. Initial reports, bad. Lots of our guys."

"KIA?" I texted back.

"Don't know yet."

Forward Operating Base Chapman was located just outside the town of Khowst, in an area controlled by the Taliban, close to the border with Pakistan. Named after Special Forces sergeant Nathan Chapman—the first US serviceman to die in combat in Afghanistan—it sat on an arid three-thousand-foot-high plateau and was surrounded by high mountains. The area was under the political and military control of warlord Jalaluddin Haqqani, who had spent years during the Soviet war on the CIA payroll and was still a close friend of Osama bin Laden. Haqqani, as I had learned, was a complicated and difficult character, less interested in ideology, theology, and nation building than in maintaining his lucrative drug-smuggling empire. In a land of shifting allegiances and vendettas, he was currently our enemy.

The CIA station in Khowst was tucked inside the much more expansive military base, separated by its own high-security fence, and patrolled by ex–Special Forces civilian contractors armed with automatic weapons. I knew several young CIA officers assigned there and had trained with them at the Farm—the Agency training facility in southern Virginia, where we had all been sent to learn the basics of running clandestine operations.

I was currently in Chicago, not DC, so I couldn't march into headquarters and offer my assistance. Nor was I geared up to deploy. In fact, HQ had me scheduled to ship out in June 2010. In the intervening six months, I was slated to receive the weapons and other types of training required before going to a forward base.

So I sat amid tables of people drinking, eating, conversing, and watching college football on TV and considered the implications of an attack on a place they had never heard of, and probably couldn't pronounce.

Most likely they thought, like most Americans, that the Agency had thousands of officers deployed all over the globe. But they were wrong. Even in a hot spot like eastern Afghanistan we had only a handful. So losing even one or two would be a severe blow. There were sources to run and valuable intel to gather on the Taliban and al-Qaeda. The safety of tens of thousands of US and NATO troops depended on it. Political pundits might argue and would be correct to assert that an attack like the one at Khowst could actually compromise the security of the United States.

Kate, who had been rambling on about the Kardashians, noticed the change in my demeanor and stopped.

"Is everything okay?" she asked.

I lied: "Yeah."

"You don't look okay."

"Really?"

"Yeah, Doug. What's wrong? You feeling nervous about meeting my friends?"

"No. Not at all. I guess my stomach's feeling a little funny."

"Who are you talking to?" she asked with a little more edge.

I lied again: "My brother."

"What's he want?"

I knew where this was going, so I lied a third time. "He wants me to come see my niece, at some point while I'm in Chicago."

"Oh."

The suspicion in her eyes told me that she thought I was carrying on with an ex-girlfriend. That's what usually happened when I was caught in situations like this where I had to dissemble in order to maintain my cover. James Bond didn't have these problems.

I tried to steer the conversation back to the reality show she'd been telling me about, even though part of my mind was occupied with the logistics of getting to Khowst. The truth was that I was dying to get into the field and finally do what I had signed up to do—take the fight to the enemy.

September 11, 2001, I was a freshman at the University of Indiana starting to pursue a course of study to become an optometrist. That night, as all of us were in shock and trying to process what had happened, I discussed the attacks on the World Trade Center with my roommate. I remember him saying, "It's probably the work of bin Laden."

I responded (believe it or not), "Who's that?"

I knew nothing about the bombings of the US embassies in Kenya and Tanzania, or the attack on the U.S.S. *Cole,* and I had never heard of al-Qaeda. 9/11 became a major turning point in my life, and caused me to do a one-eighty, change my major to political science, study Japanese and Chinese, and dedicate myself to learning more about the world around me.

Suspicion lingered in Kate's eyes.

"So they're interesting, huh?" I asked, referring to the Kardashians.

She gazed past me to the TV over the bar, where a TSU running back had just scored a touchdown. The camera panned across exuberant faces painted white and blue and cheerleaders bouncing up and down. "Who?"

"The Kardashians," I answered as people near the bar high-fived one another.

"Yeah."

"What's the name of the show?"

She still wouldn't look at me. *"Keeping Up with the Kardashians."*

"So you keep up with them?" I asked, trying to inject a bit of humor.

She didn't even crack a smile. "Yeah," she said, giving me the proverbial cold shoulder.

What had promised to be a fun day was turning into a headache.

"What's your mom doing for New Year's?" I asked.

"Going out."

"Really? That's a surprise."

Sarcasm didn't work, either. Then the food arrived. She tore into her eggs. I had no appetite for mine. Here I was sitting in an upscale bar drinking Bloody Marys, while my buddies were on the other side of the world piecing bodies together.

Part of me wanted to grab her by the hand and explain the whole situation—the fact that I was a CIA operations officer ████████ █████████, and was worried about my colleagues. But I couldn't, not because Kate wasn't much interested in foreign affairs (she wasn't), but because I was under oath not to reveal the truth about my employment to anyone.

So I tried to console her, and in so doing pretended to be the self-deprecating boyfriend who had been withholding embarrassing information that wasn't true—a role I hated and made me feel like a total douche.

I said, "Hey, Kate, sweetheart, look at me and stop watching television. Hey, you know I love you, and I'm not trying to be difficult. I'll be honest with you, it's a little embarrassing, and I haven't told you this because I've been fighting with my brother a lot lately and it's really upsetting me, because he's ignoring our most recent fight and just expects me to forget about it and come visit him."

It was a total lie—a self-inflicted punch to the gut. My brother and I never fight, nor do I let things like that upset me. But I delivered the words with conviction and they worked, because now she turned her beautiful blues eyes toward me and asked, "Really?"

"Yes, sweetheart. But I'm going to turn my phone off now, and focus on you."

"Okay," she answered sweetly. I loved her. I did. Two years earlier, I had lost another girlfriend when I had to leave abruptly ████████, and couldn't tell her where I was going or how long I'd be gone.

I didn't want to lose Kate. She was special. One day I hoped to marry her and start a family.

Slowly, Kate warmed up to me again and we started to talk about meeting her friends later and possible places for dinner.

But Afghanistan kept nagging me like a bad rash. Every twenty minutes or so, I excused myself to go to the bathroom to check my phone. Ben Z. didn't have much to add, except the fact that the attacker had been a CIA source.

My head was filled with questions: How had he managed to smuggle a bomb onto the heavily fortified base? Who was running him? Who at headquarters had authorized the meeting?

I texted a couple of my other colleagues to find out what they had heard. Most of them didn't even know about the attack, which had happened only a few hours earlier, and hadn't been reported by the media yet.

After brunch, Kate and I returned to our room in the Wit Hotel so she could freshen up. As soon as the door closed, she threw her arms around me and kissed me on the lips. I kissed her back. We were two young lovers anxious to release the earlier tension. Soon we were on the bed pulling each other's clothes off.

The trouble was that part of me wasn't in a romantic mood, and the one thing I couldn't fake was a state of arousal, which was not happening in my highly distressed state of mind. A psychiatrist later explained that in order for someone to perform sexually, their sympathetic and parasympathetic nervous systems have to be operating at the same time, which isn't possible when your brain is on operational overdrive.

I didn't know that then, so I suggested instead that my unresponsiveness was probably a result of the three Bloody Marys I had sucked down at brunch.

A frustrated Kate started to scold me for drinking too much. Awesome. Now she had pounced on my least favorite topic.

I felt an impulse to grab a beer out of the mini fridge and down it. As that would only add fuel to her argument, I considered fleeing the room and walking the frigid streets of Chicago.

"Doug, you need to face it!" Kate shouted.

Not now. Thanks.

Retreating to the bathroom, I reminded myself that I was with the woman I loved and told myself that I had to focus for the next two days on making her happy.

Somehow, I managed to make it to the bar on Sheffield Avenue and put on a friendly face for Kate's friends. I usually look forward to meeting new people, but this day was difficult, and the celebratory frivolity clashed with the dark force field of death, fear, and expectation that followed me wherever I went.

As much as I tried, I couldn't pretend that everything was cool, because it wasn't. Even as Kate's pretty, enthusiastic friends pressed around me to ask perfectly reasonable and innocuous questions like "How do you like living in Washington?," "What's it like working as a contractor?," "Where did you go to school?," I kept glancing up at the TV where I saw Wolf Blitzer's serious face against the background of a map of Afghanistan. The legend running along the bottom of the screen read, "Attack on U.S. base in Afghanistan."

I heard him say something about American casualties. Reflexively the muscles in my chest and shoulders tightened.

"So, you must be a Hoosiers fan," one of Kate's friends said.

"I am. Yeah."

"You miss Bobby Knight?" She had big light brown eyes, flawless pale skin, and a smile to melt the hardest of hearts.

On the TV, I overheard a Pentagon spokesman say something about a man wearing a suicide vest. A dozen questions burst in my head simultaneously like fireworks. How thoroughly had the source been vetted? Had anyone met with him before? Who the fuck allowed him through the CIA perimeter without searching him thoroughly?!

"You know who Bobby Knight is, don't you?" Kate's friend asked.

"Of course I do," I countered with a smile. "I was just glancing at the report on TV. Sorry."

"I know. I noticed. Afghanistan," she said with a shrug. "I don't understand it. Yuck."

I could have explained its torturous history—including invasions by Alexander the Great, Genghis Khan, China, Pakistan, the Ottomans, the British, the Soviet Union. Now we were trying to "secure" it, and prevent it from being used as a base for Islamic terrorists. According to the Obama administration, we were also working to stabilize the wobbly Karzai government, rebuild its army, and bring its people out of the thirteenth century where they had gotten stuck after centuries of fighting, repression, and neglect.

Now to make things even more difficult my ex-girlfriend Hannah started texting me. She was the only person besides my brother who knew what I did for a living. I had never informed her directly, but the ███████ ██████████ who introduced us had told his girlfriend about ██████, and she had blabbed to Hannah.

Hannah texted: "Please God, tell me you're safe and not in A right now."

I texted back: "No. I'm still Stateside."

Less than a minute later, my phone pinged again. "You know any of the people killed?"

According to Wolf Blitzer, the names of the dead Americans hadn't been released.

I texted back: "Don't know. You know as much as I do at this point."

I started to worry about Kate. She had met some of my colleagues who had been sent to Khowst. When their names were released, she might put two and two together and figure out where I really worked. I saw her across the room waving me over to the jukebox, where MGMT's "Electric Feel" was blaring. She wanted to dance.

I pointed toward the bathroom to indicate that I had business to take care of first. Checking to see that I was alone in the green-tiled room, I proceeded to delete the text messages from Hannah. Figuring that Hannah would probably continue texting me throughout the night, I changed her name on my cell-phone contact list to Tom. That way if Kate ever looked at my phone she'd think I'd been texting with one of my buddies back in DC.

The following day—New Year's Eve—more dire news trickled out of Khowst, and I did my best to secretly process it while maintaining an upbeat demeanor. That night as I was dressing in my rented tuxedo, I saw Kate step out of the bedroom in a skintight blue gown.

"Wow. You look beautiful," I said.

Our eyes met, and it hit me: What was I going to tell her when we returned to DC? If HQ decided to send me to Khowst immediately to replace one of the officers who had died, how was I going to explain?

In that moment, I realized I was probably going to lose her. Even though Kate was an amazing person and I loved her, and was hoping to marry her someday, I'd be gone for a long time, maybe years. All I could hope for was that when I returned from Afghanistan and was ready to quit the Agency, she hadn't married someone else. Then, maybe, I'd get a chance to explain and set things right.

Possibly because Kate sensed the heaviness in my heart, she walked over, bussed me on the cheek, and said, "I expect to be kissing you in a few hours when the ball drops, so I want that face smooth."

I retreated to the bathroom and confronted the reflection in the mirror. What I saw looking back at me was a paler, less confident version of myself. I had lobbied to be sent to the tip of the spear, and now I was going to get my wish.

"Hurry up," I heard Kate say through the door. "I want to get there early so we can find the best table."

"I'm coming, love. Just a minute."

As I lathered up and put the razor to my skin, I remember thinking that this was probably the last time I'd be doing this for a while.

I was right. I didn't shave again for two and a half years.

2

ONBOARDING

The untold want by life and land ne'er granted,
Now, Voyager, sail thou forth to seek and find.

—Walt Whitman

I grew up a studious kid in a rural county in eastern Indiana— home to twenty-two thousand people. According to the 2014 census, 98.1 percent of the population was Caucasian and only 9.5 percent of residents over twenty-five graduated from high school. So the odds of a kid from there becoming a CIA officer and deploying overseas were roughly the same as the Chicago Cubs winning the World Series.

My family was large, white, and German Catholic. Dad worked as the plant manager at the local steel factory, where they turned molten steel into smaller forgings. He had thirteen brothers and sisters and grew up so poor that all they got for Christmas was socks and underwear.

My father was a quiet Vietnam vet who rarely spoke to us until we turned sixteen. Weekdays, he'd return home from work at 4:30 p.m. in his industrial clothes with his name sewn on the pocket, and sit down to dinner. Barely a word was said as we ate. After dinner Dad would go off to his shed alone, or take my brother and me outside to chop wood. It fueled the furnace that burned from September to April.

He would fell trees with a chainsaw, and my brother and I would split the wood, load it into a truck, stack it, load in it a wheelbarrow to take into the house, and stack it again. It was monotonous, hard work, and I hated it, even though it made me strong.

During baseball season, Dad would lie on his bed in his shorts and listen to Joe Nuxhall and Marty Brennaman broadcast the Reds games on the radio he'd owned since he was sixteen.

When she wasn't cooking or minding the house, my mother took odd jobs at nearby Bear Creek Farms, which was a rural theme restaurant with a small amusement park. When I turned thirteen, I got my first job there busing tables. Then I graduated to dishwasher, making three dollars an hour. And after that I became a carney and ran the Tilt-a-Whirl ride, which was fun except for the times groups of Amish visitors, stuffed with fries and hot dogs, puked all over it, and I'd have to shut the ride and hose it down.

At sixteen, I got my driver's license and a stock-boy gig at Walmart. My redneck buddies would come in while I was on duty, stand right in front of the security cameras, say, "Hey, Doug, look," then stuff DVDs down the front of their pants. I had the choice of either turning them in or not saying anything to my supervisor and risking getting fired. I choose the latter.

When I wasn't working or going to school, I got drunk with my friends or read books. Most of my buds lived in trailer parks and were always getting into trouble. I didn't want to end up in jail, or married with a child at the age of nineteen, farming, or working at the steel plant.

My mentor was my eighty-nine-year-old grandmother, who had sixty-three grandchildren. I spent many a Friday night with her eating tenderloin sandwiches at the local American Legion hall. Even though she could barely read a newspaper, she had lived through wars, death, marriages, and every other human travail and had gathered some hard-won wisdom along the way.

I once asked her what it was like having three siblings in World War II and three sons serve in Vietnam. She said, "I had to stay calm and move on so my six younger daughters didn't panic and the chores on the farm were completed."

By my senior year in high school, I'd never flown on an airplane or seen an ocean, but I knew I wanted to do something that got me out of rural East Indiana. At that time, 2001, the iPhone and Facebook were nonexistent, so the aspiration of becoming a Palo Alto entrepreneur like Steve Jobs wasn't on my radar. Instead, I saw myself becoming a more typical doctor or lawyer.

One night a few months before graduation, I was sleeping on the ground floor of our house when I woke up surrounded by smoke and flames. I managed to roll out of bed and climb out a window. My dad fell through some rafters trying to put out the fire and almost died. Both he and my mom suffered from serious smoke inhalation.

Our house burned to the ground because squirrels had gotten into the attic and eaten through some wiring. My parents were badly shaken, so I tried to be the strong one as friends and relatives gathered to help us pick through the ashes for personal mementos.

I remember breaking away from the group, taking a long walk into the woods, and saying to myself, *You're over it, Doug. What did you lose? A Nintendo and some other dumb shit? You're alive. Stay calm, move on.*

The opportunity to move came a few months later. Despite the poor quality of my schools and the incompetence of my public-school teachers, I managed to gain admittance to the University of Indiana. I was there about a week planning to pursue a course of study that would lead me to become an eye doctor when the September 11, 2001, attacks occurred. I remember seeing kids from the East Coast around me crying and thinking, *Wow, this is a lot bigger than I thought. Doug, you need to amp up your shit and learn about the world.*

I changed my major to political science. Four years later I entered my senior year and started attending interviews with prospective employers—large global companies like Chase, Price Waterhouse, Nikko Salomon, and DHL. I even spoke with a marine recruiter about entering their officer training program.

One day after class I stopped to look at the listings on the job board and I saw a notice from the Central Intelligence Agency. I submitted my name, and a few days later received an invitation to attend an information session on campus. At the appointed time I sat with thirty or forty other seniors listening to an overweight guy in a black suit. He told us that ops officers work overseas, collect information, and are an important part of national security.

It sounded bureaucratic and abstract. All I knew about the CIA was what I had learned from Jason Bourne films. At one point one of the students asked about the CIA's Predator-drone program.

The sixty-year-old guy answered gruffly, "That isn't what this is about." He invited those who were interested to apply online.

Sometime in March, I checked out the CIA website and applied online. A ▮▮▮▮ later I got a call from a woman named Mary who left a message ▮▮▮▮▮▮▮▮▮▮▮▮▮▮▮▮▮▮▮▮▮▮▮▮▮▮▮▮▮▮▮▮▮▮ ▮▮▮▮▮.

I called back and left a message on her machine. "Hey, Mary," I said. "I think you got me confused with someone else. And in the future you might want to leave a more detailed message, because I have no idea who you are."

Fifteen minutes later my phone rang.

"Hi, it's Mary with ▮▮▮▮▮▮▮▮▮▮▮▮▮▮▮▮▮," the voice announced. "Is this Doug?"

"Yes. But I don't know who you are." "Wheelz of Steel" by Outkast was blaring over my stereo.

"My name's Mary, and you filled out an application online at ▮▮▮▮▮▮▮▮▮▮▮▮▮▮▮▮▮. Does that refresh your memory?"

"No. Not really."

"It was for a position in Washington, DC."

"I think you have the wrong person," I insisted. "It wasn't me."

"We're actually situated outside of DC in McLean, Virginia," Mary offered.

She must have thought I was an idiot, because I still didn't know what she was referring to.

"I'm with an organization in McLean that some people refer to as ████."

"Oh," I blurted out. "You mean you're with the CIA. Yes, I did fill out an application. Yes." I muted the music.

Mary said, "Why don't I call you back after you've had some time to think about it. I'll call you tomorrow ████. But we're not going to mention the name of the organization. Okay?"

"Okay, Mary. Fine."

████████ my phone rang. I answered hungover from a frat party the night before.

Mary immediately started peppering me with questions: "████ ██ ██ ████?"

I answered the best I could, but floundered in places.

At the end, she said, "Doug, you sound like a nice guy, but you don't seem up on current events. So I would suggest that you start reading the *Economist* and visit some of the top news websites like the *New York Times* and *Washington Post*."

"Why didn't you ask me about China or Japan, two countries I've studied?" I asked.

"██ ████████ We'll be in touch."

That summer, armed with a college diploma, I took a job with DHL based in Colorado. Six months into my employment there, I learned that there was a possibility I could be posted to Japan. Then out of the blue I got another mysterious call. It was a man who said he was with a ██████████ ████████████████████ ████████

███

████████████████

██████ Later I found myself in a colorless conference room with ██ other young men and women ████████████████. A tall man entered and passed out ██████ tests, which he told us to fill out.

After finishing mine, I was called into an office where a guy in a suit started firing questions. "██████████████████████████████ ████████████████████████████████?"

As I spoke he took notes. Then he handed me a piece of paper and said, "I want you to go to this location tomorrow. We might have a few more tests for you to complete."

"Okay. But if I pass the tests, will I be offered a job?"

"I can't tell you that," he answered.

The next morning I got stuck in traffic and showed up at the address ten minutes late. As I entered a room, I saw a fifty-year-old man standing by a projector that was beaming slides onto a screen. ██████ other young men sat in metal folding chairs watching.

I said, "Excuse me, but I was told to report here to answer some questions."

Without saying anything, the man flipped back through three or four slides until he reached one with a big ██████ emblem on it. "Is that what you're here for?" he asked snidely.

"Yes, sir."

"One of the things you'll learn in this presentation is the importance of being on time. Take a seat."

This is lame as hell, I said to myself. *They keep inviting me to interviews and asking me questions. But they haven't told me anything.*

After the presentation, we were given more tests to fill out, then told to report to another location the following day.

Some of the attendees protested. One guy said, "We have jobs. We can't keep making up excuses to miss work."

"If you can't lie to your boss, how are going to succeed at this?" the presenter responded.

Another day, another anonymous office. This time I sat across from a middle-aged African-American woman. She said, "Today we're going to assess your ██████████ intelligence."

I had no idea what she was talking about.

███
███
███
███
████
████████████████████████████████
██
██████████████████████████████
██
███
█████████████████████████████████████
████████████████████████████████
██████████████████████████████
████████████████████████████████
█████████████████
██
████████████████

We were seated in a tiny office with a desk and two chairs, and I wasn't good at pretending. ████████████████████

Looking exasperated, she ended the exercise. "Don't you understand the purpose of this?" she asked. █████████████████
███
██████████████████████████████
███████████████████
████████████████████

I was ready to leave and return to my job at DHL. She wanted to test my response to ███████████████. I didn't handle them well, either.

Finally, she said, "Your file says that you've been assessed as someone who is capable of thinking fast on his feet. But you failed today, Doug. I was expecting you to do better. Why do you think you didn't do well?"

"I guess I wasn't prepared." I was being honest. "I don't know anything about the State Department or CIA, and I don't understand how these operations work."

████████████

████████████████████████████████████

████████████████████████

She frowned. "Haven't you read any books about the CIA and how we operate?"

"Not really."

"Well, you failed ██████████, Doug. But you never ████████████ ████████████████████. So I'm going to recommend that you be moved to the next stage. But in the interim I suggest that you read some books." Then she handed me a number to call if I had any questions.

I called every two weeks for the next three months. Each time I'd leave a message and get no response.

██████ later, I was about to give up and called one last time. This time a woman answered.

"How can I help you?" she asked.

"My name is Doug Laux. I've been calling for over ██████ to find out if my application has been accepted, and nobody has told me anything."

"Oh," the woman at the end of the line said. "I've got you scheduled for an interview in Washington, DC, next week."

"Come again?"

"Didn't anybody call you?"

"No, ma'am. I had no clue that my application had moved forward."

"Well go ahead and ████████████████████████████ ████████████████████. When you get here, call this number and we'll tell you where to meet."

I lied and told my boss at DHL that my dad was sick and I had to return home. Once in DC, I called the number and was told ███████ ███████

██

██

██████████████████████████████.

██

██

██

██

████████████████

███████████████████████████

He said, "You've failed, which is too bad, because everything you've been through so far has been for nothing."

Part of me thought he was bluffing. Another part of me wondered if he just wasn't very good at this job.

I left thinking, *Fuck them. If they call me, fine. But I'm not going through any more bullshit like this.*

████████████████████ passed before I got a call informing me that they were going to initiate ████████████████████████████

██

████████████████████████████.

██████████████████████████████████████

████████████████████████████████████

██

███████

That's when I realized that I had to start building a cover on my own. And I had to do it fast.

Since I was still employed by DHL, I told my friends and family that I had filed for a security clearance to ride as an unticketed passenger on DHL cargo flights. It seemed to work.

██

██

A couple of hours later my phone rang. Thinking that it was probably my boss, I let it go to voice mail. I reasoned that once I heard what she said, I could figure out the best way to respond.

She said, "Hey, Doug, I had a very interesting ███████ about you today. I'd like to talk to you about it. Give me a call when you get a chance."

I called her back a half hour later.

"Anything you want to tell me?" she asked.

"Yeah. Have you ever heard of the *Economist*?"

"You mean the magazine?"

"Yeah, the magazine. I'm writing a paper for them that might get published."

"You?"

"Yeah, me. The *Economist* wants to make sure I'm not a total douche-
bag who is going to ruin their credibility so they're doing a quick
████████████████████."

It sounded lame the moment I said it.

"Really?" she asked. "That sounds like a lot to go through for a magazine article."

"Have you read the *Economist*?"

"Well, no. But the gentleman said you were applying for a job with
the US government."

"That was an excuse. The article is about national security."

She thought about it, then said, "That kind of doesn't make sense."

"I don't understand it, either. ███████████████████████
████████████████."

My lie ended up working even better than I ever imagined. In fact,
my boss spread the word throughout the company that I had written an
article that was about to appear in the *Economist*. My story was picked
up by the company newsletter and got the attention of the big bosses.
Undoubtedly this was part of the reason I was named District Salesman
of the Year.

Luckily, none of this reached the *Economist*. As the weeks passed and
I heard nothing from the CIA, I had to explain to my bosses why the
article wasn't out. So I told more lies.

Finally, in ████████████████████████████████,
I received a phone call from a woman from ███ telling me that they
were offering me a job. She said, "We're going to send you a letter saying that we're offering you a job with ██████████████████. It's
going to say we'll pay you ██████ a year and move you to DC. But it's
up to you to establish your own cover."

Now I had to tell my friends and parents that I was leaving my six-figure job at DHL to work for a ███████████████ (company) that doesn't exist. My parents looked at me like I was stupid.

I couldn't blame them. It sounded ridiculous to me, too.

3

TRAINING

Life is what you make it. Always has been, always will.

—ELEANOR ROOSEVELT

Langley wasn't what I expected from reading Robert Ludlum novels. I'm not talking about the architecture or the impressive, state-of-the-art hardware. I thought I'd be entering an organization that was super organized and efficient in terms of the way it trained its personnel.

Instead, managers spent a couple of days showing me and the other new recruits around the building, then pointed to a cubicle in a large room where I was to learn what operations officers do in the field and how to support them. My boss, whose job was to train me, was responsible for covering a whole region of countries and didn't have the time or inclination. So I sat behind a computer wearing a suit and a new pair of leather shoes, thinking, *I didn't sign up to be a glorified clerk.*

People stopped by from time to time and said, "Doug, I need you to do a ▉▉ search for me."

"Doug, send this report over to ▉▉▉▉."

"Doug, I need you to make copies of this for me, pronto."

I'd seen the Colin Farrell movie *The Recruit* and thought that in two months I'd be sent down to the Farm (the CIA training base in ▉▉▉), where I would learn to kick ass like a ninja and transform myself into a version of Jason Bourne.

What I found out is, one, Jason Bourne doesn't exist. Not even close. And, two, it generally takes recruits ███████ to get to the Farm. ██████████! And all new recruits were lobbying hard to get there sooner. I wasn't a hot chick who could blow someone to get pushed to the top of the list—which happened.

Trying to stave off boredom, I went to the internal library in my spare time and read everything I could get my hands on about conducting real operations—how to run sources, create explosives, conduct interrogations, stage ambushes, and ascertain if people were telling the truth. And I taught myself how to speak Arabic.

Around my clerical duties, I wandered the halls looking for someone who wasn't wearing a suit and could advise me on how to get a job in the field. One day I ran into a grizzled-looking guy who'd just returned from the war zone. I told him I wanted to be doing the kind of stuff I was reading about in the newspapers—like recruiting sources and tracking terrorists.

He said, "Doug, you've got to think about your career. You need to get the desk experience you're getting now in order to advance."

"Fuck the career," I responded. "I want to do exciting, tip-of-the-spear kind of stuff. Send me to Iraq or Afghanistan."

"All right," he said, looking me over. "I'll put you in touch with a couple of people in ████████████████."

When I met with them, they told me, "The chances of you going to a war zone with us are slight."

"Why?"

"Because you're not a SEAL or Delta, which means you don't have tier-one operations experience."

What the fuck is that?

I learned that the CIA would rather take a guy who had been a Navy SEAL and teach him how to become a case officer than select someone like me who was learning to become a case officer and give him weapons and combat training. I found out later that this was completely ass-backward. It's a hell of a lot harder to teach charm and empathy than it is to instruct someone how to fire an M4 at a target.

In other words, if you're a friendly, open-minded person who generally likes other people it's pretty easy to adapt to a foreign environment and get along. On the other hand, if you're an emotionally shut-down individual, you're going to have problems relating to some Taliban dude on the Afghan border.

I was disappointed. I didn't sign up to spend most of my time sitting behind a desk answering cables and trafficking reports. To my surprise, I found out that most of the new recruits around me loved what they were doing and thought they were the coolest people on the planet to be working for the CIA. They wanted to do what most case officers do—be assigned to an embassy overseas, work the cocktail circuit, and maybe ████████████████.

For them, establishing a cover was easy. They told their friends and family that they were working for the State Department. And they rarely socialized or dated outside the Agency.

I made up my mind that I was either going to a war zone to do black ops or I would quit. And I didn't want to hang out with my coworkers and talk about work. I was a twenty-three-year-old dude who liked to get a little rowdy sometimes, drink some whiskey, and pick up chicks. Because of the drug and partying restrictions for selection into the Agency, most of my colleagues were straitlaced and boring. There were a smattering of bookworms and lots of Mormons from Utah.

Since their religion forbids drinking, smoking, or doing drugs, and they've usually served an overseas mission where they learned another language, Mormons perfectly fit the CIA profile.

The problem is that they generally make shitty ops officers, because they have no experience dealing with a wide range of people, especially the lowest-common-denominator types who generally become sources and are willing to trade their deepest, darkest secrets for cash.

Determined to lead my own life, I found a roommate named Austin, who was a wild man from Ohio. Six nights a weeks we went out to bars and partied. But every time the drugs appeared, I had to split.

The fun nights in Georgetown weren't enough to make up for the boredom I experienced at work. After a year as a ████, I decided to take all of my accrued leave at once and go somewhere as far from DC as possible. Two weeks later I woke up in an *uyangiin ger* ("home of lyrics," or a Mongolian tent) in the Gobi. I spent the next month riding camels and horses across the Gobi and Mongolian steppes. At night I ate horse meat and drank *airag* (fermented mare's milk, the Mongolian alcohol of choice) to the point where my guide started calling me Airag ni Khan (King of Airag). I called him Orel, which was Russian for "eagle." Orel taught me how to hunt gray marmots and wolves with his pet golden eagle. He was a hardened dude.

After a month of playing cowboy, I returned to the daily grind of Langley and started dating a sweet brunette named Hannah, ████████ ██ ████████████████████████ ████████████████ ████ ████████████████.

Determined to maintain my cover, I told her, Austin, and my other friends that I worked for a ████████████ (private company), which she knew was a lie creating instant distrust.

Meanwhile, back at headquarters, I spent every hour of every day trying to figure out how to get to the Farm, where I'd finally be trained to do ops. One day a hotheaded chief of station (COS) arrived in our office from the country of the desk I was assigned to. He told my boss (the group chief) that he wanted a report typed up on a particular terrorist group and he wanted it on his desk in fifteen minutes.

The group chief said, "That's unrealistic."

"The fuck it is!" the COS shouted back. "I sent you a cable two weeks ago requesting this. Where is it?"

The red-faced group chief walked over to my desk and tried to imply that it had been my responsibility. A typical cover-your-ass maneuver.

I said, "Actually, Chief, I saw that cable and started drafting something two weeks ago. I'll have it on your desk in ten minutes."

Five minutes later I put the draft report on the chief's desk. He ran out, found the COS in the hallway, and handed it to him.

The COS wandered back into the vault about an hour later with the report in his hand. "This is really good analysis," he said. "Thanks."

My group chief took all the credit. Later that afternoon, he pulled me aside and said, "Hey, Doug. I appreciate what you did. I won't forget it."

███████████████████████████████████

███████████████████████████████████

██████████████████

Finally, I was headed to the Farm!

The sad part was that meant I would probably have to end my relationship with Hannah, because I was going to be there for four months and following that expected to be deployed overseas.

She had recently taken a job in New York. So I drove up to see her and sheepishly informed her that I was being transferred to Newport News, Virginia. She didn't say anything the first night, but woke me up early the next morning.

"Doug," she said, "I know you aren't ████████████████. That's a fact. So please don't lie to me right now."

It was hard to try to ignore her when all she had on was a tank top and a thong.

"Doug, you work for the CIA."

"Come again?"

"Doug, I know you work for the CIA. I get that you can't talk about it, but I love you and I want to be with you. If you have to leave because of your job, just tell me, but don't give me some bullshit excuse about moving to Newport News."

"Hannah, I'm sorry but I don't know what to say."

"Stop it, Doug. Just stop it, okay? If you just tell me the truth about what you are doing and where you are going, I'll wait for you. But I need to know what's going on. I need to be a part of this, or we need to end this and move on."

I felt tremendous compassion for her, but also realized that if I told her the truth I would have to trust her with my secret, which she'd have to carry the rest of her life. If I didn't, she'd continue to have plausible deniability. It was a difficult decision and one that I've reexamined a thousand times since.

"Hannah...I don't work for the CIA, but I *am* moving to Newport News. It's going to be really difficult for us to maintain what we have now...and I think...I think it's best if we just end this instead of dragging this out into a long good-bye."

I felt awful. Hannah couldn't speak. I gave her a long hug and suggested I go back to DC. She nodded, holding back tears.

I didn't hear from her for the next two weeks and used that time to sell my car, get rid of my furniture, and donate my electronics to my friends. The weekend before I was scheduled to leave, Hannah texted me from Reagan National to tell me that she had flown down from New York to say good-bye.

Before I took the Metro to the airport to pick her up, I stopped at a flower shop in Georgetown to buy a card and a single red rose. The woman behind the counter asked me who I was purchasing the rose for.

I said, "Just trying to be a nice guy for once."

"Don't try," she responded. "Just be."

When Hannah entered my apartment, she saw that it was completely empty except for a mattress on the floor.

"What's going on?" she asked. "Did you already move your furniture?"

"No, I sold it."

"Why?"

I had to start lying again. "My employer is giving me a furnished place."

"A furnished place? Does that mean that you got a promotion?"

"Sort of. Yeah."

"That's great."

We spent Friday night and Saturday together. Sunday, after lunch, I had to get her to leave because a colleague from work was going to pick me up at four p.m.

She had actually met this guy before and he'd told her that he worked for the State Department. How could I explain that some guy from the State Department was driving me, a ███████████, four hours south to Newport News?

Hannah, being the sweetheart she was, asked, "Can't I wait with you until he picks you up?"

"I'd rather you didn't," I answered, throwing my mattress off my balcony into the dumpster below.

"Why? Who's really picking you up? Is it another woman?"

"No!... Of course not. I would never do that to you, Hannah."

She started to cry. "You're lying about your job again. Goddammit, Doug. Why are you doing this to me?"

As if our breakup in New York hadn't been bad enough, now I felt like the worst human being on Earth. I went to my closet and grabbed the single bag I was taking to the Farm and the card and rose I had bought for her. As soon as Hannah saw them, she went into hysterics. I remembered that I had given her a single red rose on our first date.

I started crying, too, as I walked her outside and hailed her a cab.

"Hannah, I ... I'm sorry I've been such a nightmare to date," I said, choking down serious tears. "I uhhh ... I do love you, Hannah. And you're the first woman I've ever loved so this is really, really hard for me. And it sucks. But I gotta go. And ... I got this rose and card for you. Please don't open the card until you're back home in New York."

"Okay, Doug. Good-bye. I love you. Please be safe."

I had read once that the magic of your first love is the ignorance that it can ever end. Watching Hannah's cab pull away down M Street, the finality of our relationship hit me hard.

Four hours later, just as I was about to surrender my cell phone to the security guards at the Farm, I got a text from Hannah: "I read your card. You're devastating me, Doug. You're the love of my life but I can't do this any longer. If you ever leave Newport News, let me know. Otherwise, I can't talk to you anymore. Good-bye. And thank you."

Instead of feeling sorry for myself, I tried to focus on the tasks in front of me. Initially, there were lots of classroom lessons—like learning the agent life cycle, which includes spot, assess, develop, handle, terminate. They taught us what each step meant and how to paper everything. I learned that for every meeting you had with a source, there were approximately ▬▬ forms to fill out and ▬▬▬▬▬▬▬▬ to write.

There was a lot of role-playing, where you'd act like an officer interviewing and developing a source. In the beginning, if I was dealing with a sixty-year-old white guy who was playing the role of an Islamic terrorist and had to gain his trust, I'd walk in and start talking about some passage in the Koran. Very quickly his eyes would glaze over.

What I learned is that even though the instructors were pretending to be agents, underneath they remained themselves. So I started to play the actual guy instead of the person they were pretending to be. If I'd heard that a certain instructor loved football, I'd start talking about the Redskins. Even though it was messed up, my results improved dramatically.

One of my favorite parts of training was learning to run SDRs (surveillance-detection routes). ▬▬▬▬▬▬▬▬▬▬▬▬▬▬▬▬ ▬▬▬▬▬▬▬▬▬▬▬▬ Given the lousy neighborhoods they took place in, you often encountered some fucked-up shit. One time I was in a city where it was raining nonstop. Miserable and soaking wet, I ran into two bums kicking the crap out of another bum. They knocked him down so that his head hit the curb. Then one of the bums continued to stomp on him.

My instinct as a fellow human being was to help the guy on the ground. But since I was ▬▬▬▬▬▬▬ I didn't have a cell phone, ▬▬▬▬▬▬▬▬▬▬▬▬. Having trained in Brazilian jujitsu, I knew I could probably take both bums in hand-to-hand combat. What I didn't know is whether or not one (or both of them) was carrying a knife or gun.

So I picked up a rock and threw it, hitting one of the assailants in the back. He turned and shouted, "What the fuck?"

"Fuck you!" I shouted back. "I'm calling the cops."

The bums shuffled away cursing me and my mother. The guy on the ground was bleeding and unconscious. I asked some of the locals who had wandered over to see what was going on to call the police. None of them responded.

So I walked a block and found a pay phone and dialed 911.

A few months later, I was in an East Coast city being tailed by a countersurveillance group. ████████████████████████ ██ The key was not to let them know that I knew they were back there. I had to lull them into complacency, so they would make a mistake.

I'd been dinged previously for stopping in a Starbucks and talking to a fellow customer.

██
████████████████████████████████████
██
██████████

I wanted to nail this one. It was a long SDR that had taken me from one end of the city to the other, using multiple modes of transport—buses, taxis, subway. Now I was walking through a real bad neighborhood and stopped at an outdoor fruit stand to buy a bag of oranges.

As I proceeded down the sidewalk, I saw a six-foot-eight crackhead standing in my path staring me down. I didn't want to cross to the other side of the street, because that would be considered "alerting."

When I got within ten feet of him, I noticed that he was holding a plastic pen that had been carved into a shiv.

Great. I'm going to be stabbed to death in my own country because I don't want to alert the countersurveillance behind me.

From four feet away, I said, "Hello. How are you?"

He held up the shiv and looked like he wanted to kill me.

I said, "I'm going to walk around you. Okay?"

Apparently not, because he lunged at me shiv-first. I slammed the oranges into his gut and grunted, "Here, have some oranges!" ███ At the corner, I glanced back and saw the guy checking out the oranges.

After a week of runs, I had my evaluation. The officer rating me said, "You got an unsatisfactory grade of the run on Tuesday because you had contact with what we believe was your source and handed him a bag of oranges."

"I didn't hand them to him," I explained. "I hit him with the oranges, because he had a shiv in his hand and was about to attack me."

"We didn't observe that."

"Didn't you have surveillance on me? Didn't you see what was going on?" I asked.

"Well, maybe you got excited and started seeing things, Doug."

Whatever.

Days at the Farm were long and demanding, generally starting at ████████████████████████████████████. Every morning when I ran at six, I'd see women and guys coming out of each other's rooms. Dipping in company ink didn't appeal.

Instead on the alternate weekends we got off, I'd travel back to Washington and meet up with my buds. On one of these weekends, two months into my time at the Farm, I met Kate. Although we hit it off immediately, I was reluctant to get too involved, because I was still getting over Hannah and figured I'd soon be deployed.

Prior to graduation from the Farm, my classmates and I were asked to fill out forms listing the divisions we preferred to join. Most men chose East Asia Division. Most women wanted Europe and Africa. I wrote my preferences in this order:

1. Whichever division is willing to immediately send me to Afghanistan.
2. ████ cooking division. (They provided the cooks in the cafeteria.)
3. ████████████████████████ (The Agency's internal security escorts.)

This list became a topic of conversation among the other trainees, who couldn't believe I had the balls to turn it in.

The day after graduation, we were instructed to visit our division's personnel chief. Since I hadn't listed a specific division, I was sent to HR. Now that I was an officially certified case officer (CO), I was determined to let management know that my days of licking boots were over. So I walked into HR wearing a T-shirt and jeans—which I had never done before and wouldn't do again.

The severely overweight lady who greeted me sweated so profusely that her glasses kept sliding down her nose. She said, "We got your paperwork, Doug, and because you didn't list anything, we're sending you to Baghdad with the recommendation that you'll be eventually transferred to the Near East Division."

"That's incorrect," I answered. "I listed Afghanistan, not Iraq. I don't care which division sends me as long as I go there ASAP."

She pushed her glasses back and rasped, "You're not in a position to make the decision, honey. So, whether you like it or not, you're going to Baghdad."

"I'm not going."

"Excuse me?"

"Look, if you couldn't tell by the way I filled out the form, I'm not in the mood to fool around and want to be sent to one of the FOBs [forward operating bases]. Ninety-nine percent of officers beg *not* to be sent there. I want to go, so this should be easy. Forget about Baghdad and deploy me to Afghanistan. Either that or give me the LWOP [leave without pay] forms now and I'll go skiing for a year while you work it out."

With that, I walked to my car, cranked up Audioslave's "Show Me How to Live," and drove home full throttle.

My tactic worked. A few days later I was put directly into a Pashtu-language program and told that I would be deploying to a FOB at the completion of the course.

It was during my year of language training that Kate and I started getting serious, going out four or five nights a week, and spending nights at each other's apartments—proof that I had learned nothing from my experience with Hannah.

The inevitable questions followed. "Where do you work?" she asked.

"I'm a consultant, working on a program to update ███████████ ███ computers." (A lie.)

"Where's your office?"

"It's in Rosslyn." (Another lie)

"Oh, then I'll give you a ride. I'm going in that direction."

"That's okay. I like taking the Metro."

She looked at me like I was crazy, because I complained about the slowness of the Metro all the time.

I also faced the problem of where to hide certain things that I didn't want her to see like the shirt I had that featured a sewn-in pocket for a pistol, or my thirty or so Pashtu-language books. Those I stored in the basement, which meant I couldn't study when she was around.

Other things that I used daily, like my Agency badge, reports, and pamphlets, were stored in a drawer in my dresser that I trapped with a penny placed in the exact same position every time. That way if someone opened it, the penny would fall out.

I figured it was only natural that at some point she'd snoop around. The first time I found the penny on the floor, I didn't say anything. The very next day, the penny was on the floor again.

One night a couple of weeks later, after we had finished eating take-out Chinese, Kate turned to me and said, "I think you're lying about what you do."

"Why would you say that?" I asked back.

She said, "Don't get mad, Doug, but I was putting away some of your laundry the other day, and when I opened your top drawer I saw a lot of strange stuff in there."

"What'd you see?"

"I don't know. You've got strange writing in there and some books on the Middle East."

"If it bothers you, why didn't you say something before?"

She said, "I just saw it yesterday."

"No, you didn't. You were in there two weeks ago."

"No."

"Yes, you were in there Thursday the fourteenth and Friday the fifteenth."

"How do you know?" she asked. "Do you have a surveillance camera?"

Realizing that this was a strange conversation to be having with my girlfriend, I stopped myself. Kate stood and walked to the door. As she left, she said, "You're freaking me out, Doug. I've got to think about this whole relationship."

I ran after her and walked her home. We'd been dating for eight months and I was falling in love with her. Torn, I asked myself, *Is it better if I break it off now? What should I do? I can't tell her the truth. I don't want this to end like it did with Hannah.*

A couple of days later, she called and said, "Tell me what those things are for."

I lied and said, "I'm working on another contract that I can't talk about. We're working with the military on IED stuff."

"What about the strange writing?"

"That's Arabic," I answered, lying again. "I'm curious to learn it."

"Tell me the truth," she said. "Are you a terrorist?"

"No, Kate. Come on. I'm a white guy from Indiana."

The next time she came over she went into the drawer again. Since I had told her about the penny, she replaced it, but put it in a different spot. In the interim I had moved everything out of there, except my badge.

My badge didn't name which agency I worked for, but on the back was a PO address to send it to in case it was lost and found. Kate Googled the address and discovered that it was a PO box used by ███████ (my real employer).

She didn't say anything until two months later when we were out one night with friends. After a couple of vodkas, she turned to me and asked, "When are you going to tell me that you're really a spy for the CIA?"

I nearly fell out of my chair. "What?"

"I Googled the PO box on the back of your badge and that's what I found."

Shocked and not knowing what to say, I walked out of the bar. If the Agency discovered that I told people where I really worked, I could get fired.

When Kate caught up with me, I explained that I didn't work for the CIA, but the badge allowed me to get in their building and other government offices around town.

She bought it. But the lies started to mount and so did the pressure. One afternoon we were out walking in Georgetown and I ran into a friend who asked, "How's the ███ contract going?"

"Oh, it's fine."

As soon as he left, Kate turned to me and said, "Why did he say ███ contract? You told me you were working on an ███ contract."

"Why? Because he's in the ███ and he's not supposed to know."

"Oh."

Another time, I was taking motorcycle lessons because the Agency thought it was likely I would need to ride one in Afghanistan. I didn't tell Kate, because I was afraid she'd worry. But I'd mentioned it to another friend.

Later, when we ran into him at a restaurant he asked, "When you buy a bike, are you going to get a Honda or a Harley?"

Kate stared at him and said, "Doug doesn't even know how to ride."

"Yes, he does, and he's been taking motorcycles lessons."

She turned to me and asked, "Really, Doug? When do you have the time?"

I scolded myself for telling him about the lessons in the first place. It was almost impossible to keep my stories straight.

I found out later that many of my friends thought I was deliberately being mysterious to make it appear that my life was more interesting than it was. Ironically, some of them thought that I wanted them to think I was a spy.

As the end of 2009 approached, I was debating what to do about Kate. I cared for her deeply, but was scheduled to deploy in the summer of 2010. Keeping her waiting for a year or more wouldn't be fair.

Then Khowst happened. The Agency immediately enrolled me in a two-week weapons course and told me I would be out the door in less than a month. As soon as the course was over, I returned to DC to quickly pack my gear and give away everything in my apartment again.

I also informed Kate that my contracting job was sending me to Hawaii and I was leaving in four days. Not surprisingly, she took the news badly.

"Who in the fuck moves to the other side of the world in four days? Fuck you, Doug! How long have you known about this?"

"Kate, I swear I was just informed." We argued back and forth for the next five hours. Actually, it wasn't arguing. It was more like Kate asking perfectly logical questions and me giving evasive answers.

Rightfully pissed off, she shouted, "I should have left months ago when I thought you were a terrorist. You're not just a bomb-making terrorist, you're an *emotional* terrorist, too!"

With that, she stormed out of her own apartment and slammed the door.

The next morning when I reported to CIA headquarters, I received another surprise. Instead of going to Khowst, I was being sent to Wadi Base (not the real name), which was a secret, extremely dangerous base ██████████ very close to ██████████████████ (another country).

My superiors explained that after the bombing in Khowst, the COS in Afghanistan had decided to change the strategy and take the fight directly to the people who were killing our troops with suicide vests and IEDs. Believing that most of these devices were coming ████████ ████████████████ (across the border), they wanted me to relieve the ████████████ we currently had at Wadi.

██

██

████████████████

"Yes, sir," I answered, expecting that once in Afghanistan I would be given a more thorough briefing and a clear set of targets and objectives.

Boy, was I wrong.

4

WADI[1] BASE

One cannot plan for the unexpected.

—AARON KLUG

The bombing in Khowst was a catastrophe from the CIA's per-spective. As the dust settled, we learned that the bomber was an al-Qaeda triple agent named Humam Khalil al-Balawi. A seemingly mild-mannered Jordanian doctor who treated poor women and children in Palestinian refugee camps, he had become a mild celebrity on jihadist websites for his highly inflammatory rants against the West. In January 2009, he was picked up by the Jordanian intelligence service, the General Intelligence Directorate (GID), and interrogated. The Jordanian intel officer who was running his case, Ali bin Zeid, quickly calculated that Balawi could be useful because of his status among jihadists, and possibly could be turned.

Supposedly swayed by the promise of earning a large amount of money, Balawi offered to travel to the tribal area of western Pakistan to attempt to penetrate al-Qaeda. Despite the fact that he spoke no Pashtu and was from pro-Western Jordan, he appeared to succeed. In the fall of 2009, Balawi sent bin Zeid a video of himself sitting with a close aide

---

[1] This is a fictional name and one not used in official communications.

to bin Laden. A month later, he claimed in an e-mail that he was treating Ayman al-Zawahiri, al-Qaeda's second-in-command.[2]

The Agency, which had never successfully penetrated al-Qaeda and was concerned about a rumor that the terrorists were in possession of a dirty bomb, jumped at the opportunity that Balawi seemed to represent. Despite the warnings of some, including the COS in Jordan, they invited the Jordanian to meet with officers at Camp Chapman, where they planned to discuss a plot to kill or capture Ayman al-Zawahiri. Both DCIA Leon Panetta and President Barack Obama approved the meeting.[3]

On December 30, 2009, Balawi was picked up by an Afghan driver working for the CIA on the Pakistani border and driven to Camp Chapman. Because of his perceived value as a spy and the danger of him being identified by one of the Afghan soldiers at the gate, he was allowed to enter the base without being searched.

When the car stopped inside the CIA compound, Balawi exited and detonated the thirty-pound suicide vest he was wearing under his *patoo* (a large shawl) and *kameez* shirt. He and nine others were killed, including CIA base chief Jennifer Lynne Matthews, two other CIA case officers, a CIA targeting analyst, three CIA security contractors, Ali bin Zeid, and the Afghan driver and chief of security. Six others were seriously wounded.

It was the second-worst single-day loss in the CIA's history, after the 1983 bombing of the US embassy in Beirut, Lebanon, and an enormous blow to our ability to collect intel on the ground in Afghanistan.

I arrived in Kabul two weeks later armed with some training, near-fluent Pashtu (or so I thought), and no field experience. As I entered the airport terminal, a young man stepped forward and asked, "Are you Doug?"

---

[2] All this information regarding Ali bin Zeid, and Humam Khalil al-Balawi and his activities, is taken from public sources, including *The Triple Agent* by Joby Warrick (Vintage Books, 2011).

[3] This was also written about in *The Triple Agent*.

"Yes, I am."

"The chief of operations wants to talk to you tomorrow, so you need to spend the night in Kabul."

"No problem."

I grabbed my bags and followed him outside to a waiting SUV. It was so dark that I couldn't see much, but my first impression was of a city that was as cold as hell and smelled like human shit.

There was reason for this, which I learned later. The Afghans burn their feces to stay warm, which is why Kabul is considered one of the most polluted cities in the world owing to the tremendous amount of fecal matter in the air.

So I was not only smelling it, I was literally inhaling it.

It was after midnight when we arrived at the CIA base, which featured a number of low-slung prefabricated structures packed with desks and laptops. Nobody there had a clue who I was or why I was there.

"Maybe you should wake up the support guy," I suggested.

Minutes later a half-asleep man walked in and asked, "Are you Doug?"

"Yes."

"We have some shipping containers in back with mattresses in them. We use them when people are visiting. You can sleep in there."

They were called pods. Some, including the ones used by the embassy, were nicely outfitted with heaters and TVs. The one I was escorted to contained a bed with a mattress and a desk, but no sheets and no chair. The support guy handed me a blanket and said, "See you in the morning."

I spent the next three nights trying to sleep in the pod as rats crawled over me. The good news was that they generally didn't bite, since they were looking for food. But they made sleeping problematic. Every several hours I'd wake, shake the rats off, and try to fall asleep again.

I found the conditions somewhat appalling considering that I wasn't in some far-flung base. I was located in the capital of the country, where the Agency had maintained a strong presence since 2001.

The next morning I returned to the office and said, "I'm supposed to talk to the operations chief."

"He's busy," the support guy answered.

"Do you have any idea when he will be available to see me?"

"Sorry. Don't know."

Three days later the operations chief showed up, a fifty-year-old guy with a white goatee and a potbelly. He said, "Nice to meet you. I just wanted to put a face to a name."

"I'm Doug. I'm going to Wadi Base. What's going on?"

"Wadi Base, yeah.... Best of luck down there. Go knock 'em dead."

He struck me as a used-car dealer trying to sell me a lemon.

I cleared the disappointment out of my throat and proceeded, "Sir, I thought you'd have some guidance to give me in terms of what we're trying to achieve there, what I should expect, the threat level, et cetera."

He studied his fingernails, then looked past my head to the opposite wall. "To be honest with you, yeah.... You're the new guy. You're going out there to give it wings."

What? I had never done the job to this point. The operations chief admitted he'd never been to Wadi, and didn't seem interested in what was going on at this important forward base.

He said, "If you want to know more, go talk to our targeter slash desk officer. Her name is Karen. She manages that account."

I found her in an adjoining building. Karen said, "Yeah, it's new. No real sources are run out of there. We're looking for you to get us up and going."

"Who's the shadow governor?" I asked, having read that the shadow governor was the Taliban ruler in a particular province. He had huge influence among the Pashtuns and what he said was considered the rule of law.

"We don't know," she answered.

"What about the district governor?"

She shook her head. "No information."

"What about al-Qaeda?"

"We don't know that, either."

I tried to keep my cool. "There's a military base down there, correct? What are they telling us?"

"They don't go out," the desk officer answered. "The IED threat is too pervasive. Every time they leave they don't go more than two kilometers before they're hit by an IED. They just kind of stay on the base, really."

Real useful, I thought.

"When's my flight out?"

"Just go to the airport."

"When's my flight?"

"We don't have a scheduled flight to Wadi."

I spent the next two days at Bagram Airfield, sleeping in a shipping container with no TV, and nothing to do except read a book about economics that someone had left behind.

I finally flew out on a ██████████ plane to Kandahar. There I faced another CIA support guy who wasn't expecting me, and didn't know my name.

"You're going where?" he asked.

"Wadi."

"Really? We have a base ████████ there?"

Was this typical of how the Agency operated in the field? Or was I stuck in some weird version of *Groundhog Day* and didn't know it?

I learned quickly that most of the Agency support people in Afghanistan were like tellers in a bank. They completed the tasks in front of them, but didn't bother trying to understand the bigger picture—like what was going on at the forward bases, or what it took to run human assets. Their sole concerns seemed to be their safety and careers.

On first impression the entire US military and security operation seemed hugely flawed. You had military units that rarely left their bases, and CIA support people who didn't know where their operations officers were deployed. It explained why we were losing.

I found an abandoned golf cart and drove around Kandahar

Airfield for two days. Within a heavily armed perimeter was a vast makeshift city that featured a number of Canadian fast-food joints including a Tim Hortons—which is Canada's version of McDonald's—a PX the size of a Walmart, and stores that sold DVDs.

As I watched soldiers enter and exit, I thought, *How is it that they can keep these establishments stocked, and they can't figure out how to get me to my base?*

Two days later, I boarded a helicopter flight to Wadi. The amped-up flight crew informed me that they only flew there ▮▮▮▮▮ because the area was so dangerous. They clutched ▮▮▮▮▮▮▮ machine guns, wore body armor and NVGs (night-vision goggles), and flew with the doors open to better return enemy fire. One of the soldiers handed me a pair of NVGs as the frigid air burned my skin.

Thirty minutes later we landed in the middle of a ▮▮▮▮▮ desert.

"Good luck, buddy."

"Thanks."

I had to give back the NVGs because they belonged to the helo. Now I couldn't see more than two feet in front of me, and the sand from the spinning rotors stung my eyes.

As I slipped on a pair of ski goggles that I had brought with me, a huge man emerged from the darkness and shouted over the roar of the helicopter engines, "Are you Doug?"

"Yes, I am."

"I'm the chief. I'm going on R and R. I'll be gone for a ▮▮▮▮▮▮▮. Get her done, son."

He slapped me on the shoulder and boarded the helicopter behind me.

I stood with my two bags and an M4 slung over my shoulder, asking myself, *What just happened?*

The helicopter with the chief aboard took off and ripped into the ▮▮▮ sky. I was scared shitless in the middle of the desert reminding myself that I'd never been in a firefight before. My sphincter tightened even further at the sound of a vehicle approaching. In my mind I pictured me blindfolded while some guy with a huge black beard shouted angry slogans at a camera as he raised a sword that would lop my head off.

Two heavily armed guys in digital camo fatigues jumped out of the truck and shouted in English, "Get in, dude. We're going to take you to the base."

I hopped in the back of the truck, where one of the guys explained that it's SOP for security guys like them to wait ███████████ ████████████████████.

"Understood," I gulped.

They drove me past rolls of razor wire, concrete barriers, and heavily fortified guard towers surrounding the base perimeter and pointed out the various containers that were used for washroom, gym, and dining facility. There was also a mosque for our Afghan guards that also functioned as a hospital.

The ██████████ (place where I lived and worked) was a separate concrete two-thousand-foot prison that had been built by the Soviets in the eighties. It consisted of twelve cells and an office area. One of the cells became my bedroom.

As I lay staring at the ceiling I tried not to imagine the horrors that had been inflicted there in the past. The next morning, eager and somewhat rested, I met the staff, which consisted ██ ████████████ ████████████████████ who had been recruited to man the post while the chief was away. He was sixty-four years old and on the verge of retirement; I was twenty-six and just starting my career.

He said right off the bat, "We have a few sources, but nothing is really happening." He also didn't speak Pashtu, rarely left the base, and made it clear that he didn't think there was much we could accomplish given the fact that we were surrounded by Taliban.

Great, I thought. *I'm in a very dangerous place with no idea what I'm doing, and this guy is giving me no direction or encouragement.*

All I knew was what I had gleaned from ██████████ reports that indicated that there was an IED network operating in the area that was killing hundreds of Americans.

I was also aware that Wadi was just about the most dangerous place on the planet for someone working for the US government. According to the United Nations Department of Safety and Security map, which color-coded the entire country for risk for UN operations, the area we were in was "extreme" red. In fact, the red extended throughout the province into neighboring Helmand, Zabul, and Urozgan provinces and farther southeast.

Taliban and an allied billion-dollar opium cultivation and trafficking network controlled the entire southeast border of the country. From there opium was smuggled west to the Balkans, via Iran and Turkey, or shipped out of Karachi to the Gulf states and Africa.[4]

The drug trade had helped fund the CIA-supported mujahideen war against the Soviets in the 1980s. After the Soviets left Afghanistan, opium production increased fourteenfold, from 500 tons in the mid-eighties to 6,900 tons a year. The United States had made some efforts to curb its production a few years earlier and failed. Now it flourished, aided by the Taliban, local tribesmen working for the Haqqani network led by warlord Jalaluddin Haqqani and his son Sirajuddin, and corrupt officials in the Karzai government.

It was *Deadwood* with rocket launchers, pickup trucks, and AK-47s. Adding to the corrupt and Wild West nature of the area was a very active and lucrative goods-smuggling trade along the highway from Wadi to ███████ ████████. Under the Afghan Transit Trade Agreement, signed in 1965, Pakistan allowed Afghanistan-bound goods to traverse its territory duty-free. Used cars and other cast-off goods bought mainly in Japan were shipped into Afghanistan via duty-free Dubai, then smuggled across the border into Pakistan, where they were sold for a large

---

[4] This is open-source material mentioned in Matthieu Aikins, "The Master of Spin Boldak," *Harper's,* December 2009, and other publications.

profit because they were exempt from Pakistani taxes and custom fees that could double of even triple their cost.

The shipping containers used to haul in products bound for Pakistan—which included used microwaves, ovens, DVD players, car stereos, camcorders, toys, clothing, and even motorized wheelchairs—stood alongside Highway 4, a four-lane asphalt road that snaked through the desert from the ███████ west to Wadi and Spin Boldak, then northwest to Kandahar. The Afghanis had converted them into dwellings and workshops, which formed a makeshift town known as Wesh.[5]

My immediate mission wasn't to try to curb the drug trade, or the smuggling of cars, or even to help police the border. I was at Wadi to help figure out how to stop the traffic in IEDs that were coming in from ███████ and killing American soldiers.[6]

I had almost nothing to work with, but I did have the freedom to learn by trial and error. The problem was that I wasn't starting a small business where it didn't matter if I ordered the wrong ink cartridges for the printers. I was in a war zone conducting espionage. If I fucked up it could result in people being killed.

Not knowing where to start, I walked over to the military J2 intel office and huddled with a lieutenant.

He said, "We know all the weapons, Taliban fighters, and IEDs are coming in through ███████ [a town across the border] but we're almost powerless to stop them."

"Really? How come?" I asked.

---

[5] Matthieu Aikins, "The Master of Spin Boldak," *Harper's,* December 2009.

[6] The fact that the US government (including DOD, DOS, Department of Homeland Security, and other US agencies) was trying to stop IEDs coming into Afghanistan from ███████ Pakistan is substantiated by GAO report "U.S. Agencies Face Challenges Countering the Smuggling of Improvised Explosive Device (IED) Materials in Afghanistan/Pakistan Region," the GAO-produced video "Smuggling of Improvised Explosive Device (IED) Materials from Pakistan to Afghanistan," and testimony by US Army general Michael Barbero before the Senate Subcommittee on Near Eastern and South and Central Asian Affairs, October 13, 2012.

"The Afghan border police monitor the road. They're not only corrupt as hell, they also don't stop anyone unless he's carrying an AK-47, and they very rarely ask a driver to open a car trunk or inspect a truck's cargo. Nor do they check people's IDs. All you have to do is tell the soldiers at the border that you have a family member living in Afghanistan and they let you in."

"It sounds to me like we need to run some sources into ██████ so we can get a picture of what's going on," I said. "Have you developed anything like that?"

"No, we haven't. We rely primarily on intel we get from our liaison services, namely the Afghan police, border patrol, and army."

The more he spoke, the sharper the picture came into focus. Local DOD J2 officers were concerned with protecting the base and determining the location of specific IEDs. They weren't interested in monitoring the people and weapons crossing the border, even though it was a major Taliban supply route.

With no one else to turn to for help, I spoke to my Afghan interpreter (terp), Jon. Born and raised in the area, Jon, whose real name was Hassan, loved America and had been working with US Special Forces until the Agency snatched him up to be our terp at Wadi. It became apparent right away that he knew more about the Pashtun culture and what was going on in the area than our American intel officers. So I started to hammer him with questions. Who can I speak to who knows what's going on at the border? How should I make contact with people? What will I do that will piss someone off in a meeting, and how can I avoid that?

I realized that the Pashtu I had learned in Washington was a northern dialect called Harto and wasn't spoken in the South. The structure and verbs were the same in the local dialect, but the nouns were completely different. It was like a foreigner who had learned English trying to understand the lyrics of a rap song like "Hustlin'" by Rick Ross. "Mo' cars, mo' hoes, mo' clothes, mo' blow."

Determined to pass as a local, I grew a foot-long beard and purchased Pashtun clothes—*shalwar kameez* (loose pajama-like trousers and a long

tunic), vest, and sandals—from a market in the town ███████████.
But my northern Pashtu was going to be a problem. So I spent my first
three weeks in Wadi with Jon learning the southern dialect and vent-
ing my frustration on the pistol range.

With my Pashtu rejiggered and up to speed, I started to attend
local *shuras* (which literally means "consultation" in Arabic) in the
nearby village. The military was in the habit of sending a lieutenant or
captain and interpreter to these weekly meetings of community elders,
usually to apologize for some kind of damage they had caused.

I showed up tanned with a long beard, wearing my body armor
under my *shalwar kameez* and speaking Pashtu. The elders were mesmer-
ized, because none of them had ever heard someone who wasn't from
Afghanistan or Pakistan speak Pashtu. Although I introduced myself as
a US official, I didn't look or sound like an American.

The first couple of meetings, I shook hands and listened. By the
third week, I told them that if they needed things done they should come
talk to me at the old Soviet prison.

Even though I worried that the prison might not have a positive association for local leaders, since some of them and their relatives had
probably been detained and tortured there by the Soviets, members of
the *shura* started to stream in. I told them all the same thing. "I'm sure
you can tell that I'm not like other Americans. I can help you, if you tell
me what you need."

Usually they wanted someone to help them dig a well, or lend them
a tractor to work their little plot of land.

I'd listen, then respond, "You know what can get you the things you
want? Money. I can give you that, but first you have to give me what I
want."

That approach might be considered rude in the US, but it worked
in Afghanistan. People there understand that nothing comes for free. I
later found out that when USAID workers built roads and schools, it
scared the Afghans. They showed up at the *shuras* and asked, "What are
the Americans going to want in return? Our firstborn sons?"

I made it clear that I ran operations like the mafia. "You want a favor from me, fine. But I'll ask you for one in return."

Afghan *masheran* (elders) would say to me, "Give me the money first."

"No," I'd respond. "You do me the favor first."

"How can we trust you?" the *masher* would ask.

"Here's the deal.... You know I have the money, endless amounts, but you're not going to get it unless you do me a favor."

He'd listen and nod, then ask me what I wanted.

"I want you to put me in contact with one of your sons, cousins, or nephews. Someone who is between eighteen and thirty years old and has either been to ███████ or lives there now. If you bring him here, I'll pay you. And if I like him, I'll pay him, too."

The *masheran* were enterprising. A vast majority of them responded. Many of the young men they brought had rarely traveled and knew very little. I paid them a modest sum and sent them on their way.

But some were useful. And one in particular turned out to be key.

5

ABDUL

Never underestimate the power of the State to act out its own massive fantasies.

—DON DELILLO

I had arrived in Afghanistan in January 2010, at the height of the US military surge—trumpeted by General David Petraeus and adopted by the Obama administration. By the end of the year we would have roughly 98,000 troops in-country. Sadly, 2010 also saw the highest level of US casualties and IED attacks. According to the *Washington Post,* Taliban insurgents planted 14,661 IEDs in 2010, which amounted to an increase of 62 percent over 2009. Of the 711 coalition soldiers who died in action in 2010, 368 were killed by Taliban IEDs. The previous year 448 foreign soldiers died in action, 280 the result of IED attacks.

From the US perspective, 2010 was the bloodiest and costliest year of the Afghan war that had started in 2001 when US boots first touched the ground. In October 2001, in response to the terrorist attack on the World Trade Center, President George W. Bush sent a collection of CIA teams and Special Forces troops to work with the Afghan Northern Alliance forces. Backed by US airstrikes, the makeshift alliance managed to drive the Taliban out of power and take over the central government in Kabul.

Subsequently and with an assist from the UN, we helped install a transitional government led by Hamid Karzai. In 2004, President Karzai became the first democratically elected leader of Afghanistan with 55.4 percent of the vote. In his inaugural address, which was witnessed by the country's former king, Zahir Shah, and 150 former dignitaries, including Vice President Dick Cheney, Karzai pledged to open a "new chapter" in his country's "hard and dark" history.

Unfortunately, that hadn't happened. Maybe it was never in the cards. It didn't help that the United States and other major international players who made up the International Security Assistance Force (ISAF) in Afghanistan had diverted troops and a portion of promised reconstruction aid to Iraq starting in 2003. As a result the security situation in Afghanistan worsened and the Taliban was able to regroup. Due to the reemergence of the Taliban, the rapid growth of the poppy trade, and charges of rampant corruption in his administration, Karzai barely won reelection in 2009. And even then his opponents cried fraud.

Up until October 2003, the ISAF security mandate hadn't extended beyond the boundaries of Kabul. At that point it consisted of approximately five thousand troops and had three working helicopters. By 2006, when it became clear that the newly reconstituted Afghan National Security Forces (ANSF) couldn't secure the border with Pakistan, the ISAF mandate expanded to include the southeastern part of the country.

Now in 2010, the Taliban controlled most of the southern and eastern provinces, including the provinces of Kandahar ████████████ ████, Helmand, Nuristan, Kunar, Logar, Paktika, Zabul, Kabul, Wardak, Urozgan, and Khowst.

Given the level of Taliban expansion and violence against Americans, what I was learning defied all logic. In the eight years since 2001, when Operation Enduring Freedom was first launched, the Agency hadn't developed a single reliable ████████████████████████ ██.

How do you explain this astounding oversight?

I struggled with the answer myself as I sat in my former Soviet prison cell perusing numerous studies and cable traffic back and forth to headquarters. What I found was a tunnel-vision focus on al-Qaeda and almost zero regard for the Taliban, which was in the process of re-taking the country.

Yes, members of al-Qaeda had attacked us on 9/11. Its Fifty-fifth Arab Brigade, organized by Osama bin Laden and made up of some-where between one thousand and two thousand mujahideen fighters from the Middle East, Central Asia, and Southeast Asia, were based in Afghanistan from 1995 to 2001. But Operation Enduring Freedom re-sulted in the imprisonment and death of the majority of them. Those members of al-Qaeda who survived snuck across the border into Pakistan.

As of 2009, according to the *Washington Post,* senior US military and intelligence officials estimated that there were fewer than one hundred al-Qaeda members remaining in Afghanistan. Those same officials es-timated that there were approximately three hundred al-Qaeda hiding in the tribal areas of Pakistan. These numbers compared to tens of thou-sands of Taliban insurgents on either side of the border.

During sleepless nights in Wadi, I learned that the Taliban was a much more organized, well-funded, and lethal organization than al-Qaeda. They were based in Quetta, Pakistan, and protected, funded, and provided with logistical support by Pakistan's notorious and very competent intelligence service, Inter-Services Intelligence (or ███). An Islamic fundamentalist political movement, the Taliban had actually been founded by the ██ in 1994 to establish a regime in Afghanistan that would be favorable to Pakistan, especially in any dispute with their strategic rival India.

They had taken over the country in September 1996 and governed it according to a strict interpretation of Islamic Sharia law until they were ousted in November 2001. Almost nine years later they remained highly organized throughout Pakistan and Afghanistan and disciplined, from their top spiritual and military leaders to the recruits responsible for maintaining their websites. Throughout every province in Afghanistan they maintained a shadow government complete with district managers and governors.

By contrast, al-Qaeda was a loose association of Sunni jihadists with practically no internal discipline or central control. Any group of angry Sunni radicals in any country who pledged allegiance to the al-Qaeda call to action could call themselves al-Qaeda. Their goal was to attack the West and drive it out of what they considered to be Islamic territory. But AQ was not an integrated network. It didn't have an intelligence service to fund and support it, which meant no access to detailed reports on US deployments in Afghanistan.[7] ███████████████████ ███

As British prime minister Tony Blair stated after the 2005 London bombings, "Al-Qaeda is not an organization. It's a way of working."

Yes, al-Qaeda was extremely violent and opportunistic, aspired to have global reach, and had attacked targets in the United States, the United Kingdom, Somalia, Yemen, Saudi Arabia, Iraq, and other countries. In no way did I think that we should discount the threat it posed. But as much as I tried, I couldn't explain why the Agency had a special branch ██████████████████████ dedicated to tracking al-Qaeda and its activities and not █████████████ focused solely on the Taliban.

It made zero sense. In terms of the damage they were doing daily to NATO and ANSF troops and Afghan civilians, I considered this a tragic oversight. It's an opinion that I expressed almost daily in the following manner: "Guys, if we come across an al-Qaeda cell, let's destroy it. But we know where the Taliban headquarters is located and we know that their fighters and IEDs are coming from across the southern border at █████ and killing our troops. So let's get rid of them first."

While individual US military commanders in the field agreed with me, their hands were tied by their counterparts at CENTCOM. And the Agency's view was that al-Qaeda and the Haqqani network were

---

[7] This is open-source material found on Wikipedia and in other news sources.

more important concerns. All I could do was point out why I thought they were wrong and take action myself.

Unfortunately, I was only one of a ██████ of operations ██████ deployed at the forward bases. We had a ton in Kabul, where they weren't needed. And, because of the dangerous nature of the forward bases, the officers that we did have there served for only a year. This gave birth to a saying that was painfully on point: "We haven't been in Afghanistan for ten years. We've been in Afghanistan one year, ten times." ██████ ███████████████████████████████ Each officer who arrived at a forward base had to learn the same lessons, in terms of developing sources and running them.

I also learned that the Agency generally sucked at supporting the military in a war zone, and conversely, the military wasn't good at collecting actionable intel. Yes, they had brave men in Special Forces and SEAL teams who were great at going up against the enemy. But they relied on us to provide target packages, when most of our officers reacted to events like journalists instead of being aggressive and developing sources that could tell them what was going on in the field.

They wrote great reports about who was responsible for launching a specific RPG attack or suicide bombing, but were not good at developing accurate, timely intel. As a result, the Taliban was killing hundreds of US, NATO, and ANSF soldiers a year in and around Wadi. I was determined to stop them.

With no one to train me or give me direction, I began attending local *shura* meetings, where I sat among the thirty or so Pashtun elders, listened, and started asking them if they had younger relatives who wanted to work with me.

If the *shura* was scheduled for a village square at noon, men would start to show up at 12:30 and take their places in a large horseshoe. The person who called the meeting to resolve a land dispute or another local issue would sit at the front with his aides and various flunkies and interpreters to his left and right. By one p.m. most of the elders would have assembled. If the *shura* was called by a US military official, sodas would be passed out. If not, the beverage offered was green tea.

At around two, the person leading the meeting would try to silence the group, which took some effort. Then he'd announce the purpose of the meeting. Immediately, men would start to shout their opinions or grievance, and inevitably four or five men from a particular clan would storm out, creating a big scene.

They wouldn't leave the area, but would stand outside, shouting angrily about how they had been insulted for whatever reason. Within the *shura* there would be much discussion as to whether or not those five individuals should be invited back. Sometimes they were, sometimes they weren't.

In the area around Wadi, *shuras* were particularly contentious because of the centuries-long blood feud between the two major local Pashtun tribes, ███████████████████████. Because of this enmity very little was ever resolved. Nor was there any mention of religion or any prayer.

The guy with the most forces behind him or the most amount of money usually forced his decision down everyone else's throat. The rest of the attendees walked away expressing their displeasure and planning some sort of revenge.

I generally sat in back and watched the assemblage. If I heard someone express something that piqued my interest, I would tap that individual on the shoulder and invite him to talk outside.

The more I attended the local weekly *shuras,* the more the *masheran* who attended grew comfortable with me. They knew I was a US intel guy, but didn't care which agency I worked for, which was cool because it meant that I didn't have to request permission to ██████████ and tell them who I really was.

Most of the guys who attended were in their sixties and seventies. About once a month, a guy of about ████████████████████ ████████████████████████████████████ ██ and always wore a dark gray or tan *shalwar kameez* in the style of the South.[8] Leaders chose not to wear white, as I did, because it stained easily.

I assumed at first that he had no authority. Abdul's father had died ███████████████████████████████ he acted as the patriarch and leader of a village and a whole family network that extended through southeastern Afghanistan into Pakistan.

One day, he walked up to me as the *shura* was breaking up and asked, *"Tsinga yay? Zeh Abdul yum."* (How are you? My name's Abdul.)

"I'm Zmarai," I answered in Pashtu.

Abdul got right to the point. "I hear you work for the US government."

"Yes. That's correct."

"I have something to sell you."

"Okay, Abdul. What is it?"

"A Stinger missile."

Stingers, aka FIM-92A, aren't RPGs, which were found all over Afghanistan. It's a much more sophisticated and lethal shoulder-fired missile that uses an infrared signal to lock on to the heat from an aircraft's exhaust. It has a range of about eleven thousand feet, costs about $40,000 per missile, and is used by jihadists for ███████ ██████████████████████████████.

I thought there was slim chance Abdul had one. But like someone who runs into a kook who says he knows someone who is about to assassinate the president, I had to follow up.

I asked, "Are you sure it's a Stinger?"

"Yes."

"Okay, Abdul. Come visit me at my facility and bring me some pictures or a video."

A week later, at an arranged time, he met me outside of Wadi Base. Since I was still learning the local Kandahari dialect, which was

---

[8] Abdul is a made-up name. His description has been altered to preserve his anonymity.

different from the northern Pashtu dialect I had been taught, I brought Jon with me.

We sat in the backseat of a ████████ armored Land Rover with a group of heavily armed former SEALs, code-named Scorpions, who were now my bodyguards. Each of them carried an ████████ assault rifle with ██████ magazines stashed in the vests worn on their chests and ██████████████████████████████. For sidearms they favored ████████████████████ mags and carried an assortment of very lethal knives, including switchblade stilettos that they liked to pop open in front of unsuspecting people's faces for amusement.

I had a ████ propped between my legs and a Glock strapped to my waist. ██

██

████████████████████████████

Hopefully with Abdul they wouldn't be needed.

██

████████████████████ My focus was on a set of approaching headlights. I instructed the Scorpion sitting in the front seat, call sign Hillbilly, to kill his iPhone blasting Billy Currington's "Good Directions."

From fifty meters I made out a white sedan like the one Abdul said he'd be driving.

"That's him, guys," I offered. "Let's see if he flashes his headlights the way he was told."

The sedan headlights flashed once and paused, then illuminated again three times.

"Well, done, Abdul."

I relaxed a little. Now it was time for Jon, our terp, to get out ██████████ and talk to the source first.

I turned to him sitting behind me and said in Pashtu, "Okay, Jon, get your fat ass out there and try not to get blown up. We're having eggplant for dinner tonight and I know you don't want to miss it."

"Staa morr kuss, Zmarai." (I'll have your mother's pussy, Zmarai.) Zmarai, which means "lion," is a popular name in southern Afghanistan.

"Teh hum lapara meena larim." (I love you, too.)

I spoke Pashtu with the terp for two reasons. One, to practice the uniqueness of the southern dialect. And, two, to talk shit about the Scorpions without them knowing, which was a favorite pastime of Jon's and mine. Through the open door, I heard pieces of the Pashtu conversation in front of me.

"Where is Zmarai?" Abdul asked.

"Zmarai is in the car waiting," Jon answered. "Did you bring any weapons with you tonight?"

"No."

"Are you carrying any bombs with you, or in the car?"

"No. Absolutely not."

If you ever wondered what the most dangerous job in Afghanistan was, it was being a terp for the US government. "Good, because the foreigners will kill you if you do anything stupid. ██████████████ ████████████████████."

"But I don't have any explosives on me."

"██████████████ Now get out before the foreigners shoot you in the head."

Abdul exited the vehicle. Jon ███████████████, then turned and gave us a thumbs-up.

The two heavily tattooed Scorpions got out. The one who had been driving, call sign Lolita (yep, that's how he got his name) trained his ████████████ sight on Abdul's chest. Simultaneously, his colleague Hillbilly did a pat-down.

Thankfully Abdul didn't speak English, because Lolita asked, "Is this shitbag packing heat, Jon?"

"No, he's clean. But he had a book of matches on him for his cigarettes. I'll keep them in my pocket."

"All right. Tell this motherfucker to walk slowly to the truck and don't do anything that might cause me to sneeze or flinch and execute his ass by mistake."

Jon translated something more lighthearted and Abdul laughed nervously. They walked to the ███████ together and got in.

I greeted him with "Abdul, peace be with you. How are you today? Thank you for coming. God is great. God has willed it." As I did, I held a hand to my heart to express sincerity. I knew that if he was religious he wouldn't want to shake my hand.

During the drive back to the base, I chatted with Abdul about the local weather and the haboobs (dust storms). This gave him an opportunity to do something southern Afghans loved to do, namely lament about the terrible conditions they lived under.

I made it a practice not to talk operationally until we got back to the shipping container where I held my meetings. Afghans usually take a long time getting to the point, and I wanted to make them comfortable and make them forget that they were talking to an American.

The container was outfitted with tile flooring covered with Afghan rugs. The furnishings consisted of a beat-up leather sofa and a matching leather chair with a folding chair beside it. I directed Abdul to sit on the sofa.

Jon took his place in the folding chair. He did this on purpose. Previously, when the container held two leather seats and no steel one, the source was more comfortable talking to the terp than to me. To change that circumstance, Jon suggested that he sit on a steel chair to indicate his lower status.

It seemed to work. In the middle of the chairs and sofa sat a table with a bowl of mixed nuts. I never touched them, because sources tended not to wash their hands. I'd seen some pick at their toenails in front of me, then grab a fistful of cashews.

With all of us seated in our designated places, Abdul was offered something to drink, and chose Diet Pepsi. He lit up a local cigarette and puffed incessantly. He also had an unpleasant habit of sucking his teeth as he thought.

Abdul seemed hesitant to show me the pictures he said he had, which made me think he was bluffing and trying to extract money out of me for nothing.

After some prodding on my part, he played a video he had taken on his cell phone. It contained images of an RPG.

I said, "Thank you, Abdul, but this isn't a Stinger. Do you know what one looks like?"

"No, Zmarai, it is a Stinger. I'm sure of that."

"No. I'm sorry, Abdul. It isn't."

He shifted on the leather sofa, chewed on his bottom lip, then asked, "Is there something else I can do you, Zmarai?"

"I don't know, Abdul. That depends on who you know and what you're willing to do."

He sat up. "It's like this," he said. "I'm in charge of this large group of people. I'm in debt and I'm willing to do anything."

That was music to my ears. "Tell me more."

"I've got this big network in ▇▇▇▇▇▇ [a town across the border] and lots of relatives living in ▇▇▇▇. If you want something, just tell me what that is."

I said, "All right, bring me Mullah Omar's head." (Mullah Mohammed Omar is the spiritual leader of the Taliban. He hadn't been seen by US officials since late 2001 and was rumored to be hiding in Pakistan.)

Abdul smiled and said, "That might be difficult, but if you pay me enough I'll get it for you."

He seemed eager and motivated, but I had to vet him first. So I said, "Go back to ▇▇▇▇ and speak to your sources there. I want to know the names and locations of the top ▇▇ recruiting madrassas, and I want to know where the IED manufacturers are located."

I already knew all the information from other sources.

He called me back the very next day and said, "I've got your information. Can I come in and see you?"

In most cases I would consider his speedy response a bad sign. But Abdul had an ingenuity about him that was intriguing. Knowing he would be thoroughly searched by the Scorpions and not allowed to drive a vehicle onto the base, I said, "Okay."

When we reunited in the shipping container, he provided all the information I had asked for, and all the names and locations checked out. I later learned that everyone in ███████ (the town across the border) knew where the IED factories were located because they blew up about once a month. But the US intelligence community didn't, until a couple of weeks ago when I found out.

Knowing that Abdul had told me the truth and figuring that he had probably known all this information already because he had produced it so quickly, I decided that it was time to ask him for something I didn't know.

I said, "Good, Abdul. That was easy for you. Now I want you to find out who is in charge of these facilities. I want pictures of these people and I want phone numbers. I want video if you can get it. And I want to talk to someone else you know who can get information for me."

"Yes," he answered. "I can do that."

A week later he called and said, "I have the information for you."

I was like, *Wow!*

True to his word, he brought names of the leaders of the madrassas, the head mullahs, their assistants, and their assistant's assistant. He provided me with their genealogies and gave me photos of them he had taken with his cell phone. He also said that he had a ███████ (relative) he wanted to introduce me to, who he thought might be helpful.

Part of me thought, *We're moving and shaking.* Another part kept reminding me about the disaster in Khowst and warned me to be careful. *What is his connection?* I asked myself. *And how did he get access to the top mullahs who are actively training jihadists?*

So I asked Abdul how he had accomplished that. He explained that he simply called the top mullahs and told them that he had a gift for them and wanted to stop by and give it to them in person. The gift itself was straightforward: ████████████████████████████.

"And they weren't suspicious?" I asked. "They didn't ask you where ███████ [the gift] came from?"

"No."

The phone numbers were worth their weight in gold. Since internet service didn't extend into ███████████, members of al-Qaeda and the Taliban couldn't send coded messages over the web. Instead, they talked on their cell phones all the time, trading gossip, names, and information.

Within a few hours of receiving the numbers, I was able to ██████ ██ ████████████ and we were able to prevent a number of Taliban attacks. Headquarters got excited. Abdul was quickly becoming an important asset.

6

HAJI JAN[9]

The donkey will remain donkey wherever it goes.

—A PASHTU PROVERB

Pashtuns make up about 50 percent of the Afghan population and have dominated the southern part of the country south of the Amu River since the first millennium BCE. Their homeland extends along the eastern border and into what are considered the tribal areas of Pakistan. According to the *World Factbook,* published by the CIA, there are actually more than twice as many Pashtuns living in Pakistan than in Afghanistan—29,342,892 in Pakistan versus 12,776,369 in Afghanistan.

In terms of religious beliefs, Pashtuns are Sunni Muslims and follow a nonwritten ethical code called *Pashtunwali.* Its main principles include *Melmastia* (hospitality and respect for all visitors regardless of race, religion, nationality, or financial status), *Nanawatai* (offering asylum or protection from one's enemies), *Badal* (the practice of taking revenge against a wrongdoer), and *Turah* (bravery).

In general, I found them to be friendly and primitive. The more I interacted with Pashtuns, the more I realized that to think of them as

---

[9] Haji Jan is a made-up name, like all the names of friends, sources, and fellow CIA officers in this book. His description has been altered to preserve his anonymity.

anything more than members of a fifth-world country was a mistake. They exit the womb in survival mode and continue to struggle that way until they die. Many don't make it. According to the World Health Organization's *State of the World's Children,* southern Afghanistan's under-five mortality rate is 257 deaths per 1,000 live births, which makes it the third-highest in the world, surpassed only by Angola and Sierra Leone.

Death is so ever-present that it's expected at any time and accepted. Some people claim that's because of Islam, but I found that not to be true. Even the Taliban guys I met weren't religious fanatics. Sure they prayed five times a day and went through the motions, but they were too uneducated to really understand the religion, and too occupied with daily survival to concern themselves with esoteric things.

Life to them was a constant battle for survival, and that reality dominated their thinking. The constant struggle to stay alive might explain why Afghanistan has one of the highest rates of heart disease and heart attacks in the world.

Given the harshness of their existence, any possible monetary gain that might give them a little relief was tremendously appealing. That provided me with the opening I needed.

Once I got them to speak to me, and started giving them money, I had to establish two things: one, I was in control, and, two, I was a capable leader. Those things accomplished, I could get the Pashtun sources I developed to do practically anything.

Even though I had gained their respect, I understood that they would never trust me, and conversely, I couldn't entirely trust them.

I spoke Pashtu, which was a definite plus, but I was still a foreigner (a *harajan*), and foreigners had tried to dominate them since the days of Alexander the Great. From their perspective, I could have been an Iranian, a Syrian, or an alien from outer space. We were all *harajan* and suspicion ran deep.

Dealing with them was like riding a horse in a sense that you always had to let them know who was in control. Many of my colleagues didn't understand this, and misinterpreted cooperation for trust. If you gave an Afghan an inch, they'd take a mile by failing to deliver on promises and by lying.

They were hard and fearless, and had to be enterprising and manipulative in order to survive. Espionage to them was a means to a better life. There was no ideology, morality, or religious belief involved.

The enterprising Abdul continued to bring me valuable information about Taliban activities in ▇▇▇▇▇ (the town across the border) and haggle with me about money. I learned to place the ▇▇▇▇ I gave him in a sealed envelope and hand it to him at the end of our meeting. Otherwise, he was likely to count it in front of me and complain that it wasn't enough.

Mindful that he was a greedy bastard and had provided solid, reliable information so far, I started to think that I could use him to build a spy network that could hopefully extend into the Taliban itself. A couple of weeks after we met, Abdul introduced me to his twenty-year-old ▇▇▇▇▇ (relative). Ajmal[10] stood six feet tall and was extremely skinny. He had a shy manner and wore a short, black beard and a three-quarters prayer cap instead of the traditional Pashtun head wrap, which signified that he held no authority.

As with most southern Afghans I encountered, I was the first American he had ever met, and the fact that I spoke Pashtu flummoxed him at first. Turning to my terp Jon, he asked, "Is he Pashtun or a foreigner?"

"Zmarai can understand you," Jon answered. "He is American. Now stop talking to me and speak directly to him."

His eyes registering disbelief, Ajmal asked, "How does he know Pashtu?"

"Because God has willed it. He is a very important man and is in charge of this whole area for the Americans. Thank God that you are meeting him. Now stop talking to me and talk to Zmarai before he gets mad at you."

---

[10] Ajmal is also a made-up name. His description has been altered to preserve his anonymity.

The only exposure Ajmal, like many young Afghans, had had to Americans and US culture was through bootlegged Hollywood movies dubbed in ██████████████████████████████. He spoke pretty decent ██████ as did a majority of the young people in ██████. Since we were meeting in the evening, I had the base cook prepare a traditional southern Afghan meal of *palao* (rice with raisins and carrots), *chapli kebab* (fried hamburger), naan (flat bread), and yogurt.

After the meal, we got down to business.

"Ajmal, I am pleased you are here today. Your ██████ speaks very highly of you and says that you're a skilled mechanic. He also tells me that you live across the border in ██████ and you use your truck ████████████████████ to your neighbors once a week."

He nodded, lit a cigarette, and puffed vigorously. "Yes, thanks be to God."

"He says that you buy ████████████ in Afghanistan and then transport them across the border. He tells me that you have a good relationship with the border guards and they let you pass freely without stopping you. Is all of this true?"

"Yes."

"Thanks be to God," I said. "These facts make me very happy. Tell me, did your ████ tell you about me? Why did he tell you I want to speak to you?"

"He said that the foreigners need a ████████ driver. I own a truck. I can ████████████████████. Is this not what you wanted?"

"Ajmal," I answered, "that is exactly what I want. I want you to be my deliveryman. And I want to pay you for it. And you can keep your old job, too. In fact, I will pay you to continue your old job while you work for me. But, Ajmal, I want you to deliver information to me. I have enough ████████. Do you think you can bring me information, Ajmal-sahib?"

He nodded. "Yes. Yes, I can. What information do you want?"

"It is very simple, Ajmal, and you will love doing it, because you will make a lot of money. What I need is for you to take your truck and return to ▮▮▮▮▮ and deliver ▮▮▮▮▮▮. Then I want you to drive your truck to a specific neighborhood and look at everything there and memorize it. I want you to tell me who lives in the neighborhood, and who is the elder in charge. What kinds of shops are in the neighborhood? What activities are going on? Are there men walking around with weapons? What type of weapons? Where were they standing when you saw them with weapons? This is what I want to know."

He frowned, lit another cigarette, and said, "It is not permitted to walk around ▮▮▮▮▮ with a weapon."

I had heard this objection before from other sources and knew how to brush it aside. "Yes, thanks be to God," I answered, my eyes starting to burn from the smoke. "But we both know that certain kinds of men disobey this law and walk around with weapons."

"Yes, but they are Taliban," Ajmal said. "And they control that area."

"Yes, I know, Ajmal. That's the area I want you to drive in."

"But I don't live there."

"No, Ajmal. You do not. But you are about to begin delivering ▮▮▮▮▮ to that area. That is, if you accept my offer of ▮▮▮▮▮ a week."

The dance had begun. Ajmal came to me thinking that he was about to become the delivery man for a US base transporting ▮▮▮▮▮. Now he was being asked to deliver ▮▮▮▮▮ to a Taliban-controlled area of ▮▮▮▮▮.

He hadn't expected that and understood that the job involved a certain level of risk. On the other hand, the ▮▮▮▮▮ a week was too tempting to pass up.

Ajmal probably told himself that he would do it for a short time and back out if things got too risky. I had my own agenda. I planned to start him out asking for information that he could assess easily, get him addicted to the money, then pressure him to deliver higher-level intel.

That tactic usually worked. In Ajmal's case, ▮▮▮▮▮

later I had him embedded in ████████████████ that provided him and other young Pashtuns with weapons training in preparation for jihad.

My superiors back at Langley were thrilled. For the first time ever, we were getting information from inside ████████ about what was going on in a Taliban ████████ and specifically how young uneducated Muslim kids were transformed into martyrs prepared to attack the Great Satan. It was fascinating stuff, but I wasn't a journalist or a sociologist. I wanted to stop what was going on, not document or study it.

I had told Abdul from the beginning that I wanted to get to someone inside the Taliban and talk to him. He generally played his cards close to his vest. But one day, during one of our meetings, he said, "Zmarai, I have a friend who I grew up with. He's very religious. He was in the Taliban. Now he owns a ████████████████████████ ████████████████ [religious institution]. I think I can tell him what I'm doing and he'll work with you."

"Okay," I responded, trying to hide my excitement. "If you think he'll respond positively, I'm ready to see him. What's his name?"

"Haji Jan."

Abdul told me where he lived and described his pattern of travel. Then we worked out a plan to bring Haji Jan ████████████████. We'd meet in a ████████████, where we would do what is called in Agency speak "a war-zone brief encounter." In other words, search him carefully before we brought him back to Wadi.

Khowst burned vivid in our minds. Caution was required. What we didn't need was another catastrophe and more dead bodies. And I didn't want to be one of them.

At eleven on a windy night, the two Scorpions (Lolita and Hillbilly) and I staged about ████████ from the designated site. We sat in our ████████████████ (vehicles) nervous and alert scanning the rough landscape with our NVGs.

Hillbilly muttered, "Great fucking place for an ambush."

Lolita asked, "Who is this guy again, and why are we meeting him?"

"Guys," I answered. "Relax your sphincters. We'll never get inside the Taliban unless we talk to them. We've got to take this chance."

"You get us killed, and we'll be pissed."

I laughed. "I'll be pissed, too."

We saw a car approach in the distance and wind its way around an outcropping of rock, then descend into the ravine.

"That's them," I muttered.

The car stopped and flashed its headlights three times just like I had instructed. The Scorpion at the wheel gunned the vehicle and drove down ███████████████ with the high beams on. Through my NVGs I saw two individuals sitting in the front seat wearing *patoos,* which were thick, long shawls. The only features visible were the slits of their eyes.

Lolita got out and walked to the car with his ███ ready, while Hillbilly covered him. I heard him shout at the car's occupants in English to get out. Then he used hand signals, which they responded to.

A gust of sand and dirt blew by, obscuring the men for a moment. Then I recognized Abdul's voice explaining to the other dude in Pashtu that they were about to be █████████.

Everyone was extremely on edge. Once the two Afghans entered our vehicle, I introduced myself to Haji Jan and tried to put him at ease with banter about the weather. The terror in his dark eyes was intense.

At forty, Haji Jan was the same age as Abdul and stood about five foot nine and wore a medium-length black beard. On his head sat a three-quarter prayer cap, and he was dressed in a cream-colored *shalwar kameez.*[11]

When we entered the base and he saw that we were headed for the old Russian prison, he looked like he was about to jump out of the vehicle and run.

Inside my tricked-out shipping container, he drank tea, smoked, and

---

[11] As mentioned before, Haji Jan is a made-up name. His description has been altered to hide his identity.

started to settle down. He was exactly as Abdul had described him, except for his fluttery feminine hand gestures. Soon, he was naming all the Taliban leaders who came to his █████████████████, which put me in a good mood.

I said, "Thank you, Haji Jan. But in order for us to work together, I'm going to need proof that you actually know these people. I need their cell-phone numbers and I need photographs of them."

Abdul, the clever man he was, had prepared him. Haji Jan proceeded to give me the cell-phone numbers of the Taliban leaders who frequented his ███████.

I thanked him and told him that I was going to ████████████████ ████ establish that they were authentic. He said that his Taliban friends were aware that the Americans could tap their phones. A lot of the lower-level Taliban soldiers communicated only via Icom radio. The senior guys used cell phones, but changed them █████████████████████.

Clearly, the Talibs were much more sophisticated in terms of security than the mullahs. While the mullahs were mainly recruiting, the Taliban leaders were planning and launching operations. █████████ ██ ██ ████████

Our meeting stretched into the morning. By the time we drove the two Afghans back to their car the sun had started to rise behind us, turning the desert shades of orange and gold.

I watched them turn the car around and head back to ██████████. Back at the base, I spent the rest of the day writing reports and sending messages back to headquarters.

General Stanley McChrystal, who was the commander of US and ISAF forces in Afghanistan when I arrived, had a sign hanging above his doorframe that read "17-5-2." Meaning seventeen hours for work, five hours for sleep, and two hours for PT and eating. As a small unit entirely self-sufficient and reliant upon one another for everything, we lived and breathed this motto at Wadi Base.

One of the reasons we never took a break was the understanding that the Taliban wasn't going to relax until they had achieved their objectives. We were hugely outnumbered and in danger of being overrun at any point. With the return of the chief at the end of January, our base consisted of ██████████████████████████████, which meant our footprint was small.

In order to avoid the near-nightly mortar indirect fire that most bases in Afghanistan experienced, it was imperative that we keep our presence and sources off of the Taliban's radar. In Agency parlance, we were "in the black."

Even though the workload was exhausting, Wadi was where I wanted to be, workwise. I liked that we were lean and mean, and could move quickly and with fluidity according to the dictates of our dicey environment. Wadi was the tip of the spear and I liked living on the edge.

Every other morning, I'd drive over to the military base nearby and swap info with the J2 shop from 0600 to 0700. I'd show up in my Dri-FIT running shirt and shorts, which the military guys referred to as "Ranger panties." After the meeting I would run laps around their base for ninety minutes and then shower and be back in my cell (my office) by 0900 to start the day.

Those runs proved to be essential. As I circled the base, I'd consider where I was in terms of the assets I was developing and the picture they were painting, where I wanted to go, and, most importantly, how I could possibly get there.

Working and PTing to relieve the stress proved an effective combo, because the exhaustion was the only way I could get my mind to shut off at night. The nights I wasn't completely spent, I'd lie staring at the ceiling of my former prison cell and begin second-guessing. *Am I prepared for the events of tomorrow? Will the source remember his bona fides? Will he sell me out or try to kill me?*

During waking hours there was literally no time to worry. There were too many reports to write, e-mails to dispatch, calls to make to sources, meetings to set up or attend. Lolita gave me a piece of advice from his prior days as a SEAL HALO (high altitude, low opening) instructor: "Plan your jump, jump your plan. Period." It meant have a plan and execute it accordingly. If things go sideways, know that you've been trained to handle that, too.

Lolita and his crew expected the unexpected and dealt with it like it was no big deal. The other shit—the constant danger, sandstorms, bureaucratic snafus, freezing-cold nights, etc.—were considered, as Lolita would put it, "just another peaceful Sunday drive."

Although the pace at Wadi was nonstop, my mind often traveled back to Kate and Hannah seven thousand miles away. I know it sounds bad—me thinking of two women at the same time—but I couldn't help it. Both had played an important role in my life, and both relationships had ended abruptly and badly.

Kate remained foremost in my mind. We had dated twice as long and had developed a much more intimate relationship. Hannah, on the other hand, was the only person in the world besides my brother who knew what I really did for a living, and where I had been assigned.

Working from a ▇▇▇▇ (secret) site in Afghanistan sucked in terms of developing a relationship with a woman, or maintaining a social life. Not only were there extremes of heat and cold, sandstorms, unrelenting danger, and no female contact, but the local women I did have occasion to see in town were completely hidden under burkas.

During the small windows of time I was allotted to use the internet, I checked my Gmail and Skype. Because I was convinced they thought of me as a lunatic, or a complete clown for leaving so abruptly, I was too embarrassed to Skype with my parents or Kate. Instead, I sent them occasional e-mails.

When Skype was available, I'd ring Hannah and hope she was home. Her pretty if somewhat concerned-looking face was a welcome sight. I usually appeared wearing a *shalwar kameez* and caked in mud.

"Hey, Hannah, sorry I'm so goddamn dirty. We had another giant haboob today. Blacked out the sun for a good forty-five minutes. Couldn't see anything and almost collided with a jingle truck."

"You look tired, Doug. What's a jingle truck?"

"You look *real* good."

"Thanks. What's a jingle truck?"

"It's kind of like something a Walt Disney animator might imagine while he's on acid."

"What?"

"They're these colorfully painted trucks that look kind of psyche-delic and are tricked out with chains and pendants on the bumpers. They're driven by madmen with head wraps and used to transport people, produce, arms, and opium back and forth to Pakistan."

"Send me a picture of one when you get a chance."

"I will."

One thing I hadn't considered before my deployment was a living will. Now surrounded by Taliban, drug traffickers, Islamic terrorists, and Afghans who either hated Americans or would happily betray one at the right price, I realized it was probably a good idea. Hashing one out with my brother over Gmail was a strange experience. The following is one of the e-mails I sent him during this exchange:

Chad—Need you to print off this email and keep it in your safe. Cant have anything notarized by an attorney at this point because I cant provide enough personal info to make this a legal document. Just print it off and save it so that if some greedy fucking lawyers try to take my shit you can show this as evidence that I want it all to go to you. Sorry if this sucks to read, but if I end up getting killed you are on the books at work as my beneficiary. This means you will be getting a check for around ███████████ from the government. I also have accidental insurance so that's probably another ██████ way to predict how much I would have in my personal bank account but I did you a favor by making you a joint owner of the account which means you can take whatever you want out of it with no penalties. Other than that, all I have is in storage in the unit I gave you the key for so that shit is all yours as well if you want it. Also, not sure what the official process is of how they go about explaining things, but I requested mom and dad not be informed if I am killed. This means they will likely call you and only you. I guess I don't care much what you tell mom and dad about what I was doing since I wont be around anyhow, just give them a flag and tell them I'm sorry. Try and make sure you keep everything low key and don't go to any funeral service for me at my place of work. I don't want to be remembered for this job since no one knows I have it to begin with. Instead, please have my funeral at Holy Trinity and bury me in their graveyard with the rest of our family. Last, and I know this blows, but I would appreciate it if you kept it down to just you and your wife and mom and dad. I can imagine it would be hard on them if I get killed and they didn't even know I was here. Don't need people they've never met coming up to them and offering condolences. Anyhow, that's that. Sorry again for the depressing email. Thanks for always being my brother.

I don't know if it freaked him out, or he was too busy with his own life for it to really register. His two-word response was: "Got it."

7

COMMANDANT KHAN[12]

The risk of a wrong decision is preferable to the terror of indecision.

—MAIMONIDES

Fear runs deep throughout the Agency and inhabits every fiber of its soul. I started to see and sense that the first time I passed through the door. I saw it in the type of people they recruited, and the ideas that were drilled in our heads. It created a culture of risk aversion, which proved to be a huge impediment in the field.

It doesn't help that the Agency has become a media kick toy. One day you'll see some so-called expert calling us inhumane torturers on CNN, and the next some congressman who can't find Afghanistan on a map ranting about how we are incompetent. Conversely, conspiracy theorists worldwide talk about us as though we have omnipotent power. We're blamed for constantly screwing up, and for planning and carrying out the most complex and nefarious plots imaginable. It makes everyone inside defensive.

I arrived eager to get things done like officers had back in the fifties and sixties. What I found was an organization that was cautious and maddeningly bureaucratic.

---

[12] Commandant Khan is a made-up name. His description has been altered to preserve his anonymity.

It started with the kind of people they recruited and the Agency's outdated drug policy, which filtered out anyone who had ever smoked pot or taken illegal drugs. That immediately eliminated more than half of Americans in their early twenties. One recent survey conducted by Bowdoin College, in Maine, indicates that 73 percent of their students have smoked marijuana at least once. The 2009 CORE survey reported that slightly more than 53 percent of survey respondents said they believed the average college student used some form of illegal drug at least once a week.

According to CIA policy, anyone who has ever smoked marijuana in college or taken a bump of coke at a party isn't qualified for admission. When I was a member of a frat at the University of Indiana sitting in my room playing PlayStation in my spare time, all the guys around me smoked weed. Most of them were superpatriotic and smart.

It's easy to understand why a clandestine organization wouldn't want to employ drug addicts. But the Agency was eliminating a lot of good, adventurous, intelligent, and open-minded people. As a result, young recruits tended to be bland and squeaky clean. A majority of the people in my class were Mormons and fundamentalist Christians. They carried strict judgments about people with different beliefs and more permissive lifestyles. And they were generally not the kinds of people who would challenge the system or propose innovation.

When I looked around the larger Agency population, I saw very few Jews, Muslims, blacks, or Hispanics. Maybe tall blond-haired, blue-eyed people were ideal for ███████ assignments, but they weren't going to blend into the populations of the Middle East, Latin America, or Africa.

Before a potential candidate signed the SF-86 form giving the Agency the right to conduct a background investigation, they were warned that the penalty for lying could be up to thirty years in jail. And once offered employment you could be subjected to a polygraph test at any time. The Agency constantly reminds you that you're being watched. You take a hit of marijuana at a party or associate with the wrong people and you're out.

Young recruits live in fear of doing anything that might get them in trouble or dismissed. My first year at HQ, I started playing softball on the Mall in DC with some of my fellow trainees and started to collect money to join a league. One of the guys we played with went to the Agency regulations office and asked if that was okay. He was told: You can't combine ██████████████ employees in a team. It's forbidden.

I went to Regulations to ask for an explanation. I said, "This is silly. How are we going to operate clandestinely overseas if we can't make up a good cover story? We'll tell players on the other teams that we work at ██ ██████████."

The asshole I spoke to said, "Absolutely not. It's not permitted!"

When I threw parties at my apartment, fellow recruits were afraid to attend because booze was served and people sometimes got a little rowdy. Once I got called in and scolded for attending a movie with a colleague. The reason: We weren't supposed to be seen together.

Another time I got hold of a couple of Nationals tickets and wanted to take a colleague who was in language training. His teacher was sick, so he had the afternoon off. I said, "Come on, Jesse, you're free, so let's go to the game."

He answered, "No, the rules state that when I don't have language training, I have to go in to the office."

"And do what? Sit on your butt staring at a wall?"

He said, "I know they'll have nothing for me to do. But it's not worth throwing away my career."

People were afraid of stepping out of line and being terminated. They had no friends back home and rarely socialized. They were desperate to deploy overseas as quickly as possible so that they could have an ██████████ cover and enjoy a normal social life.

That same risk-averse mentality permeated everything from the way officers were deployed to bureaucratic hoops you had to jump through to get anything accomplished.

Once stationed at Wadi, in order to continue to meet with Abdul I had to fill out ███ forms that were reviewed by headquarters, DOJ, and the FBI. I always got a lot of whiny complaints and second-guessing from our legal department. They were afraid that something would result from our relationship that would get picked up by the press and give the Agency a black eye.

Running assets took a considerable amount of time. When I recruited a new one with ties to a terrorist network (like Abdul's ███ (relative) or Haji Jan), which you would think was something the Agency wanted, I was required to do about ███ days of paperwork to get the asset approved.

So much of my energy was devoted to covering the Agency's ass that it hindered progress. Additionally, the extensive paperwork and second-guessing from HQ acted as strong disincentives to recruit new assets. Because of the hassle you had to go through and the physical and organizational danger entailed in sticking your neck out, a lot of ops officers in the field got lazy and sloppy. They made little effort to recruit assets and they didn't bother to monitor or question the ones the Agency had been running for years.

Shortly after I arrived at Wadi, Afghans started to come in to sell information. A lot of what they had to offer was one-off type of stuff regarding names of individuals who were members of the Taliban, or Taliban fighters.

There was a group of ten to fifteen guys who had been doing this for years, selling names of people they claimed had carried out attacks against American soldiers. It was small-time stuff, for which they would receive ███ per name.

I would always ask them, How do you know about this?

A typical answer was: I heard it during my travels. Or, My son found out from one of his friends.

The information wasn't of great value, but it could provide a military target, or serve as a piece of a larger picture. The problem was that it was hard to ascertain if these guys were telling the truth.

Someone would report a name of a Talib who had participated in an ambush of American soldiers—say, someone named Mohammed Rasul.[13] I would report this to the J2 military intel officer on our base. He would respond, "Mohammed Rasul. Yeah, we've heard of him. We'll put him on our ███████████ list."

One day, three weeks into my time at Wadi, a young man I'd never seen before came in to sell information. During the course of our conversation, I asked if he'd ever heard of Mohammed Rasul.

He said, "Yes. Everybody knows about him."

"Why?" I asked.

"Because his name was reported on the radio."

He informed me that the local Afghan radio stations in the area regularly broadcast the names of individuals the US military wanted information about in relation to particular attacks. Our military counterparts had neglected to tell us at the Agency that they were doing this, and the practice had been going on for years.

I sent my handyman out to buy me a transistor radio. That night I sat on the roof and listened to a local news report. Sure enough, the US military issued an announcement asking for information on certain suspected Taliban terrorists.

So I met with the dozen or so guys who had been selling names they got from the radio for years and told them I was in onto their game.

Then I sent out a message to our other Agency ██████ informing them of this practice and recommending that they have their terps listen to the local radio news broadcasts to find out if this was going on at their ██████ too. I heard back from a number of them telling me that it was. In some cases, it had been going on for as long as ██████ years.

I blamed two things: a bureaucratic culture that discouraged developing new assets, and a lack of Pashtu-speaking officers in the field.

Our Wadi chief of base (COB), whom I'll call Nealy,[14] returned in

---

[13] Mohammed Rasul is a made-up name. His description has been altered to preserve his anonymity.

[14] Nealy is a made-up name. His description has been altered to preserve his anonymity.

mid-February. He was a friendly officer in his mid-forties and had spent his whole career in Europe. He had no experience in Afghanistan and little familiarity with the culture, couldn't speak the local language, and refused to attend the *shuras*.

What did interest him was running our small base and issuing rules. The first was that all work was to cease on Thursday night at 2100 and not resume until 1300 on Friday. He did this in order to appear politically correct and abide by the schedule adhered to by our Afghan guards and cooks. Friday was their holy day, and Thursday night was reserved for gathering with family and friends.

(This has to do with a rule about weapons.)

Lolita teased me, saying, "Dude, you don't know how to use it anyway."

"Then what was the purpose of my fucking weapons training?"

Hillbilly cracked, "I can nail a fly on a wall at a hundred feet. You'd be lucky to even hit the wall."

"Not true. Don't forget, I'm just as redneck as you, Hillbilly. I've been firing pistols since I was eleven."

The third rule pissed me off even more. Any communication that left the base had to be cleared by Chief Nealy. In my opinion, he did this in order to guard against anything that cast him in a negative light. The effect was to slow all outgoing e-mails while he reviewed them and sometimes sent them back with revisions. I alone was sending out over thirty e-mails a day.

Shortly after I met Abdul, he said, "I got a call from someone you've probably heard of, Commandant Khan."

I'd heard that Commandant Khan was reputed to be a top Taliban commander in the South.

"What did he want?" I asked.

"He got my number and told me to stop attending the *shura* meetings, because he heard there was someone who was showing up who was half Afghan." Abdul laughed and added, "People know who you are."

I liked that people had heard about me and considered me half Afghan.

"What did you say back?" I asked.

"I told him that the half Afghan is named Zmarai, and he pays money for information about the Taliban. I told him that if he was smart, he would work with you, too."

"What did he say to that?"

"He doesn't want to risk being detained," Abdul answered. "He knows that his name is on a ███████ list because he's been hitting US military targets for the last five years."

I said, "Give me his number. I'll find out where he is, and if he's close, we'll wrap him up."

███

██ and, therefore, out of reach. So I decided to call him directly. He answered on the third ring.

"Yes?"

"Commandant Khan, it's the half Afghan you were talking about with Abdul. My name is Zmarai."

"Zmarai, yes. I know who you are. We are enemies." He spoke Pashtu so fast that I had to summon Jon to help me.

With Jon's aid, the Taliban commander and I engaged in a verbal chess match, feeling each other out. I was careful not to reveal what we didn't know.

At the end he said, "I have your phone number, Zmarai. If I hear where a Taliban unit is located, I'll give you a call. But I need money."

"I have money," I replied. "Call me."

He did, several times during the next week, and the chess match continued. One day Khan said that he knew where a certain Taliban unit was located. They weren't members of his faction, so he didn't care if they were killed.

I gathered from listening to him that the Taliban was unified in terms of gaining territory and currently dominated all of southern Afghanistan. But now that they had it under their control, all bets were off and individual tribal rivalries had kicked in. Khan thought that by working with me he could accomplish two things at once: make money, and eliminate some of his competition in the South.

Khan was willing to exchange Taliban troop and arms locations for money. Now the question was who was going to provide first. Was he going to give me the information, or was I going to front the cash?

██

██
██

██████████ (I can't tell you how, but we worked out a scenario for me to deliver money.)

My question for Jon and Abdul was: Do you think Commandant Khan will deliver his side of the bargain?

Both men agreed that Khan was motivated by greed, and would therefore come through.

Before I could execute anything, I had to get approval from headquarters. When I e-mailed them, their first response was "He's got to provide the intel first."

I e-mailed back a long explanation of why we should take the first step. Someone at HQ e-mailed back, "Why do we even want to work with him?"

"Are you serious?" I wrote in my response. "The guy commands ▮▮▮ men in the South who are constantly launching strikes against us and planting IEDs."

"That's precisely why we can't work with him," someone at Langley replied.

"No, that's why we need to engage him and try to flip him," I argued. "If we don't succeed in turning him, we have his cell-phone number, ▮▮▮▮▮▮▮▮▮▮▮▮▮▮▮▮▮▮▮▮▮▮▮▮▮▮. In the meantime, we'll learn how his network works."

HQ remained skeptical.

I explained that every time one of Khan's men snuck across the border in the middle of the night and planted IEDs around our base, we lost human lives. And every time a mine-resistant, ambush-protected vehicle was hit it cost us ▮▮▮▮▮▮ to repair the roller. I guaranteed that I could destroy Khan on a budget of ▮▮▮▮▮▮.

After more haggling back and forth, the money and program were approved by HQ. ▮▮

I put ▮▮▮▮ in a sealed envelope and gave it to Abdul, who gave it to ▮▮▮▮▮▮▮▮▮▮▮▮▮▮▮▮▮▮▮. Several hours later, Khan called to tell me where some IEDs had been placed.

I rushed out there with a military team, and sure enough the IEDs were exactly where he said they would be. I thought, *Great! For* ▮▮▮▮ *we saved ourselves a minimum of* ▮▮▮▮▮▮ *and possibly some soldiers' lives.*

A week later, we executed another ▮▮▮▮▮▮. In response, Commandant Khan told me about an upcoming ambush on a US military convoy. Based on that intel, the military flanked the area where the Taliban had set up, and destroyed them.

The next two ▮▮▮▮▮▮▮▮ yielded two more IED sites, which

were then cleared. Over about five weeks of us talking back and forth, Khan's information started to peter out. I thought to myself, *Okay, it's time to zero in on this guy and eliminate him.*

Commandant Khan continued calling three times a week. During one of our conversations, he asked for ███████████ (a present).

██
██
███████████████████████████████████
██
██
███████████████████
███
███
█████████████
███
███
█████████

Later, that night Commandant Khan called and said, "I got ████████. Thanks. This is really going to help me to fight you guys."

████████████ ████ █████ ████████████
██████ ██████████████████

The dirtbag SOB was undercutting his fellow Taliban, taking my money, and still had the nerve to threaten me.

I started to ███████████████████. Every place he visited, I'd send Abdul or his ████████ to check it out. They came back with names and locations of madrassas, arms factories, and Taliban safe houses. With the help of ████████████, we mapped out the entire Taliban network in ████████████.

Khan called one afternoon and started to brag. He said, "I just conducted an attack on the Afghan army, killed ████████████ soldiers, and disabled all their Ranger trucks."

"Where did this happen?" I asked.

He had the audacity to tell me. I jumped in the Land Cruiser with the armed Scorpions and drove out to take a look. There had been an ambush and several trucks were stolen, but the number of Afghan army casualties was considerably lower than Khan claimed.

I dutifully wrote up the incident and sent it to HQ. They went nuts.

I was ordered to stop talking to Khan. Still, he kept phoning every day for the next two weeks. One morning when he called, I answered and he immediately started berating me for not picking up my phone. He threatened to end our relationship if I didn't give him ▮▮▮▮▮ immediately.

I said, "Okay. Let's end it."

"I will kill you, Zmarai."

"You first."

It was a threat I took seriously. ▮▮▮▮▮▮▮▮▮▮▮▮

(Note: I tried to locate Commandant Khan and eliminate him from the battlefield, but I am not allowed to talk about how.)

I wanted to punch someone in the face. HQ had terminated the op, not me. ▮▮▮▮▮▮▮▮▮▮▮

██

█████████████████

It was added incentive to do nothing. Once you launched an op or recruited an asset and something went wrong, your head was on the chopping block.

Agency policies and attitudes were counterproductive. It was one of the reasons we were losing the war.

STONE FIREBASE[15]

Afghanistan is more than the "graveyard of empires." It's the mother of vicious circles.

—Maureen Dowd

One morning four months into my stay at Wadi Base, I returned covered with sweat and dust from the shooting range. ███████ ███████ Dirt and cordite clogged my nostrils, and my arms were shaking. As I walked down the hallway of our base to the shower, Chief Nealy called me into his office/prison cell.

"Doug, come in here for a minute," he said, wearing his usual sandals and shorts.

"What's up, Chief?" I asked, removing my goggles.

He eased his big body back in his chair and said, "I've just been talking to COPs back in Kabul."

COPs was what we called the chief of operations for all of Afghanistan. Nealy and COPs had spent most of their careers in Europe and were buddies. Though he hadn't made a great first impression, I didn't have much experience with COPs at the time.

---

[15] Stone Firebase is a made-up name for a base that no longer exists. During the time it was in operation it was written about in detail in several articles, including ███████████████████████. It's also described on Wikipedia.

Nealy, though somewhat lazy and careful, and at the twilight of his career, had been kind enough to look after me. He saw I was full-throttle and liked that about me.

"Yeah?"

"I have a chance of a lifetime for you, Doug. Get excited."

He had my full attention. "What's cookin', Chief?"

"How do you feel about going to Stone Firebase?"

Stone Firebase had the reputation of being the most dangerous place in Afghanistan. It sat spitting distance away from the ███████ border and received Taliban mortar and rocket fire practically every night. Its position was so precarious that it had been opened and shut something like four times by the Afghans, the US Marines, and Special Forces. As a result of the 2010 surge, it had recently reopened as a CIA base and was guarded by our internal Special Forces Ground Branch (GB) and Afghan Counterterrorism Pursuit Teams (CTPTs).[16]

"Hell, yeah," I responded. "I'd consider it an honor to go there. What's the story?"

"Our guys there need your Pashtu skills," Nealy answered. "As I said before, it will be really good for your career. Everything that you report back will be read on the seventh floor at HQ. You've only been in field four months and this will be a huge opportunity, because just between you and me, Stone is focused on some high-profile AQ targets."

Even though I was already sold, Nealy kept up the pitch.

"Imagine every cable you write starting like this: CO Smith, under operational alias Zmarai, met with his big-name AQ source and communicated in Pashtu independent of a terp. Pretty fucking excellent, right?"

---

[16] For more on the CIA's Counterterrorism Pursuit Teams see "How the CIA ran a secret army of 3,000 assassins," *The Independent,* September 23, 2010. The Afghanistan Analysts Notebook also provides a wealth of info on the CTPTs in an online article published on April 28, 2013. The CTPTs are also mentioned in a story in the *New York Times,* "U.S. Military Seeks to Expand Raids in Pakistan," published December 20, 2010.

"Absolutely." Like all young officers on their first assignment, I wanted to make a positive impression and be noticed by the seventh floor.

"Well you're going to be writing that, and I'm going to make sure that it's released by COPs."

"Cool. But what about the guys I'm currently running here at Wadi?" My one concern was the assets I'd developed, including Abdul and Haji Jan.

"Call your guys and tell them to take a paid vacation for the next two or three weeks," Nealy answered. "I need you to leave immediately."

"Chief, I'm all in."

"Good, I'll get back to COPs and tell him you're excited. If you weren't, I was going to force you to go there anyway. Arrangements have already been made. There's a helo coming in to get you tomorrow night."

Turns out Stone, though only ███████████████████, was a bitch to get to. The roads were too dangerous to travel, so I took a helo ride to Kandahar, and spent twenty-four hours there before boarding a prop flight to Khowst, ████ of Stone.

Back in December, after the suicide bombing, I had expected to be assigned to Khowst. It felt weird to finally enter the base where those nine brave officers had died. The four Scorpions who were on the flight with me felt it, too.

I could tell from the deferential way they communicated with the logs (logistics) lady who greeted us and showed us to our bunks. Usually Scorpions were cocky as hell when they landed at a base and encountered a female. You could expect them to say things like: What the fuck's up? We're in the house. Show me to my room, and let's get the party started.

But upon arrival at Khowst, they were solemn, and said, "Yes, ma'am. And thanks for showing me to my room."

Shortly after ████████ I caught a solo helo ride to Stone. As soon as we touched down, I heard guys outside screaming at me, "Run! Run! Move, motherfucker. Sprint!"

There was dust everywhere. Through it, I made out Toyota Hilux trucks and heavily armed Ground Branch officers. They moved like lightning, unloading ▓▓▓▓▓▓▓▓ of gear from the helo to the trucks in less than ▓▓▓▓▓▓.

Before I had a chance to say anything, I was pushed into one of the trucks, which tore off at high speed. The helo lifted off. The ground shook.

"Welcome to Stone," one of the GB guys muttered. GB officers constituted the main force at Stone and were selected from among the baddest-ass military units—SEALs, Marine Force Recon, Air Force Parajumpers, and the Army's Combat Applications Group (formerly know as Delta Force). They wore civilian clothes and were equipped with the most advanced light weaponry on the planet.[17]

We were flying over a gravel road at eighty miles an hour. Through the swirling dust, I spotted a tall watchtower ahead and the walls of the base. A firefight was in full heat. I saw tracer rounds ripping off and zipping into the surrounding mountains.

"The CTPTs are getting their motherfucking slay on tonight," noted the GB driver nonchalantly, spitting tobacco into an empty can of Coke.

We zoomed in the gate through coils of razor wire and mounds of sandbags. The whole base was mad with energy. Fifty-cals clanged. Rockets and mortars tore into the night sky.

Holy shit! I said to myself, adrenaline coursing through my veins.

I had read reports and heard stories, and had mentally prepared myself. Now I was actually here and it was fucking awesome.

The base itself was super small and built like an old-style fortress with mud and concrete walls. On first impression, it reminded me of a Wild West outpost or like the Alamo. One of its former US commanders had dubbed it "the evilest place in Afghanistan."

---

[17] The recruitment, training, and various missions of CIA Special Activities Division Ground Branch officers has been described in detail in various print and online sites, including Wikipedia.

A sand-colored hundred-foot-long one-story building served as the Agency headquarters. Surrounding it was a maze of concrete and mud houses where the CTPTs lived. All the buildings had been hardened to withstand incoming mortar rounds and rockets, which they regularly had to do.[18]

We pulled up to the Agency spaces, and the GB guy in the passenger seat punched a code into the cipher-locked door and showed me in. I dropped my bag in the little lobby, which contained a couple of beat-up couches, and took a breath.

He asked, "Do you know who you're meeting with?"

"Yeah, I'm meeting with the chief. Don't know his name though."

There were cipher-coded doors to my right and left. The one to the right led to the workstations. The one to the left opened on the living quarters.

"Stone is pretty gangster, huh?" the GB dude said as he showed me to my bunk. When I asked him what he meant, he said nonstop action and no women.

In my four months at a forward base, I'd found the few women there to be a source of tension. Most of the guys, including me, were too occupied with work and staying alive to have much of a libido. But the Scorpions and GB guys certainly did. When there was a woman around, they wanted to know who was sleeping with her currently, and started plotting their moves so they could fuck her next.

The GB guy showing me around gave me the code to the workplace keypad. I opened the door, entered the bullpen office area, and immediately recognized three guys I knew from training. Since all of us had been given pseudonyms the day we entered service, none of us knew the others' real names. That, combined with the fact that officers moved so frequently, made it difficult to keep track of where particular people were at any given time.

---

[18] This is open-source material found in various publications, including on Wikipedia.

I high-fived my three buddies and shouted, "No fucking way!"

They hadn't heard that I was coming and shouted back, "What the fuck are you doing here?"

My friends had started to introduce me to the one officer in the bullpen I didn't know when I heard someone from behind a partition say, "I thought I heard a familiar voice."

It was another buddy of mine, Rick G., who was currently the head of GB at Stone. We'd entered the Agency together even though Rick was twelve years older than me. Because of his Special Forces background, he'd deployed to Afghanistan ███████████ of transferring to GB. Prior to that he'd been in Afghanistan since █ with ███████. He knew his way around, to say the least.

We stood yucking it up. I said, "Holy shit, I know everyone here."

So far the only two guys I hadn't met before were the chief and some guy who was running a special program, which I understood not to ask about.

Rick asked, "Have you met the chief yet?"

"No."

He showed me to an office. Sitting there was Ken Stowe, who had been the chief of a ████████ facility I had trained at.

"What the fuck!" I exclaimed.

He stood, shook my hand, and said, "When I saw your pseudo, I thought, I've seen that pseudo before. But I couldn't place it."

"This is great!"

"Your chief at Wadi speaks highly of you," Stowe said.

It was good to hear.

"He says you're really turning it out. What's this I hear about you speaking Pashtu?"

"Yeah, pretty rad, huh?"

"Close the door, take a load off your feet, and I'll tell you what I want you to do."

He had an iPod dock on his desk that was blaring "You Belong to Me" by Taylor Swift. This was remarkable for two reasons. One:

According to common practice, nothing that could be used to record information—i.e., cell phones, iPods, tape recorders, laptops—was allowed into a station. But Chief Stowe didn't give a shit, which I respected.

And, two: The song was by Taylor Swift, not Metallica or Korn, which would have been more in line with the spirit of Stone. Stowe explained that his daughter had downloaded her playlists for him the last time he was home on R&R.

"How's your Pashtu?" he asked.

"It should be okay," I replied. "I was trained in the northern dialect, which should pass well here."

"Good, before we get you in the weeds, I want you to attend meetings with your buddies and their sources and say nothing. Just sit and listen, and vet how carefully the terps are translating everything."

I was somewhat confused. "Where are your terps from?" I asked.

"The local area."

"Chief, if they're locals, they know the dialect a hell of a lot better than me. *De mor jibbay.* It's their mother tongue."

"Doesn't matter," he said. "Just sit and listen."

I was disappointed. "Is that the reason you called me here, to check on the terps?"

Chief Stowe shook his head. "I'm working on something else," he answered. "For the next week, I want you to sit, listen, and observe. Tell me what you see. Let me know if the terps are making any of our assets uncomfortable."

"All right. Cool."

When I told my buddies that I would be tagging along to their meetings, they asked, Why? What's going on?

Even though we were friends, I could tell the prospect of me sitting in on their meetings made them uncomfortable. Handling assets involved creating an atmosphere of mutual respect and trust. So I understood why they wouldn't want another person present.

I met the two terps, but didn't tell them I spoke Pashtu. One of them was a skinny young kid; the other was stocky and in his forties. I instructed them to tell the assets that I was an officer visiting from DC and wanted to meet them.

The meetings I attended went well, and I quickly learned two things. One, my understanding of the local Pashtu dialect was much better than it had been at Wadi. If I was getting 60 percent of what I heard there, I comprehended 90 percent in Stone. Two, the terps were translating everything with accuracy.

I reported this to Chief Stowe when I sat with him in his office six days later.

"Good," he said, pulling a bottle of Johnnie Walker out of his desk drawer and pouring me a shot. It was the first time I'd touched booze since my arrival in Afghanistan and it was rough going down.

I coughed and the chief laughed. As he poured me another shot, his expression turned serious.

"It sounds like the terps are fine," he said. "That's reassuring. Now I'm going to tell you what I really need you for."

I was all ears.

Chief Stowe said, "I'm personally running a source, who is probably our most important source in all Afghanistan. He's been working with us for three years and has helped us eliminate about a ███████████ ███████████ in al-Qaeda. He's not with al-Qaeda, but rubs shoulders with them, because he's a popular tribal chief across the border on ███████████. We call him Converse,[19] and I'm afraid we might have a problem."

"What?"

"He claims that he was recently meeting with some AQ fighters and one of them said something that could have only come from this base. The only people who leave the base and go into town are the terps and CTPTs. The latter aren't privy to sensitive information. So maybe one

---

[19] Converse is a made-up name. His description has been altered to preserve his anonymity.

of the terps went into town and said something to his wife that was passed around. I don't know."

I knew that there was no point polygraphing the terps, because Afghans had a tendency to lie about everything including their age, especially when they were talking to foreigners.

Chief Stowe reiterated that, saying, "If I polygraph the terps and they fail, I'll have to ████████████, which I don't want to do."

"How can I help?" I asked.

"It would be nice if I could transfer you here and you could run Converse yourself so we wouldn't need a terp."

I was totally up for that, but Stowe said it wasn't possible. He suggested instead that I come up to Stone when needed.

"I'm cool with that," I said.

"Well good, because guess what? We have ██████ coming up, so we need you now."

He named a guy in al-Qaeda (code name Scimitar[20]) who was considered the number-three man in the area, and told me that Converse had a relative who had gotten close to him. The problem was that Converse had some concerns about coming back to Stone.

The last time he was there, he handed the chief a note explaining what had happened and why he was concerned. Chief Stowe, who couldn't speak or read Pashtu, gave the note to one of the terps. At which point, Converse ripped the note back and said, "I don't want him to read it."

The day after my confab with the chief, Converse called. Again the chief used one of the terps to translate, whereupon Converse got upset and said he wouldn't come to a meeting at the base.

The terp told Converse that he wouldn't be translating the meeting, because the Americans had brought in an American who spoke Pashtu. When Converse heard this, he agreed to come in.

That morning, which marked my seventh day in Stone, I woke with cramping in my lower abdomen. Later, as I ran on a treadmill, my stom-

---

[20] This is a name that I made up for this book and not the real code name.

ach started to ache. I figured I had eaten something that didn't agree with me.

The following morning when I got up to urinate, my dick burned. Returning to bed, I saw a dark red stain on the sheets the size of a basketball. I thought to myself, *Holy shit! Have I been shot?*

But when I examined by body, there were no cuts. The only part of me that was sore was my dick, which had turned bright red. Even the pain in my lower abdomen was gone. I tried not to freak out, reasoning with myself that maybe I had passed a kidney stone.

Later, as I was sitting in the office writing a report, I felt liquid dripping out of my penis. I returned to my bunk, wrapped toilet paper around it, and hoped it would stop.

When I checked again at lunchtime, the toilet paper was soaked with blood. So I found the chief and asked, "What do you guys do if you think you ate something that's making you sick?"

He said, "There's an 18-Delta guy"—a field medic—"who has medicine for that. You'll find him at the field hospital, which is a pretty high-tech operation, because guys are getting shot here all the time."

I tracked down the 18-Delta medic later that night. He examined me and said, "I'm not a doctor, so I don't know what it is. But anytime you're leaking fluids, it's not a good sign. Don't drink alcohol or caffeine, and no PT, and come back to see me tomorrow."

The next evening Converse was scheduled to arrive. Usually, he visited ███████, but hadn't been to the base in ███████ because of the flap. I spent the day huddled with the terps practicing my Pashtu, and practicing mentally. I felt it was important that I put Converse at ease.

Scheduled to attend the meeting were Chief Stowe, myself, the secret squirrel officer from Special Activities (SA), and an intel guy from the ODA (Operational Detachment Alpha—Special Forces). The SA officer met Converse at the gate, searched him thoroughly, then escorted him to the meeting room—an Afghan-style hut containing sofas and chairs.

Converse was there when I arrived with Chief Stowe and the ODA officer. His appearance shocked me. I had pictured a vital-looking badass. Instead, I greeted a rail-thin man with a scraggly white beard who appeared to be about ninety years old and on the verge of crumbling into dust. I thought to myself, *This is the guy who's been taking down all the AQ big shots? He's got some stones.*

I sat and recited a typical Pashtu greeting: *"Assalam alaykum. Tsinga yay? Jor yay? Koranai kha dee? Ahamdillah. Zmaa noom Zmarai dai."* (Peace be with you. How are you? Are you healthy? Is your family healthy? Thanks be to God. My name is Zmarai.)

Converse threw his head back and cackled.

I continued, "Before we begin, I want to make sure that you understand my Pashtu, because I've been spending a lot of time in the South and now have *de janoobi jibbay,* the southern tongue. If you do not understand me at any point, please stop me by raising your hand. Thanks be to God my ears are good but sometimes my tongue is slow."

Converse, who was sitting on the sofa beside me, leaned over and took my hand. He placed his other hand over his heart and said, "Brother, I cannot tell you how happy my heart is that you're here."

Continuing to hold my hand, he said, "I have been waiting for this day for a long time, and have wondered why the *harajan* have not sent someone like you to work with me until now. I have had to deal with the locals, and I do not want to work with them anymore."

Chief Stowe and the other two Americans looked on with surprise at the two of us grinning at one another like long-lost friends.

"What's he telling you? Is he proposing?" the chief asked.

"He's very happy I'm here, and wants to make sure I'm at all our meetings."

"Is that why you two are holding hands?"

"Yes."

"Thank God." Chief Stowe laughed.

Converse was happy to finally be communicating directly with an American, and I was pleased that I understood everything he said. My

Pashtu instructor who hailed from ▇▇▇▇▇▇▇▇ (a nearby city) would be proud.

"Looks like you're going to be coming to Stone a lot," said the chief.

I translated his comment to Converse, who nodded vigorously and laughed. The vibe was terrific.

Converse said, "My cousin's ▇▇▇▇ has gotten close to Scimitar. He has studied his pattern of movement and knows his plans." He spoke like a CO, talking ▇▇▇▇▇▇▇▇▇▇▇▇▇▇▇▇▇▇▇▇▇▇ ▇▇▇▇▇▇▇▇▇▇▇▇▇▇▇▇▇▇▇▇▇▇▇▇▇▇▇ ▇ and had people tailing him wherever he went. He also made it clear that he hated al-Qaeda and what they were doing and wanted them all dead.

I was impressed.

He said, "We are very close. In the next week or two, Scimitar will be attending a wedding in ▇▇▇▇▇▇▇▇▇▇▇▇▇▇▇▇ ▇▇▇▇▇ I'll find out where he is sleeping and we will destroy him there."

I was so wrapped up in the moment, I didn't realize that we were talking about killing someone. What I was aware of was the blood dripping from my penis down my right leg and into my boot.

Chief Stowe said, "Tell Converse that we have to do this while you're still here. Let's do it this week if we can."

Converse replied, "I will try to do it within the next week, but it will probably be two."

The chief handed Converse several ▇▇▇▇▇▇▇▇; then Converse thanked me again and left. Whereupon Chief Stowe turned to me and said, "Doug, that was impressive. I'm going to go to my office now and write up the report."

It was three in the morning by the time I returned to my room and found my underpants caked with blood. The next morning when I awoke, the mattress and sheets had turned dark red. When I examined my dick I saw that the lining of my urethra was hanging out of my pee hole. I started to panic.

When the 18-Delta examined it, he said, "Dude, this is fucked up.

You must have something bad in your urethra, which is causing you to lose a lot of blood. If you don't want to lose your dick, we'd better get you to Kabul ASAP."

That night I told Chief Stowe about my medical dilemma. He said, "Let's get you out of here on the next helo, so you can get healed up and back as soon as possible."

The next three days Stone was under nonstop attack from the Taliban, which made it too dangerous for a helicopter to land. The exploding mortars and rockets didn't bother me as much as the fact that I was bleeding nonstop, the lining of my dick was hanging out, and it was almost impossible to urinate.

After three days of mental and physical anguish, a helo finally ferried me to Kabul, where a doctor in a Hawaiian shirt examined me. "Friend," he said, "I don't know what the fuck this is. We've got to get you on a flight back to DC so you can be examined by a urologist."

Not exactly what I wanted to hear.

Two days later, I stood in the bathroom of a 747 trying to urinate and feeling like my bladder was going to explode. As people pounded on the door wanting to get in, my belly screamed and my mind was spinning thoughts of my imminent death.

It just so happened that my buddy Ben Z. was back in DC on R&R. I called him as soon as the eighteen-hour flight ended and asked him to drive me to the ER at Reston Hospital Center, which is close to Dulles Airport. A doctor examined me, then inserted a catheter in my dick to drain out the urine.

Feeling greatly relieved, I spent the night drinking beer and smoking cigars with Ben. If I was going to punch out from a dick disease, I might as well go on my terms. The next morning I was examined by the urologist, Dr. Greenberg, who said, "You've got a bad infection. We're going to have to perform surgery on your dick tomorrow and clean it out."

All I could say in response was "Fuck."

I was sitting on the examining table, stroking my foot-long beard, hoping it was all a nightmare, when Dr. Greenberg asked, "What do you do for a living?"

"I work for ███████████████████."

The doctor thought I had an STD. He said, "If you banged a prostitute in Bangkok or some other place, that's fine. Don't worry. We'll save you. But I need to know where you've been so I can diagnose this."

I told him I'd spent the last four months in Afghanistan.

He shook his head and said, "That makes it worse, because we don't have extensive medical data on their diseases. You could have eaten something, or consumed tainted water, or you could have gotten it from having sex."

"Doc, I haven't been with a woman the whole time I've been there and I'm not banging the goats, so it's not that."

First thing the next morning, they knocked me out, sliced open my dick, and cleaned out the infection. Then they closed me up with internal stitches, gave me some medicine, and informed me that I was going to pee the color orange for a week.

That night when Dr. Greenberg stopped in my room to see how I was doing, I asked him to close the door and said, "Here's the deal, Doc. I have to get back to work. How stressful will it be for me to work in this condition?"

He answered, "You should probably stay off your feet for the next three or four days."

"Negative. I need to catch a flight back to Afghanistan tomorrow."

"I advise you to stay home and rest for a week."

"Circumstances at work won't allow that."

He frowned and asked, "Who is your employer again?"

███████████████

"All I can say is, you've got more zeal than any ███████████ person I've ever met."

"Thanks," I said. "I'll wear that as a badge of honor."

He grinned and said, "I can't tell you what to do. If you have to go back, continue to take the medicine with the understanding that if you pop a stitch it's going to hurt like the fire of a thousand suns burning inside your cock. And if the infection returns, we'll have to open you up again."

"I definitely don't want that to happen."

"Neither do I." He smiled, draped an arm across my shoulder, and said, "Hey, thanks for doing what you're doing for us out there, and good luck."

I teared up. "Thanks, Doc."

Dr. Greenberg's last words to me were "Stay safe and stop fucking goats."

9

BOB

War is life multiplied by some number that no one has ever heard of.

—Sebastian Junger

The next day I boarded a flight to Kabul. Three days later I was back at Stone, feeling better and very relieved that my equipment was intact. Chief Stowe informed me that I had returned just in time, because Converse was scheduled to meet with us the following day.

As I sat prepping, one of the GB guys—a tatted muscular dude named Wade—walked up to me and asked if I'd like to rip off some rounds with the CTPTs.

"Sure," I answered, jumping at the opportunity to blow off steam.

"You ever fire an AK?" he asked.

"Yeah absolutely, but not as much as I'd like."

"Then this is your lucky day."

We climbed into a Hilux truck with a couple more GBers and a visiting accountant from Finance and drove to the shooting range, which was set up in a dried-out riverbed. Another truckload of CTPTs followed.

Everyone at Stone, including the commo guys and clerks, had to be ███████ and ████ qualified. But most of them had never fired Russian weapons like an AK-47, a Makarov pistol, or a PKM machine gun. I had, and took the opportunity to show off for the CTPTs. When I fired an

AK one-handed and miraculously hit a target at a hundred yards, the Afghans hooted and shouted.

It was a lucky shot that I couldn't repeat in a thousand tries. When I fired the PKM machine gun mounted on the back of a Hilux, a round jammed in the barrel, which was dangerous because it could have exploded in my face. Wade examined the weapon and declared the round faulty. Then he informed me that they were getting rid of the ammo because it was ███████████ and not dependable.

Thanks, Wade, for not telling me before.

The GBs had also brought a box of grenades. Wade said, "Let's get rid of these bad boys, too."

They were different sizes and configurations. "What's this?" I asked, picking one up.

"That's a fragmentary."

I threw it over a mound of dirt and covered my ears. *Bo-oom!*

Wade turned to the accountant from Finance and offered him a grenade. "You want to throw one of these?"

"Sure," the nerdy-looking guy answered.

He struggled with the pin, so Wade pulled it for him. But when the accountant threw it, he tossed it like a girl, and the BB grenade landed barely six feet away.

Wade screamed, "Get down!"

Another GB shouted, "What's your problem, dude? Didn't you ever throw a baseball before?"

Ka-plow!

Wade, who was hugging the ground in front of me, flinched and groaned.

"You hit?" I asked.

BBs had struck from the middle of his back to his thighs. Wade, being the badass he was, climbed back in the truck and drove back. The Finance guy beside him looked as white as a ghost.

Wade turned to him and growled, "At least you didn't shoot me, kid."

The rest of us in the Hilux laughed. That night as Chief Stowe and I went to meet Converse, the 18-Delta was removing pellets from Wade's ass.

Converse had come prepared, and provided us with the precise location ███████████████ where the AQ target was going to be staying the next two days while he attended a wedding. ████████████ ████████████████████████████ He told us that he'd text us *73 when Scimitar arrived at the location.

"The rest is on you," he said.

The next day at six p.m. he texted *73. ████████████████ ███████ Twenty minutes after that, Converse confirmed that Scimitar had been killed. ████████████████████████████ ████████████████████████████████

Chief Stowe waved me into his office and handed me a cigar. "Good job, Mr. Zmarai, and thanks a lot for coming. You're going to be shit hot now because Converse loves you and only wants to talk to you."

I returned to Wadi feeling pretty good about myself, but also having second thoughts about playing a role in killing someone. At the time of the kill, I was enthusiastic about taking Scimitar out. He had helped ██ ████████████████████████████████ ███████████. So fuck him, he was a terrorist and now he was dead.

But the more I thought about it, the more it struck me that we had gotten zero intel from icing Scimitar. Wouldn't it have been much better to capture and interrogate him? That way we could have learned about future AQ plans and foiled upcoming attacks. Better yet, what if we had tried to turn him?

Sure, it might not have worked. But as I was learning from the assets I had been developing in Wadi, anything was possible in this area of the world. Even die-hard Taliban commanders and religious leaders were willing to sell info for money. So why not try to develop a source network within AQ?

My thinking quickly ran into two bureaucratic dead ends. First, Agency rules made it next to impossible to ████ a source who was classified as a terrorist or a known enemy combatant. So even if Scimitar had been willing to work with Converse or someone connected to him, we wouldn't have been able to reciprocate, because Scimitar had directed attacks against the United States. And, second, an executive order signed by President Obama on January 22, 2009, banned the Agency from using what were called enhanced interrogation techniques (EITs), including waterboarding, hypothermia, and slapping.

I had seen the intel produced from using EITs on captured terrorists and knew that it had helped us disable AQ and stop numerous attacks. ███████████████████████ with the ban, many people found EITs morally reprehensible. For political reasons it wasn't going to be revoked.

Maybe Scimitar would have spilled his guts under approved interrogation techniques. It's possible he had a son, daughter, or other relative who needed medical help or was severely in debt, and we could have traded for information. Maybe we could have gotten in his head and learned about AQ's strategy, plans, and coordination. Maybe not. Either way, none of that was going to happen now that he was dead.

A few weeks after my return to Wadi, Chief Nealy walked into my office and asked, "You got a second, Markhor?" (Markhor was my radio call sign.)

"Sure. What's up?"

Nealy said, "I wanted to let you know that you don't have to go to Stone anymore."

"Why not? I thought Converse wanted to work with me."

"Converse is dead," Nealy said.

"Oh, fuck."

"You're not going to believe this, but he was killed by ████████ ████████."

"How?" I asked. "Did he shoot him?"

"No. Converse was at a market buying apples and this █████████ wearing a suicide vest went up to him, hugged him, and detonated."

"Fuck." I sank into my chair trying to come to terms with the sick

fact that a ▮▮▮▮▮▮▮▮ had been trained and selected to take someone's life.

"I know," Chief Nealy added. "I've never heard of anything like that
before."

Fucking IEDs again, I said to myself. IEDs were killing hundreds of
American and ISAF soldiers, and hundreds more Afghan police, military, and civilians. An IED worn by an AQ triple agent had killed nine
CIA employees in Khowst in January. Now an IED had killed our best
source in Afghanistan.

The experience with Converse had taught me that it was possible
to run a network of sources deep into ▮▮▮▮▮▮ and into the heart of a
terrorist organization. I also learned that each asset I ran was its own
individual chess match. So the more I ran, the more chess matches I had
to play simultaneously. It was a tricky game that had the potential to
result in "checkmate"—or the asset ratting us out to the Taliban, which
could result in my death or an assault on our base.

Of course, I had the ability to slap the pieces off the board when
the game no longer made sense to play. Meaning, the asset was wasting
my time. With some of them, it took weeks to determine when to flip the
board over. But like anything else, the more reps I got with them, the
better and faster I was able to determine their veracity and utility.

I picked up with Abdul and Haji Jan where I had left off. I met with
them both separately and together, and then used the information I got
from each of them to vet the other. Some officers at HQ didn't want me
to run Haji Jan at all because of his close ties to Taliban leadership.
Others said I should break off contact with Haji Jan until he proved he
was who he said he was.

My response to all of them was simple: He gave us phone numbers.

▮▮
▮▮▮▮▮▮▮

The more he told me, the more the bosses at HQ started to come
around. Within a short period of time he identified dozens of Taliban

commanders living across the border ███████████. We now knew their names, their faces, and in many cases their phone numbers, which meant that we could track their movements.

Before when a special-ops unit went on a raid of a suspected Taliban safe house, they might kick a door in and find a bunch of guys who called themselves Mohammed, and have no idea who they were. Now the special-ops guys knew exactly who to arrest.

During one of my weekly meetings with Abdul and Haji Jan in the shipping container, I told Haji Jan that I wanted to stop the Taliban, and specifically their IED network. He told me that the Taliban command and the IED network were two separate entities, which we had never realized before. █████████████ assumed that Taliban leaders in Quetta purchased explosive material, which was then sent to █████████ where it was packed into IEDs and suicide vests. The vests and IEDs were then distributed to bombers recruited in the madrassas.

Haji Jan explained that the Taliban outsourced the entire IED operation through ██████████ businessman. In other words, the Taliban placed orders for a certain number of IEDs and suicide vests and the ████ businessmen fulfilled the orders.

People back at HQ found this hard to believe at first. But Haji Jan named the ████ businessman who was running the whole operation out of ██████████. I gave him the code name Wolverine.[21]

Haji Jan said, "Everybody in ██████████ [a town across the border] knows about this man. People talk in my mosques and madrassas and they mention his name all the time."

I was determined to learn everything I could about Wolverine. With that in mind, I asked, "When you see a Talib ███████████████ can you ask him about Wolverine and find out as much as you can?"

"Yes, Zmarai, I can get you that information," answered Haji Jan.

He returned with Abdul a week later and described Wolverine to

---

[21] Wolverine isn't his real code name. It was made up for this book.

me. He didn't provide a photo or a phone number, but he told me what kind of car he drove and the license-plate number.

I asked, "How did you get this? Someone you know must have seen him recently."

"Yes, the person I got this information from is a Taliban commander who sees him all the time."

"Really? How close are you to this commander?"

"I'm very close to him," Haji Jan answered. "In fact, he's ███████ [a relative]."

"Wait a minute. You have ███████ [a relative] who is a Taliban commander?"

"Yes." He provided the man's name, which I recognized. He had a reputation for being a real thorn in the side of ISAF.

Thinking this was too good to be true, I said, "I don't believe you."

Abdul, who was at the meeting, said, "What Haji Jan is telling you is the truth."

I thought back to the spy network Converse had built and how effective it had been. Planning several steps ahead, I asked, "Haji Jan, tell me why you're here today meeting with me?"

He pulled at his beard and answered, "I don't like the war. I'm an Afghan, and I don't like what is going on. I support the Taliban, but I want the war to end. I think the Taliban should negotiate a settlement."

I bought about 30 percent of it, but nodded my head as though I agreed.

"You're a wise man," I said. "And as a wise leader, what you need to do is to convince your ███████ [relative] to think the same way."

He frowned deeply and looked at Abdul.

"You're a highly respected ███████ figure, and the commander's a young man," I continued. "You need to get inside his head and convince him that the war is wrong. Tell him that you have a way out and that's the money I can provide to him and his family. You can do it. I know you can."

Haji Jan looked at me skeptically and said, "I can try."

"You can do more than that," I replied. "The reason men like him are fighting in the first place is because some mullah got inside their heads and told them that they had to. I want you to convince him to work with me. If you do, I'll give you a big reward."

He nodded and said, "Zmarai, you're asking me to convert a hardened fighter who hates the United States and has killed many of your soldiers."

"I know and I believe you can do it."

"I'll try."

The next morning, I called Abdul in for a one-on-one meeting and poured it on thick.

"Abdul-sahib, my brother, thanks be to God the merciful that he has brought you to me. I consider myself blessed to have you as my Afghan brother. You are such a wise man and I see great things for you in your future. I want to help you achieve them as well."

Abdul loved the praise and began to reciprocate. "Oh, Zmarai, it is I who thank God every night that I have met you. You are my *masher* and I will do anything you tell me. Yes, together we will have much success God willing. But tell me, what great things do you see in my future?"

"Abdul, imagine this," I began, rising from my chair to heighten the drama. "Imagine, you, on a motorcycle driving from Kandahar to Kabul followed by a caravan of supporters who cheer for you throughout the entire journey. As you enter Kabul, you are saluted by the top Afghan generals, who escort you to the Presidential Palace. Inside, President Karzai waits for you in his office along with the US ambassador and top US general. The president greets you and places a robe around your shoulders and the most beautiful white turban on your head. 'Thank you Abdul Khan for destroying the Taliban,' he says. 'You are a national hero and a true Pashtun.'"

Abdul was on his feet, too. Unable to hide his emotion, he reached for my arm with both hands. "Zmarai! Zmarai-khana! This is exactly what I want!" he exclaimed.

I stared at him for a moment, then walked over to the small box I had placed at the back of the container. Opening the box, I pulled out a dark brown *patoo* and handed it to Abdul.

I said, "When you wear this on your ride to Kabul, remember that it was because of your decision today that you were able to garner such success."

Abdul took the *patoo* and started weeping. "I will do anything for you, Zmarai. I will be just like *jamhor raiyees* Karzai."

Every Afghan knew the story. It was one that President Karzai liked to tell himself—about how he rode into Afghanistan from Pakistan on a motorcycle in early October 2001 and assisted US Special Forces in destroying the Taliban from Kandahar to Kabul. While it was as far-fetched as could be, like the line in the movie *The Man Who Shot Liberty Valance* says, "When the legend becomes fact, print the legend."

"Abdul, from this point forward," I continued, "you are my main assistant. More than that, you are now my brother. This means I need you to keep a close eye on Haji Jan and make sure that he brings his ████████ [relative] into our network. You will need to monitor both of them and report back to me what you see. *Per tul narai kay,* in all the world, however, you cannot tell anyone about our secret relationship and how I have asked you to report on your friends. Do this for me, Abdul, and I will help you realize your future."

According to Agency regulations, I couldn't promise Abdul that I would provide him with anything other than money or gifts in return for information. The only thing I had actually committed to was help-ing him in the future without defining what that help would be.

Not all the assets I worked with were as direct and as useful as Haji Jan and Abdul. But they all had something to offer, even if their characters and motivations were often suspect.

One person who fell into this category was a ████████ Pashtun tribesman named Mohammed. ████████████████████████

████████████████████████████████████

████████████████████████

Members of his particular tribe were known for their fierce loyalty and strong community bonds. I had learned that some high-ranking leaders of the ███████ were simultaneously Taliban commanders also involved with drug trafficking.

In September 2008, ██████████████████████ (the tribe's leader) was sentenced to ten years' imprisonment by a US court for manufacturing hundreds of kilograms of heroin in Afghanistan and Pakistan and importing it to the United States. According to court records, he owned five hundred acres of opium fields extending from Kandahar City into the Maiwand district. He testified that in return for his financial support, the Taliban allowed him to continue his drug-trafficking activities with impunity.[22]

The drug trade had been going on for hundreds of years. Local farmers grew poppies, slit the seedpods open with razors, collected the white sap, and sold it to middlemen who dissolved it and purified it into opium. The area I was in was the epicenter, not only for poppy cultivation but also for drug trafficking into Pakistan and the Middle East. Growing poppies provided a subsistence living for Afghan farmers, and the opium it produced funded the Taliban and tribal warlords.

For the most part, the US military turned a blind eye to the drug trade and focused instead on antiterrorism. There were numerous reasons for this, including the fact that many suspected drugs traffickers were top officials in the Karzai government and the sale of poppies was the livelihood of an estimated 3.3 million Afghan farmers. According to the United Nations Office on Drugs and Crime, cultivation, production, and trafficking of opium constitutes 52 percent of the country's GDP.

The scale of production was huge. Afghanistan remains the

---

[22] This information about the ████████████████████████ comes from open-source material, including the *New York Times,* "Afghan Linked to Taliban Sentenced to Life in Drug Trafficking Case," May 1, 2009.

greatest illicit-opium producer in the world. In 2007, 92 percent of nonpharmaceutical-grade opium originated from Afghanistan, amounting to an export value of around $4 billion. What is rarely mentioned is that Afghanistan is also the largest producer of cannabis in the world—most of which is used to produce hashish, which is then sold throughout South Asia and the Middle East.

Mohammed loved American movies and wanted to be called Bob.[23] He was around forty, stood about five-nine, was overweight, and ████ ██ ████████████████████████.

I compared Bob to an Afghan Tony Soprano—big, sloppy, crude, and violent. He wore a filthy dark brown *shalwar kameez,* sandals, and a traditional head wrap that indicated that he was an important man in his community, which in Bob's case wasn't true. His job was ████ ████████████████████, but he dabbled in the drug trade, smuggling, and other illicit activities.

I used him to get a picture of what was going on in the area and to warn me about Taliban activity—information that I would then pass on to the J2. Bob had no problem dimming out his friends in the Taliban, and did so often and with impunity.

Even though he was corrupt down to his dirty yellow toenails, his information proved accurate, and was used by the US military to target Taliban combatants and kill them.

Most of the Afghans who came to me with information made an effort not to cast themselves or their country in a negative light. But Bob didn't give a shit. If the people he dimmed out really were his friends, he showed no remorse. He'd lick his lips as he told me that he had three wives and regularly beat them, and he enjoyed having sex with young boys.

"Really, Bob?" I asked. "And you think that's okay?"

---

[23] Bob is not his real name or alias. Also, his description has been altered to hide his identity.

"Yes, Zmarai," he answered. "███████████████████████████."

Though he liked our culture and mimicked American attitudes and swagger, he regularly expressed his hatred of the United States and on several occasions told me that he would laugh his head off the day I was killed by the Taliban. He had the perverted laugh of a little girl.

Once he said, "I hope you get to meet my friend Zaman, who is a Taliban commander."

"Me, too. Why don't you introduce us?"

"Okay. When you meet him I'm sure he'll make your neck smile." He underlined his point by running a finger across his throat.

Another time he said, "I hope you get blown up someday and never make it back home to the US."

"Really, Bob? If I'm not here, who's going to pay you money?"

"I'm not worried," he answered as he picked his nose. "Your replacement will do that, I'm sure."

Part of me wanted to pistol-whip him, and another part admired his nerve. "Do you really hate me so much?" I asked.

"No. It has nothing to do with that. You're not my friend. This is just a business for me."

"I'm glad you realize that," I answered. "Because I would never have a friend like you."

He laughed.

Not an attractive individual by any measure, but the juice was worth the squeeze with Bob.

One afternoon he called me to tell me he had information to sell. The Scorpions and I met him outside of Wadi Base. Bob pulled up in his beat-up Toyota Corolla, and the Scorpions proceeded to search him. As I sat waiting in the armored Land Cruiser, I heard Hillbilly through my headset exclaim, "What the fuck is this?"

In the headlights I saw him holding up something that looked like detonating cord.

██

███████████████████

███████████████████████████████

"What's he got?" I asked.

"He says he brought some things to show you."

"What?"

"Blasting caps, det cord, and this." It was paper folded into a vial filled with some kind of explosive agent.

███

██████

I said, "Chill, guys. He's a fucking idiot. ████████████████ and let's get Bob out of here."

They tossed him in the Land Cruiser and drove him to my shipping pod. Once we were seated and ████████████████████, I said, "Sorry about that, Bob. But what the fuck were you doing?"

"I brought this to you as a sample, Zmarai. I want to show you. ████████ ███████████████████████."

I said, "Next time you're going to bring stuff to show me you should tell me in advance."

The next two meetings passed without incident. But the time after that, when Bob got out of his car, Jon asked him if he was carrying anything.

Bob answered, "I have a gift for Zmarai."

"What do you have?" the terp asked.

"This."

He handed Jon something wrapped in white computer paper. Inside was a glass vial with a piece of cloth over the top affixed with a rubber band.

The Scorpions, who hated Bob because they knew he was a pedophile, drew their guns ████████████████████.

"Why are you bringing him this?" Jon asked.

"Zmarai has asked me to follow the terrorism and the drug trails. It's drugs."

"Drugs? What kind of drugs?"

Bob explained that it was a type of acid used to process opium paste into heroin. If spilled, it could eat through human flesh. And if inhaled, it could render a person unconscious.

I had heard about this specific acid and expressed an interest in where the drug traffickers were getting it. But I had never asked for a sample, or expected Bob to proffer one.

Another time, I was wrapping up a meeting with Bob when he told me that he had recently gotten into a knife fight with a Talib over a piece of contested land and thought that he might have killed him.

I didn't want to report this to HQ, because I knew they'd freak out. So I said, "Bob, stop killing people. You're eventually going to get into a knife fight, lose, and die."

"No," he replied, "because I always have a knife on me and know how to use it."

I wasn't interested in hearing him brag about his knife-fighting skills, but knew Bob well enough to ask, ██████████████████ (if he had one on him now).

██████████

███████████████████

████████████

████████████████████████

██████████████████████████

████████████████████████████

██████████

According to regulations, I should have turned Bob over to the Scorpions, which would have been the end of Bob. But I knew he was an idiot and didn't want to lose him, because he had been giving me good information. ████████████████████████████

"Where do you hide it?"

"In my money pocket," he answered. "We all have them."

The US military had been in Afghanistan for eight years at this point, and as far as I knew, we didn't realize that most Afghan men keep their ████████████ (weapon), and a shit stick in a pocket sewn into their pants that's near their testicles. The shit stick was used to cover up their feces after they took a dump.

The pocket made sense, because of all the Afghans I had seen searched, I had never seen one with cash. They always carried cell phones and maybe a notebook and pen in their pockets but never cash. I just assumed they didn't carry money because they were afraid that we'd take it from them.

I said, *"Ma'alesh."* (Literally, "It can't be helped"; or "What the hell.")

Leave it to Bob to teach us about Afghan essentials. Because the ████████████ (weapon) and shit stick were all carried together, from that point on the Scorpions always searched an Afghan's money pocket and were damn sure to wear plastic gloves.

10

PAMPLONA

What sane person could live in this world and not be crazy?

—URSULA K. LE GUIN

It was late at night and Lolita, Hillbilly, and I were on our way back from a meeting with Haji Jan and Abdul in the desert, shooting the shit about home, girls, and football—our three favorite subjects. Hillbilly, at the wheel of the armored Land Cruiser, tore through back roads near the town of ███████. The scene ahead reminded me of something out of the Bible—a brilliant canopy of stars over undulating hills of sand.

For a moment I felt transported back in time. But the straps across my temples reminded me that I was wearing NVGs, and body armor, and had an M4 squeezed between my knees.

Hillbilly asked, "What's the difference between a shopping bag and Michael Jackson?"

"Beats me."

"One is made of plastic and dangerous to children, the other holds groceries."

"Funny."

I saw the dark outline of the watchtower ahead that marked one of the ANP (Afghan National Police) checkpoints before the base. Lolita flashed the IR strobe twice to identify us.

Instead of signaling back, the Afghans in the tower hit us with a spotlight. Since we were all wearing NVGs, we were immediately blinded.

"Fucking assholes!" Lolita shouted, hitting the brakes.

"Didn't you tell 'em we were out?"

"Hell, yeah."

"If they unload their DSHKA on us, we're Swiss cheese."

A DSHKA is a Soviet-made antiaircraft gun that fires a round the size of a man's forearm that can penetrate the armor of a tank or take down a helo. My sphincter tightened enough to cut a bolt.

We had no bullhorn in the vehicle and no way of communicating with the tower, so Hillbilly radioed ahead and told someone at the base to hop on a motorcycle and make a beeline to the tower and let them know that we were friendlies.

A tense ten minutes passed before the spotlight went out and we were waved through.

I returned to my prison cell thinking that I had been at Wadi and Stone for more than five months working seventeen hours a day, seven days a weeks, and needed a break. Except for the medical-emergency flight to DC, I hadn't taken any time for myself. Usually guys like me serving at FOBs got R&R every ▮▮▮▮▮▮▮. Since I was on a temporary assignment to Wadi, I was considered an exception.

The Agency had no logistics person in Wadi, so all requests for travel were being handled by HQ seven thousand miles away. I fired off an e-mail to a woman named Sheila at HQ, explaining my situation and asking her to schedule my vacation time and a helo flight out of Wadi by the end of June. I told her I had arrived with one bag and would leave as light, if not lighter.

I got no response, so I sent her another one the following night.

Two weeks passed with no reply. One night as I was on my computer, I noticed that Sheila was on the Agency's IM system, so I sent her a message. Again, she ignored me, so I wrote, "I can see that you're online. Please, respond!!!!!"

She immediately signed off. The next morning I went to see Chief Nealy to tell him about the trouble I was having.

He acted sympathetic and said, "Five months is way too long in a place like this."

"It's been nearly six."

"How many messages did you send her?" Nealy asked.

"Twenty-four."

"You're kidding."

"I wish I was. If I don't get a response from her by the end of the week, I'm going to go nuclear."

I could see that Nealy's mind had shifted to something else. He said, "Sure. Do whatever you've got to do."

Another week passed and still no response from Sheila at HQ. So I sat in my cell at my computer and wrote, "Dear Sheila: If I could schedule the helo flight myself, I would, believe me. Since you clearly are incapable or unwilling to do this, please refer this request to your supervisor. And give me his name so I can communicate with him or her directly in the future. Thank you. D."

Two hours later Chief Nealy got a call on his emergency line, which was normally reserved for alerting him of an impending attack on the base or an urgent message from the seventh floor. It was Sheila's boss and he was livid. He informed Nealy that Sheila was in the process of filing an EEOC (Equal Employment Opportunity Commission) violation against me for workplace harassment even though I had used no profanity and was seven thousand miles away at a black site. Everyone knew that getting an EEOC amounted to a career death sentence.

Chief Nealy called me into his office and informed me about the call from HQ and told me that I had to stop by the supervisor's office and sign Sheila's complaint when I was in Washington.

"Chief, there is no way in hell I'm going to do that. If he presents me with the complaint, I'll staple it to his forehead."

Chief Nealy blinked twice, nodded, and said, "Okay, I'll tell him."

Two nights later I boarded a helo flight to Kabul. I was scheduled for thirty days of R&R. Following that, HQ wanted me to take a one-week field-operations training class so I ███████████████████ ██████████████████████████████████, even though I had been fulfilling those tasks in the field for six months.

I arrived in Kabul keyed up, only to learn that I had just missed a flight to DC and would have to wait three days for the next one. Again, I was given a filthy shipping container to sleep in. Fighting off rats during the night made it hard to decompress.

One morning I had just finished running around the base when I spotted a contractor drinking a cup of coffee and wearing a T-shirt that had a picture of a guy looking from the scope of an M4 and the phrase "Stone Firebase: Tip of the spear, end of the line."

I went up to him and said, "Cool T-shirt. Where'd you get it?"

"Stone. What did you think?" the overweight guy answered.

"When were you there?"

The guy looked at me like I smelled bad. "Why do you want to know?"

"I was there three weeks ago," I answered. "I didn't happen to see you."

"Yeah, well I was there on assignment in January."

"And they gave you that T-shirt?"

The guy nodded with an added condescending raise of his eyebrows. "Yeah, we had them made."

"That's weird. I didn't get one. None of my friends had them, either."

"We had them made after we left."

"What program were you on? You probably know some of my friends."

"I was out there installing new plumbing for the wet pod," the guy answered.

"Oh."

In other words, he was a plumbing contractor easily making twice as much as I was and living in clean quarters with no rats.

Three days later I boarded an eighteen-hour flight to DC. I landed at six a.m. on the twenty-fifth of June and wasn't expected to report to Kandahar until mid-August. With no plans and no place to stay, I grabbed a coffee, read the local paper, and then bought a TracFone to call my old roommate Austin.

"Hey, man, it's Doug and I'm back!"

"Great, but I'm leaving for work. What's up?" Austin went on to tell me that he was still living in the same town house on Thirty-third and P Street in Georgetown, but had a new roommate.

"Can I stay with you awhile?" I asked.

"Sure," Austin answered. "I'll tell my roommate Van you're coming."

I had the cabdriver let me out on the corner of Wisconsin and M Street and started to walk uptown carrying my big camping-sized back-pack. I was hypervigilant and felt vulnerable being among so many strangers without body armor and a weapon. Passersby stared at me, which only added to my sense of displacement.

I was deeply tanned and hadn't shaved in six months. Van answered the door looking shocked. "You're Doug?" he asked.

"Yeah," I answered, dropping my backpack on the floor. "What's up?"

Van stared at me like I was Charles Manson. "You used to live here?" he asked.

"Sure did."

"When did you grow the beard?"

"The beard? Oh, a while back."

"Where have you been?"

"Hawaii."

He said, "You look really dark, man, and nothing like your photo."

I weighed 175 when I left DC and was now down to a ripped 145. Because of the daily running and working out, I was in the best shape of my life.

"You're probably pretty tired," Van said. "I'm off to work now, so I'll let you rest."

I wasn't tired at all and hadn't had any downtime in almost six months. Excited to be back, I went for a long run through Georgetown and along the Potomac. Then I showered and changed and looked at my watch. It was ten a.m. on a Friday and I didn't know what to do with myself.

With no interest in watching TV, I wandered over to the Daily Grill on Wisconsin Avenue, which was the only place open that was serving alcohol this early. With one or two exceptions, I hadn't touched a drop of booze in six months. I ordered a Budweiser with a shot of Jim Beam and continued to do so for the remainder of the afternoon.

Feeling a nice buzz, I returned to Austin's and crashed on his couch. He returned around six p.m. and, seeing me, said, "What the fuck, Doug, you look like a homeless person. What happened to you, man? You're totally emaciated."

I didn't realize how strange I looked, and had expected to pick up with my friends where I had left off.

At the bar I went to later with Austin and some friends, I was having trouble showing an interest in baseball and recent movies. Instead, my mind kept drifting back to Abdul, Haji Jan, and Converse.

One of my friends sat next to me and asked, "What's going on with you and Kate?"

I had e-mailed her before I left Afghanistan and told her I was returning. I said, "I don't know. I have to call her."

"She doesn't even know you're back from Hawaii?"

"I told her I was coming, but didn't tell her when."

He nodded and said, "Well, dude, I'm pretty sure she's dating someone else."

My heart sank. "Really?"

"I saw her on the Metro with some guy the other night and it looked like they were on a date."

Feeling anxious and a little drunk, I walked outside and texted Kate. "Hey, this is Doug on a burner cell phone I picked up. I'm here. Text me back."

A minute later my cell phone pinged with a text from Kate. "Yeah! When can I see you?"

"I need a couple of days to get squared away. I'll call."

"Okay."

I knew I wouldn't be able to sleep if I didn't ask: "Everything good with you? Anything I need to know?"

"We'll talk when I c u."

Oh, shit, I said to myself. *That's not good.*

I passed out on Austin's couch but was awakened around four a.m. by a giant tomcat perched on a ledge outside the living-room window. Unable to get back to sleep, I laced up my shoes and went for a long run. Back at Austin's I showered, dressed, and waited.

The clock read 7:00 a.m. Austin and Van were still fast asleep. I thought to myself, *Fuck this. I don't want to be here anymore.*

I couldn't relate to my friends' talk about the Nationals, girls they had met, and problems they had encountered at work. It all sounded petty and boring when I was used to dealing with matters of life and death and nights of rockets and mortars exploding around me.

So I got on the internet and booked a flight to Miami. Not surprisingly, I had pretty much the same experience with my friends there. Tried as I did, I couldn't manifest any interest in the World Cup, the economic crisis in Greece, or even the beautiful Latina women standing around us.

I told one of my friends, Chris, "I'm not happy to be back. Let's go rage somewhere. I need to blow off some steam."

Chris, who hated his job, suggested Europe.

We checked the calendar and saw that the running of the bulls was taking place in Pamplona, Spain, on the fifth of July.

I said, "That's it! That's exactly what we need to do. No question about it."

I sent out e-mail inquiries to some of my other friends. My buddy Tony, who had just gotten out of the navy, responded immediately. "I'm in. A hundred percent!"

I told Tony, "I've got to go back to Georgetown to settle my hash. Then I'll book my ticket."

My mind was on Kate. Sunday night when I returned to DC, I texted her. "Let's meet up."

She was out to dinner with some of her girlfriends, but wrote back. "How about later tonight?"

"Okay. Where do you live?"

"Courthouse, VA."

It was a six-minute bus ride from Georgetown. But since I was feeling anxious, I decided to walk.

As I crossed Key Bridge, I considered my future with Kate for the first time in six months. In some ways, my first girlfriend, Hannah, felt closer to me. I cared for them both, but Hannah was more like a friend I could trust, whereas Kate was someone I still felt passionate about.

I loved her, wanted to make her happy, and understood that like most girlfriends she wanted some sense of stability. How could I give her that when I was about as steady as a one-legged stool?

The closer I got to her place, the more passion overrode logic and common sense. As I passed the Rosslyn Metro station, I decided that I would do everything in my power to make our relationship work, even from seven thousand miles away in a war zone.

Forty minutes into my walk, I entered Kate's development and started to search for her address. It was dark and the streetlights weren't strong, so I was having trouble finding it. Then I heard Kate call out, "Doug."

I turned and saw her sitting on a picnic bench in a little parklike area. I got the impression that Austin or some of my other friends had warned her about my appearance and state of mind, and she had been watching me. I wondered if they had discussed where they thought I really was and what I had been doing.

"Wow," she said. "Look at you."

She looked great with her blonde hair to her shoulders. I felt both excitement and the onset of anxiety in my chest. That quickly blossomed into shame about the way I had left and my sketchy communications since.

When I got within three feet of her, I could see that she was on the verge of tears. "How are you doing, Doug?" she asked.

"Fine," I answered unsteadily.

"Were you safe where you were?" she asked softly.

"Yeah. I'm fine. It's great to see you."

I've always been shy around women, but now I felt almost painfully vulnerable. I asked, "Should I go?"

"No," Kate answered. "Give me a hug."

The first hug I'd had in a long time sent a shock wave through my body and seemed to awaken my sex drive, which had been hibernating for six months. I had been so hypervigilant and busy with work that I hadn't masturbated my whole time in Afghanistan.

Now I stood staring at Kate in a tight blouse and yoga pants, thinking that I wanted to rip them off right there and ravish her. Instead, I said, "It's really good to see you."

Kate smiled. "I like how you took your time before bothering to see me."

"No, it's not like that," I started. "We obviously have a lot to talk about. You want to do that here, or do you want to go somewhere and get a drink?"

"Can you shave first?" Kate asked, pointing at my foot-long beard.

"No, I can't."

"You said you were going to be here a month. So why can't you shave? What's with the beard?"

I had to reach quickly into my bag of tricks. What I came out with sounded dodgy, even to me. "I work with some of the old hands at Pearl Harbor. They let their beards grow, too. It lets everyone know that we're not in the military, so they don't talk to us like we are and try to give us orders."

She looked at me skeptically, like she was growing used to my bullshit and maybe even understood why I had to keep it up. Then she said, "I have a bottle of wine upstairs."

Minutes later we were sitting on her couch, sipping wine. I maintained some space between us because all I could think about was sex. Things were just starting to warm up, but I could no longer resist asking the question "So are you seeing anyone?"

She put down her wineglass and frowned.

"You are, aren't you?" I asked.

"Well, yes and no. I just met this guy and he's kind of creeping me out. We've gone on a couple of dates, but it's nothing serious. What about you?"

"Me, no. I've been in Hawaii the whole time working."

"That doesn't mean you haven't been dating someone there," she countered. "I mean, you didn't tell me anything, or call me while you were gone, so I figured that you were."

"No, I haven't even thought of other women. If you're getting serious about some other guy though, I should probably go."

I started to stand; Kate stopped me. "Not necessarily. No."

It was awkward and strange. "Well, how serious is it?" I asked. "Has he been in this apartment?"

"No."

"Have you been to his?"

She shook her head. "No, I have not."

I could tell that she was lying. Poor Kate. She was talking to a professional liar and didn't know it. Nor did she realize that I had been trained to be expert at determining if someone was lying to me.

Incongruent body language. Check. Lack of eye contact. Check. Avoidance of verbal contractions. Check. Quavering voice. Check.

I said, "Look, I'd love to take you out, but not if this other guy's around."

"It's okay," Kate answered. "I already told him that you were coming back."

It sounded like the truth. "Where does he live, so I don't run into him?"

She looked at me like I was nuts. "What?"

My brain was now in operational overdrive and was regarding her new beau as a potential threat.

"He lives in Bethesda," Kate answered.

Good. That's thirty miles north. Probably won't run into him accidentally.

"Why do you care?" she asked.

"I care, Kate, because I've thought about you every single day since I left. I know you hate me for leaving the way I did and for my lack of communication since I've been gone, but ... it's uh ... it's ... it's been tough."

She hugged me again. "Where are you staying tonight?" she asked.

I looked deep into her blue eyes and answered, "I honestly don't know."

"You can sleep here if you want."

I had two immediate impulses. The first was an urge to scream YES! at the top of my lungs. The corresponding impulse was to make up an excuse to leave based on the thought *Oh fuck, after what I've been through medically, I'm not even sure my equipment still works!*

Kate put me at ease on both fronts when she responded, "Good. I'll get you some blankets."

Still not knowing how to act with her and not wanting to be rejected, I settled for sleeping on the sofa. But I couldn't quiet my mind.

Amped up and not having slept a wink, I left quietly at three a.m. and walked back to Georgetown, where I laced up my sneakers and ran till it hurt.

Kate texted me when she awoke. "Where r u?"

"Sorry, I'm on a different clock. Couldn't sleep."

"Am I going to c u tonight?'

"Yes."

Waiting on my server were e-mails from Tony and Chris informing me that they had already booked tickets to Spain for July 1. I was manic all day, trying to decide if I should stay and try to work things out with Kate or escape to Spain.

We met at a sushi restaurant in Georgetown. As we were standing at the bar waiting for a table, she put a hand on my waist, and said, "You've got to be kidding."

"What?"

She lifted my shirt, and exclaimed, "Holy shit, Doug! Your abs are out of control!"

"Umm…yeah, I mean, I guess."

"Let's go back to my place now," she whispered.

We jumped in a cab, and it was on immediately. The sex was fantastic. Afterward, she quickly fell asleep.

Meanwhile, I lay in her bed, staring at the ceiling, thinking, *What's next?* After an hour of tossing and turning, I roused her and asked if she'd like to make love again.

"I can't," she answered. "You're a maniac. Go to sleep."

I knew that wasn't going to happen, so I asked, "Can I have your key? I want to go for a walk."

I wandered from one neighborhood to another looking for a quiet place to sit and think. After an hour or so, I entered a poorer Latino area with broken-down houses and trailers. Three tough-looking *vatos* approached. I stared at them hard, all the time thinking, *Go ahead, motherfuckers. Bring it on!*

They passed without saying a word. When I returned to Kate's apartment, she was getting dressed for work. She said, "You've been gone for three hours, Doug. That was weird."

I spent the day at her place, not knowing what to do with myself. That night we hooked up again. Afterward, I couldn't get my brain to stop. Again, I lay awake, feeling miserable and realizing that I had to somehow wear myself out.

The next morning, I told Kate that I was going to Spain.

Upset, she asked, "How long will you be gone?"

"A week, maybe more."

Two days later, I arrived in Madrid, where Tony was waiting. We spent a couple of days there, then headed up to San Sebastian, where we hung with some shady Nigerian dudes at a seedy casino. I longed for grit, adventure, and maybe even a fight.

Chris met us in Pamplona on the third of July and the three of us rented an apartment on Estafeta Street from an Asian British guy named Dave for an exorbitant amount of money. Dave, who was thirty-five and stood five feet tall, showed us where to purchase traditional white pants, shirt, and red sash, and a wine bladder, then took us to see the bulls, which were fucking enormous!

Tony and Chris were already shitting themselves. I was ready to get it on.

We woke up early the morning of the fifth, which marked the first day of the running of the bulls. Dave showed us the course, which was 826 meters long. He explained that approximately five hundred people actually ran it. The rest were spectators who might poke out from behind the fence for a few seconds before jumping back. Every year between two hundred and three hundred people were injured, and every couple of years someone died.

Tony and Chris found a safe spot behind the fence about halfway through the course and said, "We'll stay here."

I was determined to run the entire course. The gate stood near a statue of San Fermín, the patron saint of the festival. Only ten runners waited at the gate. Dave explained that it was the most dangerous place to be, since the bulls shot out of there mad and crazy.

He shouted, "Best of luck, Doug," over spectators singing a benediction at the top of their lungs.

"Aren't you going to run with me?" I asked.

"Hell, no. You're fucking insane."

I was the only American near the gate. The rest were Spaniards and two drunk Aussies.

As the minutes counted down, some of the men decided not to run and jumped over the metal fence. One of the Aussies near me started to tremble.

At 8:00 a.m. sharp a rocket went off and the crowd roared as the gates opened and the bulls came charging out at twenty miles per hour. It was like being at Wadi and staring down the DSHKA—the intense adrenaline rush I had been searching for.

The bulls were as massive as SUVs, weighing 700 kg (1,543 pounds), and each with sharp horns and pissed. Their hooves hit the cobblestone streets all at once with a bang. Fear and excitement electrified the air inside the clogged, narrow streets.

The Aussie kid ahead of me stumbled and fell. I saw his head hit the pavement and hurtled over him as a huge bull pushed past me on the left and caused me to scrape the wall. Six bulls blew by. I was running after them up Cuesta de Santo Domingo when a second rocket exploded behind me, indicating that six more bulls had been released from the pen.

Dave had warned me to be careful not to get trapped between the two groups of bulls because sometimes a bull in the first group would get confused and turn around, creating a situation where you could have bulls charging at you from both directions.

That's where I was now, tearing up the street as fast as my legs could take me, my heart pounding in my throat. I saw sheer panic in the faces of the people in front of me, who were looking back at the angry bulls and diving under and climbing over fences. I shouted at the top of my lungs, "*Correr rápido!* Move! Fucking move!!!!!"

Dead Man's Curve (La Curva, also known as Hamburger Wall) lay ahead. It's where the street narrowed and bore sharply right onto Estafeta. The charging bulls crashed into the wall and plowed through people. Some of the animals lost their footing and fell. One of them—a massive fucker—got confused and charged toward me. People were screaming and crying.

In the chaos, men slammed into me to my left and right. I ran with my elbows out, pushing them off, creating space to get past the bull and sprint down the long straightaway to the bullring in Plaza de Castillo. My lungs were burning.

Up ahead, I saw hundreds of drunken spectators milling in the plaza around the bullring. They let the first group of bulls pass, but didn't see the other eight bulls charging behind me.

I shouted: "*Cuidado!!* Watch out! There are more bulls coming!"

Men in white and red started to panic. Some of them crashed into each other and fell. I saw a guy get trampled.

I burst through the gates of the bullring, out of breath, thinking I was safe. Until the sand beneath my feet turned loose and thick, which made it hard to move. Furious bulls ran in behind me.

As soon as all dozen or so bulls were inside the ring, the gates closed and the bulls started dropping people left and right. A total massacre. Men screamed around me in Spanish.

I was so fired up my eyes and ears started to pulsate. My chest was pounding wildly. Men in charge of the bullring corralled the bulls, and then let out two young bulls to fuck with us further.

I climbed into the stands and laughed my head off as drunken young men from as far away as Australia played bullfighter and were knocked on their asses. I thought to myself, *Only the Spanish could allow something like this to happen.*

Exhilarated, I found my way back to the apartment, where I found Chris and Tony. Tony said, "You're the craziest mofo I've ever met. This isn't the same Doug E. Fresh I knew before."

We spent the rest of the day and night partying our asses off with a bunch of insane Spaniards. By one a.m., Chris and Tony were fried and returned to the apartment. Dave took me to some private parties where people were drinking, doing blow, and all-out raging.

At six a.m., when he and I stepped out to buy more bladders of wine, we saw people starting to assemble for the second day of the running of the bulls.

I turned to Dave and said, "Dude, I can't believe that you've lived here most of your life and never run with the bulls. That's fucking bullshit. Be a man and do it this once. What's the worst that can happen?"

"Umm... well, I could die."

"How many people died yesterday?" I asked.

"One."

"Out of five hundred? What's the odds? Come on. It will be the rush of your life. Grow up, Peter Pan. Stop being a pussy."

"You're right," he answered. "Let's do it."

I'd been awake for twenty-four hours, but was so wired that I ran the entire race again. Dave entered the course just past Dead Man's Curve and made it into the bullring with me.

After Pamplona, Chris, Tony, and I decided that we needed to keep the party going, so we hopped on a ferry and headed to Ibiza for a week, where we spent days drinking on the beach and nights going to clubs and dancing with topless chicks to Tiesto, Armin van Buuren, and Gareth Emery. While we were there, Spain won the World Cup, which added a whole new dimension of mayhem and celebration.

A week and a half later, and three weeks after I had left, I limped onto a plane back to DC feeling depressed and anxious because I was coming off a bender of epic proportions. Kate picked me up from the airport and we spent the next three days together while I convalesced at her apartment.

My departure date loomed over us like the sword of Damocles, sharp and foreboding. When the day came, Kate insisted on taking me to the airport to discuss our future together. We held hands as she drove. As Dulles Airport appeared in the distance, I turned to her and asked, "How do you want to do this? I'm tired of pissing you off and making you sad. It's exhausting for both of us."

She started to cry.

I said, "I've got this retarded job that I'm probably going to continue doing for the next three or four years, and I love you very much. But I hate what I'm putting you through. I'll be going on another vacation in ninety days, and I know I'm going to want to see you again. But that's completely up to you. I'll love you either way."

She wiped her eyes and said, "I'll see how these next ninety days go. But you need to communicate with me better. A couple of times a week, I want to hear from you, okay? If you do that, I'll be here for you when you get back, and I won't date anyone else."

She stopped the car in front of the terminal. I held her tight, kissed and thanked her, and said good-bye. It was a beautiful moment. As I grabbed my backpack from the backseat, a store receipt flew out of the car. I bent down and retrieved it before I entered the terminal.

The receipt was for two hot fudge sundaes from an ice-cream shop in Bethesda (where she said the guy she had been dating lived), purchased at 11:23 p.m. the night before I returned from Spain.

I tossed it in the trash, thinking to myself, *This trip had to end this way. It's the only thing that makes sense.*

11

CAMP GECKO[24]

We are content with discord; we are content with alarms; we are content with blood; but we will never be content with a master.

—A PASHTUN LEADER TO BRITISH MAJOR-GENERAL
WILLIAM EPHINSTONE

I arrived at Kandahar Base, Afghanistan, in August 2010—"Camp Gecko" (aka Firebase Maholic) to be exact, which ███████ occupied Taliban leader Mullah Omar's former compound, built for him by Osama bin Laden.

It was a punt away from Afghanistan's second-largest city. Founded by Alexander the Great in the fourth century BCE, Kandahar had served as the center of Pashtun political and cultural life for the past two hundred years. From 1994 to late 2001 it was the capital of the Taliban government and headquarters for al-Qaeda.

Now it was a dusty, dirty, crowded city of half a million, whose landmarks included mausoleums of past rulers, the governor's mansion, and the vast, crumbling Sarposa Prison. It lay in a flat, reddish desert with a promontory known as Elephant Mountain resting in the distance.

---

[24] Camp Gecko (aka Firebase Maholic) is described in detail in open-source material, including Wikipedia.

Most of its buildings consisted of one- and two-story mud shanties with tin roofs.

The Taliban, which had been ousted in 2001, maintained a strong and active presence, blending in easily with thousands of unemployed young Afghans who hung out on the city's potholed streets. Assassinations of Afghan National Police and other Karzai government officials and suicide bombings were routine. Because of the danger and general hostility to the country's foreign occupiers, US and other ISAF forces rarely ventured into the city even in heavily armed patrols. Instead, the ANP policed the city from green Ranger trucks with Soviet PKM machine guns mounted in back.

The region had an appointed governor and the city had a mayor. But the man who dominated political and business deal making was President Karzai's half brother Ahmed Wali Karzai, a big, affable man who spoke English with a Chicago accent and was neck-deep in corruption.

The vast majority of foreign forces in Kandahar resided at the Kandahar Airfield, or KAF, which had been built by the US in the early sixties and was appropriated and expanded by the Soviets in the eighties. The Taliban occupied it during the nineties and until US marines drove them out, in December 2001. As soon as the Taliban relinquished control, the Karzai brothers claimed ownership of the land, which they leased back to us for a king's ransom.

The base itself was the largest in Afghanistan—a vast city of tents, modified trailers, heliports, hangars, bunkers, and reinforced concrete buildings that included a $35 million hospital, numerous cafeterias, a vast PX where you could by everything from video games to souvenirs, an Italian restaurant, a Tim Hortons, a Subway, and a Burger King. Food services were provided by Sodexo, the multi-billion-dollar French company that kept the cafeterias stocked with steaks, pizza, hamburgers, sodas, Perrier, and Red Bull. Totally deluxe by Afghan standards.

The day I landed at the KAF, the airfield was in the middle of another $850 million expansion so it could house up to thirty thousand soldiers and support personnel from the US, the UK, France, the Netherlands, Canada, and Afghanistan. Surrounding it were three levels of security, and perimeters of ISAF and ANA (Afghan National Army) guards. Unlike at Stone and Wadi, rocket and mortar attacks were rare.

Camp Gecko, the CIA sector, where I lived and worked, was separated by yet another security perimeter. Mullah Omar's former headquarters, consisting of a two-tiered fountain, multiple bedrooms for his wives, and a series of underground tunnels, was in the process of being torn down. Everyone in the city knew the CIA was located at Gecko and the locals still referred to our compound as "Mullah Omar's house." A visit to Mullah Omar's house meant you were looking at either a life-changing payday or time in prison. Sometimes, one led to the other.

The chief of base, call sign Boss Man, seemed like my kind of guy. He was in his mid-fifties and had served almost exclusively in war zones and the Middle East. He backed up his officers and knew when the juice was worth the squeeze.

Usually incoming officers inherited assets from their predecessor, so the deputy COB, named Hooper, transferred two unique assets from a departing officer for me to run. I'll call them Ben and Jerry.

Ben was a skinny Afghan man of twenty-three with greasy black hair and a wispy mustache who dressed like a Westerner in slacks and a cotton short-sleeved shirt. He wasn't a member of the Taliban or associated with al-Qaeda. Instead, he was educated and had a reputation for knowing what was going on across the ██████ border.[25] After studying his file and comparing it to what I already knew about Taliban activity in the area, I came away with the impression that he had been selling us dubious information for almost four years.

The first time I sat down with him, he announced, "I'm your eyes and ears in ██████."

"Really?" I answered in Pashtu. "If that's true, tell me something I don't know already."

---

[25] Ben's name and description are fictitious so as to hide his real identity.

He'd had four case officers before me, and I was the first who spoke Pashtu. Still, I kept one of the base's four local terps in the room to put him at ease and pitch in if I needed help.

"You need me," Ben boasted.

"Really? Explain why."

"Because I'm the best."

"Best at what?"

He looked confused.

I said, "Here's what's going to happen, Ben. I want to see you again in two weeks and when I do, I'm expecting you to bring me some valuable intel. I'm not even going to tell you what I want, but I want to be impressed."

Ben smiled and nodded like he was going to show me.

Two weeks later, I drove into downtown Kandahar with the Scorpions to pick him up, but Ben didn't appear at the designated spot. Nor did he show at the alternate pickup location twenty-four hours later. Nor did he answer the burner cell phone I had provided.

With no internet in Afghanistan, and therefore no other way to reach him, there was nothing I could do but wait. Two months later, Ben called and requested a meeting.

████████████████████████████████████ I sat waiting in the Afghan-style hut that served as a meeting room with one of our terps. A glass table with tea and a bowl of cashew nuts occupied the space between my chair and the sofa where he sat.

I said, "Ben, it's been two months since I saw you last, so I'm hoping you brought enough intel to justify this month's and last month's salary."

Ben spread out a map of ████████ and started to point out certain locations. He said, "The Taliban leadership had a meeting here on the twenty-first. They held another meeting in a house near this mosque two weeks ago during the night."

Skeptical, I asked, "How do you know this? Were you there?"

"No. Of course not," he answered. "But my uncle told me."

"Your uncle? Is he a member of the Taliban?"

"No."

"Then how was he allowed to attend these meetings?" I asked.

"I didn't say he attended the meetings."

"Then he heard about them from someone else?"

"Yes."

"So what you're telling me is that your information is thirdhand."

Ben didn't know what I meant, so I explained.

Sourcing of intel is critical. If a friend comes to you and says that Michael Jordan is going to be in Los Angeles tomorrow, you're naturally going to wonder about the source of that information in order to access its veracity. So you might ask: How do you know Michael Jordan is going to be in LA tomorrow?

Your friend might answer, My brother told me, and he knows him.

If you stop there, you've verified nothing. A more inquisitive person might ask, Wait a second, how does your brother know Michael Jordan?

If your friend answers that they were roommates in college and you find out independently that MJ and your friend's brother are the same age and did attend the same college at the same time, then the information is more credible. It still doesn't mean it's true, but it gives you something to build upon.

I asked, "Ben, haven't you been asked to source your information before?"

"No," he answered. "This is how I always report to you guys."

I didn't think he was lying. Also, I'd learned enough about the Taliban and their rigorous security to know that they would never talk to someone outside their circle about a strategy session. Therefore his sources were likely crap, or he was a fabricator—the ultimate worst in the intel business.

I looked at Ben and said, "This information you've brought me is useless because it's third-source. So I'm not paying you. We'll meet again in a month. If you bring me nothing then, I don't see why we should continue working together."

Ben appeared shocked; so did the Afghan terp, who looked at me as if to say, You can't treat one of our star assets like this.

Summoning the Scorpions, I said, "Escort him to the gate. I'm not in the business of creating access for you, Ben-sahib. You've either got it or you don't."

Afterward, I stopped in Deputy Hooper's office and asked, "Have you ever looked at Ben's sourcing? He has none. In my opinion, the information he's been providing is highly unreliable. In fact, Ben might be a liar."

Hooper said, "Ben's uncle is connected. Reread the file."

I didn't want to be disrespectful. Hooper was an experienced officer in his early forties. I was twenty-eight with only six months in the field. I said, "His uncle isn't a member of the Taliban, nor is he a mullah, so I don't think he's connected to anyone of value. As far as we know, his uncle is just repeating rumors, if he even exists."

Hooper looked annoyed.

I said, "I don't want to meet Ben again unless I have the power to terminate him, because I think he's been ripping us off. If he can't source his information, it's useless."

"No," Hooper countered. "I want you to pay him this time no matter what he brings. After that we'll transfer him to another case officer at another location who might be able to better validate Ben's access."

The next time I met with Ben, he gave me more information sourced to his uncle, which I counterchecked and found to be total BS. It proved that the sneaky little bastard was lying. Still, management insisted on keeping him on the books and handing him off to someone else.

I was convinced that Ben was a waste of our time and money, but there was nothing I could do. So I turned my attention to Jerry,[26] who was considered another all-star ████████████████

████.

---

[26] Jerry's name has been changed to hide his identity.

The officer who ran him previously had departed. To prepare for the meeting I studied her notes. One of them said: When you search Jerry don't ask him to remove his turban and don't search near his genitals because he's extremely religious.

I immediately tore the note up and threw it in the trash. Bombs targeting Afghan police and ISAF soldiers were hidden under turbans all the time. I said to myself, *Who the fuck would put the CTPTs, Scorpions, and the entire Camp Gecko at risk simply to avoid offending one of our asset's sensibilities?*

███████████████████████████████████████
█████████████████████████

Then I met with the Scorpion team and instructed them to search him thoroughly. The Scorpion team leader said, "Don't you know who this guy is? You're going to cause a shit storm with management."

"Look at me," I answered as I pointed to my beard and local attire. "I'm clearly all for blending in and adopting the local culture, but I'm not on board with getting people killed. Get up in this guy's ass just like you would with anyone else. No one gets a pass."

The Scorpion leader smiled to indicate that he liked my approach. He and his men would be the first to die should a source decide to detonate. They received Jerry ████████████ searched him thoroughly, and brought him to the meeting room. I entered with our head terp, who bowed deeply before Jerry as if he was an honored guest.

██
███████████████████████████████████Jerry definitely stood out, which I immediately saw as a red flag. He also wore a large gold watch on his wrist.

Although he was highly alerting, he seemed like a jovial fellow. I wanted to like him. Then he removed his shoes and started stuffing cashews in his mouth while picking his toenails.

Now I was disgusted. Trying to maintain a cordial demeanor, I said, "Jerry, it's great to meet you. May God bless you and your family and your home. Please tell me everything about yourself."

He smiled and launched into a long speech about how he loved America, which immediately struck me as odd. All of the other assets I'd run were Afghans who wanted the United States out of their country ASAP. And they all made it clear that they were cooperating with us strictly because of the money.

Jerry concluded by saying, "We're in this fight together, friend."

He was trying so hard to win me over that I suspected he might be an ■ or Taliban plant. Also, *How is this guy not pissed at me for having his balls grabbed for the first time?*

I said, "Let's get down to business, Jerry. *Tseh khabaroona dee?"* (What's the news?)

"Okay, Zmarai," he responded. *"Staaso de loomrai* intel *da dey."* (Here is your first intel.)

I almost fell out of my seat. *Did he really use the English word* "intel"?

The terp looked at me as if to say: Isn't he smart?

By the time Jerry got to his fifth intel, it was clear to me that he couldn't possibly be telling the truth. Some of the information he had was about senior Taliban leadership meetings and was so intimate that the person reporting it had to have been in the room.

Jerry told me that he got the information from a friend.

"What's your friend's name?" I asked.

"Mohammed Kashar."

Mohammed Kashar was a well-known senior commander. "How do you know him?" I asked.

"We're friends."

"Childhood friends?"

"No, he's a neighbor."

"Do you know his phone number?" I asked.

"Yes," Jerry answered.

"Then call him now. I want to hear you talk to him."

Jerry told me that the number was on a cell phone that he didn't have with him. I asked him to bring me a photo of the two of them together. Afghans loved to take pictures of themselves with friends.

If Jerry was so closely connected to a major Taliban commander, I was pretty sure I would have heard about Jerry from one of my other sources. And since Jerry wasn't a member of the Taliban, why would someone high up in the Taliban be telling him what went on in a clandestine meeting?

When we reached the end of our session, I said, "Jerry, I'll give you this month's money. But next time I want you to bring me some firsthand information."

He rose slowly to his feet, smiled at me in a condescending way, and said, "I know it's your first time, my friend. You will soon understand what is going on. Next time don't have your men frisk me so hard, and tell them not to remove my turban."

I said, "Thank you, Jerry. Now, please understand that you are *not* my friend. You're my employee and I'm your boss. If you were my friend you would be doing this for free."

Jerry turned to the terp and asked, "Why is Zmarai talking to me like this?"

I immediately ordered the terp out of the room, which caused Jerry to look more bewildered. Clearly, no one had spoken to him like this in years.

"Do you want to give me the money back? And call this a friendship?" I asked. "Or do you want this to remain a business relationship?"

Jerry placed the envelope of money in his vest pocket. "This is fine, Zmarai."

Between our first and second meetings, I asked HQ to send me everything they had on Jerry. ██████████████████████ ██ ██████ Unbelievable.

A month later when Jerry and I met again, he told me an elaborate story about how he was asked by a friend to pick up someone in Quetta and drive him to a village in northwestern Pakistan. This person turned out to be none other than Taliban supreme leader Mullah Omar—who was the second or third man on the US military's most-wanted list after OBL.

Jerry's story seemed highly improbable given the fact that Mullah Omar had not been seen in three years and was surrounded by tight security. It was even harder to imagine that Mullah Omar would travel anywhere in the Northwest Frontier Province, which the Taliban knew was within a preapproved zone for US strikes.[27]

"Was he alone when you picked him up?" I asked.

"Yes."

"Did you ever see his face?"

"No," Jerry answered. "He was covered from head to toe in a long white shawl."

"Then how do you know it was Mullah Omar?"

"I could tell from his hands. He was holding them in such a way and praying the whole time."

"Really? That's interesting. Where did you drop him off?"

"In the village."

"Then what did you do?"

"My friend and I left."

"Mullah Omar didn't say anything?"

"Maybe he said, God bless you. I don't remember. But it happened only two days ago, so he's probably in that same village."

I was almost certain it was a load of crap, which I explained to Deputy Hooper.

He surprised me by answering, "You should consult with the targeters who know more about Mullah Omar."

I spoke to another officer at the base, who said, "Send those locations back to HQ immediately."

---

[27] The existence of Pakistani-approved kill zones for drone strikes has been described in detail in several articles, including "The Rise of the Predators," the *New York Times,* April 6, 2013, and "Drone Strikes in Pakistan," The Bureau of Investigative Journalism, thebureauinvestigates.com.

I did, but wondered why anyone was taking what Jerry said seriously. Had I been smoking Afghan hash without being aware of it?

Things got even weirder when headquarters wrote back excited. They wanted me to sit down with Jerry immediately and pump him for more info about Mullah Omar.

Of course, as soon as I did that, Jerry knew he had us hook, line, and sinker. He sat across from me smiling and pouring out more BS. The stories he told grew more far-fetched and bogus.

When I couldn't take it anymore, I said, "Jerry, you hurt my heart." It was a big insult to an Afghan, but Jerry took it without blinking.

"Let's stand down for a couple of months," I continued, "unless you have something important to tell me. When I'm ready to see you again, I'll contact you."

"Will I still get paid?" he asked.

"Yes. Of course."

I went to see Deputy Hooper and argued vehemently that Jerry be terminated. Instead, he assigned Jerry to another case officer and we continued to buy his crap, which highlighted a major problem that I would see again many times. Once a station recruited an asset and he was on the books, management was unlikely to fire him, even if he wasn't producing. Why? Because ████████████████████████████████ ████████████████████████████████.

There was no incentive for terminating bullshitters. Instead, you could just reduce their salary and meet with them less frequently.

Ben and Jerry aside, sometimes people who made terrible initial impressions turned into valuable assets. A man whom I'll call Kabir[28] fell into this category. I came across his name in the cable traffic coming out of Kabul Station.

Kabir, I found out, lived near ████████ but was traveling once a month to meet with an officer in Kabul—a friend of mine named Christopher.

---

[28] Kabir is not his real name.

I called Christopher and asked about him. He told me that Kabir wasn't a member of the Taliban, but had good access to the Taliban operating in the ▮▮▮▮▮▮▮▮▮▮ of Afghanistan through some friends he had grown up with. I understood that Christopher wanted to recruit Kabir because it would look good in his file. I was happy to give Christopher credit, but pointed out that it made a hell of a lot more sense for Kabir to meet with me in Kandahar than to travel to Kabul each month.

Christopher agreed and ▮▮▮▮▮▮▮▮▮ down to Kandahar to hand him over. As in the case of Ben, Kabir didn't show up at the prearranged pickup site, which was an immediate red flag. Two days later, he called to say that he ▮▮▮▮▮▮▮▮▮▮▮ had been in a coma.

Two days after that, he showed up outside the base gates in a taxi. The CTPTs searched him thoroughly, then radioed back: He's clean, but he can't walk.

I sent the Scorpions to escort him to our compound. They lifted him up out of the taxi and loaded him into their SUV. Turned out that Kabir was another large man, standing five foot eight and weighing 230.

The Scorpions carried him into the room where Christopher waited with the terp and sat him down on the sofa.

Kabir informed the terp that he was in tremendous pain because his leg was shattered. The terp and Christopher examined it but didn't see any swelling or bruises. Thirty minutes later, they called me in.

I found a rotund man in a *shalwar kameez* sitting on the sofa with his hands over his face muttering to himself.

"What's wrong with him?" I asked.

"I think he's wasted on pain medication," Christopher answered. "He says his leg is broken."

I introduced myself in Pashtu.

Kabir was so out of it that he mistook me for an Afghan. He said, "Shame on you, Zmarai, for working with these Americans. You're an Afghan brother. You shouldn't be doing this."

I said, "I'm an American. You're the Afghan. Shame on you."

He was so fucked up, he didn't understand. Nor did he make sense.

With the meeting going nowhere, I said, "Let me get you some crutches, so you can walk out of here."

One of the Scorpions brought him a pair from our clinic, but Kabir couldn't figure out how to use them. He fell over four times.

I said, "Okay, we're going to put you in a cab and send you to a hotel so you can rest and continue this tomorrow."

"First," Kabir muttered, "I have to use the bathroom."

Since he couldn't walk with the crutches, Christopher and I got on either side of him and carried him down the hall to the john. We held him up in front of the toilet, and I said, "Okay, Kabir, take a pee."

"No. No, Zmarai. I have to do the other one."

I turned to Christopher and said, "You're not going to believe what we have to do now."

Kabir was so loaded that we had to pull his pants down and lower him onto the toilet. We stood on both sides supporting him while he did his business. It was the most putrid thing I have ever smelled in my life.

Trying not to gag, I asked, "Kabir, are you done?"

He nodded. "Yes."

As Christopher and I started to pull his pants up, Kabir screamed in Pashtu, "No. No. I'm still dirty down there."

I'd reached the limit of what I was willing to do. I said, "That's something you're going to have to live with, Kabir."

"No, you must, Zmarai."

"Not a chance, friend."

The Scorpions wrapped him in a big Afghan blanket and carried him to a cab, which dropped him off at a downtown hotel.

A month later, a now-sober Kabir returned limping badly and us-ing a tree branch as a crutch. ███████████████████████
██
███████████████████████████

Feeling sorry for him, I gave him a ██████████ cane I found on base ███████████████████████.

The third time I saw him, he walked in with a branch again. I asked, "Where's the cane I gave you?"

"I sold it."

"Greedy bastard."

He laughed.

Later, when I handed him a lighter to fire up one of his cigarettes he slipped it in his front pocket and said, "This is your gift to me, Zmarai, for making friends. I'll carry it near my heart."

There is a term in Pashtu, *chalak,* which means "clever" but in a shifty, self-benefiting sort of way. Kabir was *chalak* to a tee.

Kabir's ▮▮▮▮▮▮▮▮▮▮▮▮▮▮ but he ended up doing incredibly valuable work for us against the Taliban. Unlike Ben and Jerry, in his case, the juice was worth the squeeze.

12

MAHMUD[29]

You miss a hundred percent of the shots you don't take.

—WAYNE GRETZKY

With Ben and Jerry out of my hair and very few other assets to run, I went to see Deputy Hooper for guidance. He said, "You speak these people's language. So why don't you just do what you did in Wadi, and start turning over rocks."

"Happy to," I answered, appreciating the freedom I was being given to operate on my own. "Thanks."

The first person I called was Abdul, whom I hadn't spoken with since I left Wadi in June. ███████████████████████████████
██
████████████████

Since my Pashtu was a little rusty, our one female terp made the initial call, while I listened on speakerphone. We caught Abdul as he was driving in traffic.

As was typical of many cell-phone calls with Afghans, we heard thirty seconds of him shouting *Owwraay? Owwraay? Owwraay?* It was their version of: Can you hear me?

---

[29] Mahmud is a fictitious name. His description has also been altered to conceal his identity.

She said, "I'm calling on behalf of Zmarai."

"Who Zmarai? Which Zmarai?" Abdul asked.

"Do you remember when you had a friend down near the border named Zmarai?"

"I don't know what you're talking about."

"He used to pay you. He was your friend. You were working together on something," the female terp continued.

"Wait!" Abdul exclaimed. "Are you talking about my brother, the American? Is he here?"

"Yes. He's returned to Afghanistan."

Over the cell phone we heard Abdul scream with joy and honk his horn. "This is the best day of my life!" he shouted.

I met him a week later and told him I wanted to develop a network of spies to penetrate the Taliban's command and support structure in ██████████. While Abdul chain-smoked local cigarettes, I explained, "You're going to be my point man. You're going to be my eyes and ears and help me recruit a whole group of spies. Then you'll help me keep tabs on what they're doing."

Abdul sipped from a can of Diet Pepsi, smoothed down his Ron Burgundy–style mustache, and nodded. "This will be difficult and dangerous, Zmarai. But I can do it."

Although he wasn't in the Taliban, he liked money and through his large family network knew people who knew things. I understood that if I wanted this to work I'd have to give him a cut similar to what I paid to the sources he recruited.

At the end of the meeting, I told him that I wanted him to contact his friend Haji Jan and Haji Jan's ██████ (relative) Mahmud, who was an actual Taliban commander and, therefore, could provide great access. Haji Jan ██████████ wasn't a problem, Abdul answered. But because it was summer, Mahmud was busy fighting US troops.

Great, I thought. *Chances are the guy will get smoked, and I'll never get a chance to develop him.*

The following week, Haji Jan arrived at our compound and sat with

me in one of the meeting rooms. He was still running a ███████████
███████ ████████████████████████████████████
████████████████ (religious institution).

As he had done in the past, he voiced his philosophical opposition
to the war, then provided more names and cell-phone numbers of Taliban combatants, which I passed on to the US military ██████████.
Both he and Abdul were hesitant to go beyond identifying Taliban,
because they both thought that I'd leave again.

I met with them together twice a week for a month, sharing a big dinner each time, and warming them up to what I wanted to do, which was map
out the entire Taliban operation in ████████ ████ ████████—leaders,
madrassas, mosques, storage centers, and IED makers and suppliers.

Both men started to understand that the key to understanding the
military command structure of the Taliban was Haji Jan's ██████,
Mahmud. He was the guy with the credentials—he'd been a Taliban
fighter since the age of sixteen and a commander for three years, and
he had a reputation for hating Americans.

Turning him would be the challenge, but I had three weapons:
Abdul, Haji Jan, and cash.

I told Haji Jan to place a call to his ██████ and ask him to stand
down. Mahmud wasn't willing to quit the fight, but he did curtail his
activities. By November when the fighting stopped for the winter, and
I had met with Abdul and Haji Jan approximately ██████ times and
was quickly approaching the limit of what I could do with them,
Mahmud informed Haji Jan that he was willing to meet.

Late one afternoon, he arrived at our base with Abdul and Haji Jan,
looking tense and smoking like a chimney. Since he was a known enemy
combatant, he thought we were going to arrest him.

Mahmud's appearance surprised me. Although he had the look of
a hardened fighter, was dirty, and wore a short beard and a *shalwar kameez,* he was also tall, fit, and good-looking. Clean him up, and he would
immediately be popular with the single women at the bars I used to fre-
quent in Georgetown.

Trying to put him at ease, I asked him about his background.

"Is that why I'm here?" he snarled back. "You want to know about my background?"

"Why don't we start there."

He told me ███████████████████████████████

██

██

██

██

████████████████████████████. It was clear right away that he was a serious, no-nonsense, intelligent man.

The second time we met, he seemed a tad more comfortable. We sat across from one another in one of Mullah Omar's former rooms outfitted with prayer rugs, sofas, and a glass table that held pistachios and cups of green tea. As an active Taliban commander, Mahmud found the location to be wildly amusing.

A meal of *seek kabab* (lamb kebab), *palao* (steamed rice with lentils, raisins, and carrots), and *mantu* (dumpling) was served. As we ate, Mahmud asked me about American food. He was curious to try pizza, hamburgers, and fries, which he did on subsequent visits.

After thirty minutes or so, I asked him to help me understand his operation.

He told me that he lived in ████████ but the ████████ fighters he commanded were stationed in ████████ ████████. ████████████

██

██████████████████████████

"How does that work?" I asked.

He stared at me with arms crossed and asked, "Why do you need to know that? What's the point?"

"I want to understand how you supervise and supply your men."

"Why? If I tell you, how much will you pay me?"

I gave him a figure. He scowled, puffed on his cigarette, thought it over, and said, "I have deputies who stay with the fighters in ████████

I monitor finances and show up once a month to make sure everybody has equipment and has been paid."

"So you're not really fighting."

"That's what everybody does. I'm a commander. I don't fight. Are you kidding me? I have other people who do that."

Basically he directed his troops via cell phone, made sure they were properly equipped, and funded them by collecting a cut from the poppy harvest in the fall.

When I reported this to HQ, the analysts there were skeptical. They asked, "Really? Is this true? It's hard to believe a Taliban commander operates that way."

What was harder to believe was that we had been in Afghanistan for ten years and didn't have that knowledge.

I tasked Abdul and Haji Jan with asking Mahmud the same questions when they were alone with him. He gave them the same answers, and I corroborated his information through other sources.

Progress with Mahmud was slow. The third time we met, I said, "I want you to visit your troops and give me their names and phone numbers."

"Why?" he asked.

"So I can catalogue them and track their movements."

"They're not fighting now," he answered. "So you don't need to know that information."

I had to be patient. I told him that I wanted to understand the fighting season, how the troops were supplied, and who supplied his IEDs. He explained that he placed his orders for the components he needed, including calcium ammonium nitrate and blasting caps, from a businessman who was part of the Wolverine network in ███████ ███████ then sent one of his fighters to pick it up at the border.

He described the different kinds of IEDs he used in different parts of the country and why they were deployed in specific places. It was immediately apparent that he knew how to build them, which isn't a simple task.

If you asked me to make a pressure-plate IED and handed me a manual, I'd probably blow myself up. And these guys weren't using pre-made explosives like C-4 and Semtex. They were mixing their own chemicals.

How were they trained? Mahmud claimed that he received instruction in IED making at ████████████████. The more I got to know him, the more I learned to appreciate how intelligent he was. Was he an exception, or were other Taliban commanders equally talented?

I did more research and spoke to guys on the DOD recovery team who conducted forensics on every IED explosion. They had discovered that command wire and det cord were being used in the construction of the devices. The also found commercial-grade blasting caps. All three materials were very difficult to purchase and expensive. Yet some of the IEDs they recovered were wrapped in several feet of det cord to make them more deadly.

The det cord they were using was traced to manufacturers in ████, ████, and ██████. Those countries carefully monitored the people they sold it to. So how was it getting into ████████? Was the ████████ ████████████ helping to put commercial-grade explosive materials in the hands of terrorists?

I went to my DOD counterparts in Kandahar and said, "Let's investigate and prove it if it's true."

Their response was "That's your job, Bond."

I took up the challenge. Through the network of sources I developed, I learned that Wolverine was one of a group of ████████ businessmen who operated like criminal gangs, smuggling explosive materials into ██████ and using them to build IEDs that they sold to the Taliban. Wolverine was the biggest operator, moving and supplying 90 percent of the product. His motivation for doing so was profit.

Whether ████████████████ (another country's intelligence service) was aiding and abetting Wolverine and his associates was unclear. If ███ was involved they were very carefully hiding their hand.

Patiently and painstakingly, using one source to reach another, I learned of a wealthy businessman who worked closely with Wolverine. This individual, whom I'll call Hassan, would purchase demolitions materials from Russia, India, and China claiming to own a large construction firm ████████████. Wolverine worked with twenty or thirty individuals like Hassan.

Hassan and the other businessmen who purchased the explosive materials would then sell them to another group of individuals, or cutouts, so they could wash their hands and hide their association with the end users.

These cutouts or middlemen would then transport the chemicals, det cord, blasting caps, and other explosive materials to ████████ and sell it to Wolverine, who stored it in one of eleven warehouses he had in ███████████████████████ (a town across the border).

The Taliban demand for IEDs was so high that Wolverine was buying these materials from the middlemen as fast as he could. He employed a group of deputies, all of whom were unsavory characters and some of whom were former Taliban. The deputies served to find and vet buyers for the IEDs. For every sale they made, they took a cut. Many of the deputies were buying the IEDs from Wolverine, smuggling them into Afghanistan and marking them up 200 percent.

It was a very profitable enterprise, and the end products were expensive.

So where were the Taliban fighters in Afghanistan getting the money to purchase the IEDs? The lion's share came from the sale of opium and other narcotics, and a smaller amount derived from taxes levied on villagers in Afghanistan the Taliban claimed to protect.

I also kept hearing rumors that ████████████████ was secretly funding the Taliban's purchase of IEDs ████████████. If substantiated, these allegations could have powerful and far-reaching implications because of the ██████ government's cozy relationship with the US. But they were almost impossible to prove, because the money was changing hands directly and therefore impossible to trace. But I kept trying.

The Agency and DOD had assumed for almost ten years that the entire IED operation was funded and managed by the Taliban. They had also theorized that ███████████████ was selling the Taliban blasting caps and other materials.

I found out that neither of these assumptions was true. Wolverine had been in business since ████. There had been other suppliers before that. Although he had four or five minor competitors, he currently produced 90 percent of the IEDs that went into Afghanistan and earned millions of dollars a year.

The network he had created was complex, involved hundreds of people, and extended deep ████████ (into a country that wasn't Afghanistan). He used fifteen different cell phones at any time.

Now that I understood the network and how it worked, there was no question in my mind that it needed to be destroyed. To achieve that, I came up with the idea of inserting Mahmud into Wolverine's operation. As a well-known Taliban commander he had the bona fides. All I had to do was convince him to take the plunge.

With the spring 2011 fighting season rapidly approaching, I was forced to move fast. In a mid-March meeting with Mahmud in our compound, I told him I wanted him to stop buying IEDs from a middleman and deal directly with Wolverine's deputy.

"Why should I do that?" he asked.

"Because I want you to start picking up the product yourself."

He looked skeptical. "Why should I take the risk?"

"Why? Because I'm paying you and I'm asking nicely."

He laughed. Over the last several months, Mahmud and I had developed a friendly relationship to the point that we could joke with one another.

On the QT, I had Abdul and Haji Jan meet with him and convince him that this was his route out of a life of constant warfare and almost certain death. If he helped me penetrate the Wolverine network, they explained, Zmarai would pay them all a lot of money, which would enable them and their families to leave ▮▮▮▮▮ (the country they lived in) and pursue a better, more peaceful life elsewhere.

Abdul had already proved himself to be a master manipulator, but now he pulled out all the stops. Even though he wasn't a religious man, he knew that Mahmud was ▮▮▮▮▮▮▮▮▮▮▮▮▮▮▮▮▮▮▮▮▮▮. So Abdul started praying with Mahmud and reciting passages from the Koran that spurned the path of violence.

Slowly Mahmud started to warm to the idea I had proposed. ▮▮▮▮ ▮▮▮▮▮▮▮▮▮▮▮▮▮▮▮▮▮▮▮▮▮▮▮▮▮▮▮▮▮▮▮▮▮▮▮▮▮▮ ▮▮▮▮▮▮▮▮▮▮ After he gave me the IEDs, which I then turned over to the DOD forensics team, Mahmud told me that he didn't want Abdul to attend any more of our meetings.

So I started to meet with him individually and provided him with a burner cell phone so he could contact me directly. He told me that his main contact in ▮▮▮▮▮ was in touch with Wolverine directly. Not wanting to raise suspicion, I had Mahmud's contact facilitate meetings with Wolverine's three deputies first—code-named Iceman, Cyclops, and Polaris.[30] It turned out to be easier than I thought, because they considered Mahmud to be one of them and were willing to supply him with anything he wanted for the right amount of money.

Things were starting to develop with Mahmud, but Abdul was miffed. He wanted to know what Mahmud and I were discussing. I had to find ways to placate him, because I still wanted to use him to meet with Mahmud in private to keep him in line.

Meanwhile, Haji Jan still served the important purpose of identifying people with access to the Taliban's inner circle and Wolverine's network who might be willing to work with me.

Within six months of arriving in Kandahar my plate had become completely full as I managed multiple assets, conducted daily meetings,

---

[30] All of these names have been made up for the purposes of the book. They are not official code names.

and worked seventeen-hour days, seven days a week. Mahmud was my main asset, and the paperwork around his case was overwhelming. Because he was a known enemy combatant, HQ wanted me to be cautious. ██████████████████████████████████

I met with Boss Man in his office and said, "I know I'm taking a big leap with Mahmud. If it doesn't work, it's on me. It's my career."

"Go do it," Boss Man responded. "The possible payback could be enormous. I've got your back."

At the beginning of April, the spring weather arrived, and Mahmud announced that he was returning to the front.

I said, "No. I need you to become more friendly with one of Wolverine's deputies first."

In the back of my mind I hoped that one day Mahmud would get a chance to replace one of them and start working with Wolverine directly.

(This redacted section describes our search protocol.) ████████

██

██

██

██

███

██████████████████████████████████████

█████████████████████████████████

███

███

██

██

██

██

██████████████████

So we proceeded with caution. ████████████████████

██

██████████████████████████████████████

██

███████████████████████████████

███████████████████████████████████████

████████████████████████████ After another search,
Mahmud would get in an armored vehicle with me and the Scorpions
and we'd drive to the meeting room.

I always had a meal waiting. We'd eat and exchange pleasantries for
half an hour, then get down to business.

I always started with, *"Tseh khabaroona dee?"* (What's the news?)

He might say something like, "I met with Polaris on the eighteenth,
and I saw Wolverine on the twenty-first. He was screaming about something that he didn't like."

I'd stop him and ask, "Does Wolverine yell a lot? What does Polaris think of him? What does Wolverine think of Polaris? When they
meet who sits next to Wolverine? Is he paranoid? Has he ever mentioned
anything having to do with ███████ [another country's intelligence
service]?"

As Mahmud answered my questions, I'd record everything in a
notebook. He'd be drinking tea and chain-smoking cigarettes the entire time.

I liked to joke with him, but Pashtuns generally don't understand
sarcasm. So after I made a humorous comment, I'd add, *"Ows zeh Shaitan
kawum."* (That's me being the Devil [joking])

Only then would Mahmud laugh. If he didn't understand something
I said, he'd simply shake his head, whereupon the terp would jump in
and explain what I was trying to tell him.

After he reported all his new intel, he'd show me the materials he
had brought and tell me who he had purchased them from. We'd discuss the type of people using this specific product, where the components came from, and how it was being smuggled into Afghanistan.

██

██

███████████████████████████████████████

███████████████████████████████████████

█████████████

Our meetings were conversations. If I tasked him with something I wanted him to get from Wolverine directly, Mahmud might warn me that he didn't think he should because it might make Wolverine suspicious.

I would answer: Okay, let's figure out another way to get that information.

Then we'd game-plan together. It was all off-the-cuff and in-the-moment. If something he wanted to do involved getting support from the US military, which I knew would involve complicated approvals, I'd have to make a snap decision. Sometimes, I'd say, "Okay. Let's do it." And I'd get the official okay later.

At one meeting Mahmud said, "Wolverine is meeting with ████████████ [a foreign intelligence service] in three days. What do you want me to say? Do you want me to see if I can participate in that meeting?"

I had to decide: Was it worth putting Mahmud at risk? Did I want ████████ to be aware of him or not?

There was always a danger that Mahmud could make a mistake that could cause him to be discovered. If that happened, Wolverine would surely have him killed.

One time he arrived with photos of a meeting with Wolverine and his deputies that he had taken surreptitiously. When I asked him how he accomplished that, he told me that he asked another person in the room for his cell-phone number and when he appeared to be entering it in his phone, he was really snapping pictures.

I confirmed through other sources that the man in the photo really was Wolverine. Then I tested all the assets we had on the books who were telling us that they knew Wolverine by showing them ten photos and asking them to pick out the right one. Knowing about Wolverine was common in ███████. Actually knowing what he looked like was very different.

A number of them failed and were dismissed. Mahmud, meanwhile, kept burrowing deeper into Wolverine's network, to the point where people on the seventh floor of HQ started to take notice. Boss Man and Hooper asked me to file the paperwork for recruitment, which was a big deal bureaucratically ████████████████████████████████████ ████████████████████████████████████.

People in the intelligence community often compare the USG to a gigantic warship that takes a really long time to turn around but when it does, it's fully focused on its target, and isn't turning back until the target has been obliterated. In other words, watch the fuck out.

Mahmud had now officially turned around the warship. The game was on.

13

MULLAH SALAAM[31]

He who does his duty as his own nature reveals it, never sins.

—LAO TZU

Mindful that delivering an HVT or big shot in the Taliban could earn him a large bonus, and that Mahmud was now meeting with me alone, the enterprising Abdul was constantly on the lookout for new assets. During one of our meetings, he asked, "Zmarai, have you heard of the Quetta Shura?"

"Of course," I answered. The Quetta Shura, founded in 2001, comprised the militant leadership of the Afghan Taliban and included supreme leader Mullah Omar.[32]

Abdul said, "If you want I can arrange a meeting with Mullah Salaam."

"Okay. Who's he?" I wasn't familiar with the name.

"He's from ▮▮▮▮▮▮▮▮▮ [a city in another country] and is one of the Taliban's military chiefs. ▮▮ ▮▮▮▮▮▮▮▮▮▮▮▮▮▮ ▮▮▮▮▮▮▮▮, so he's real important. And he's close to Mullah Omar."

---

[31] This is not a real name. It was made up for the purposes of this book.

[32] The information on the Quetta Shura is open-source and available on various news sites and on Wikipedia.

"Sure," I said. "Bring him in. I'd like to meet anyone close to One-eyed Jack."

I ran Mullah Salaam's name through our system and found no match. Analysts at headquarters hypothesized that he was likely someone who we knew as Mullah Tariq. If that was correct, he was a big-time player.

Next time I saw Abdul, I mentioned the alternative name we had for Mullah Salaam.

Abdul looked skeptical, then responded, "I've never heard him referred to as Mullah Tariq, but I'll check."

The names created a lot of confusion back at HQ. Some people speculated that Abdul was trying to sell us bogus information. I doubted that, since everything he had given us so far had checked out. I wondered, instead, if we had the right name.

There was one way to figure it out, and that was to schedule a meeting with Mullah Salaam and find out who he really was.

A week later, at our next session, Abdul said that he had spoken with Mullah Salaam and he was willing to meet. Since he was a very high-level guy, he had to do it incognito.

"I'll bring him ████████████████ [to the border]," Abdul suggested, "but he doesn't want to come to Kandahar where he might be recognized and he wants to meet with your chief."

I spent a week dialoguing with the big shots at Kabul Station. None of the chiefs there wanted to participate. Instead, they proposed that I hold the initial meeting in Kandahar and smoke him out.

Mullah Salaam wouldn't agree to that. So I proposed that I meet him in Kabul with another officer, who would pose as a chief. Kabul Station agreed and selected a friend of mine named Dan, who spoke no Pashtu and was under thirty.

I wrote back, "This isn't going to work for obvious reasons. Can't you give me someone in his late forties or fifties? If Mullah Salaam is who Abdul claims he is, it will be worth it."

"Tough," Kabul replied. "That's the way it's going to happen. It's going to be Dan."

Fine, I said to myself. *I'll go to Kabul and make a warm introduction, then peel off, let Dan handle him, and hope for the best.*

I traveled to Kabul by helicopter a few days later. When I arrived at the station I quickly realized that dozens of people, sensing that Mullah Salaam could be an important score for us, had gotten involved. Included were midlevel guys in their forties who wanted to be in on the planning. But when I asked if one of them was willing to attend the meeting posing as the "chief," all of them declined.

Their political thinking was obvious. If the meeting went well, they could say they planned it; and if the meeting went badly they could blame Dan and me—a combination of risk aversion and glomming credit.

Over the next few days, they put Dan and me through the ringer, and refused to commit the Scorpions to pick up the mullah before he was vetted.

I argued, "Look. Abdul brings me new people all the time. I pick them up on the streets of Kandahar in a fucking Corolla. It simply wouldn't work if we put them through a Moscow-style surveillance-detection route!"

One of them answered smugly, "Well, that's how we do things in Kabul."

To prove their point, they came up with an elaborate cloak-and-dagger plan straight out of a bad sixties spy novel. It called for me to ███ ██.

I got it: No one wanted to get blown up by sacrificing security. But I also knew what my sources were capable of and realized that this was beyond their skill set.

On the night of our meet-up, I sat with two Scorpions in an SUV parked in a pitch-black alley with NVGs on. ███████████████ ██ ███

By the time we picked them up, an hour and forty minutes later, both Abdul and Mullah Salaam were scared to death. Then one of the Scorpions proceeded to frisk Mullah Salaam, while the other held a ██ to his face. Abdul was subjected to the same welcome.

Both men trembled with fear and anger. Mullah Salaam was a thin man in his sixties with a long white beard. As soon as I introduced myself, both he and Abdul started screaming at me in Pashtu.

Abdul said, "Zmarai, we're Pashtuns from the South and you just walked us through a Hazara neighborhood. Don't you know that they're our mortal enemies? We are ████████. Are you deliberately trying to kill us? We don't speak Dari! Do you see my turban? Do you see Mullah Salaam's beard?!"

During the drive to the meeting site, I tried my best to calm the two men.

Any good I might have done disappeared the moment we entered the room and they saw twenty-something Dan sitting with a female terp.

I thought to myself, *Could we make a worse initial impression if we tried? This guy's on the Quetta Shura and ultrareligious, and Dan has to bring a female terp? What the fuck?*

Mullah Salaam immediately expressed his displeasure with Dan and the fact that he didn't speak Pashtu. To make matters worse, Dan turned to me and said, "You need to go with Abdul to another room, while I conduct this meeting with the mullah."

"What are you talking about?" I asked.

████████████████   ████████████████████████

Now I was pissed. "What the hell are you talking about, Dan?" I asked. "I can help you. I'm from the South. I speak the language. You don't even understand what's going on down there."

He said, "The bosses told me to do it this way."

"Of course. Thanks, Dan, good buddy. You might have alerted me ahead of time."

Abdul and I sat in a nearby room discussing business. After three hours, one of the Scorpions stuck his head in and grunted, "Let's go."

When I saw Dan, I asked, "How did it go?"

He shrugged and walked away. As soon as Mullah Salaam spotted Abdul, he started laying into him.

The female terp pulled me aside and said, "That didn't go well. The chemistry was bad."

"Why? What happened?"

"Well, two-thirds of the way through the meeting, Dan asked the mullah to draw a map of his Taliban compound ▮▮▮▮▮▮▮. And the mullah asked, 'Why? Are you going to attack it?'"

I found Dan in the station cafeteria and asked, "Why did you do that?"

"Obviously, so we can ▮▮▮▮▮▮▮▮▮▮," he answered.

Trying to hold back my frustration, I said, "Dan, that's not what the guy wants to hear at the first meeting. The point is to hook him, and then get everything he knows—names, strategies, safe houses, plans, supply networks, et cetera."

"Or we can just arrest him and all his buddies," added Dan.

I couldn't control myself any longer. "Are you really this fucking stupid?" I asked.

"Maybe we do things differently here," Dan shot back.

"Or maybe you're a bunch of idiots who don't know shit."

The following day we sat with the senior people from Kabul Station. Dan reported, "Mullah Salaam wasn't cooperative. In my opinion he's a complete waste of time."

The COPs rubbed his chin and nodded. "Well," he said, "we didn't think he was Mullah Tariq anyway. He probably doesn't know anything. Therefore, we don't need to make any future contact."

I sat biting my tongue, thinking, *He probably is a senior guy who is close to Mullah Omar, and now we'll never get anything out of him. It's like finally getting a chance to meet the woman of your dreams and puking on her shoes.*

As the post-mortem was breaking up one of the senior officers turned to me and said, "I don't know how you do things down south, but here in Kabul we have standards. I suggest you take what you learned here, bring it down south, and stop wasting people's time."

I wanted to punch him in the mouth.

The next time I met with Abdul, I asked about Mullah Salaam.

Abdul sighed and shook his head. "He thinks Americans are mo-rons," he said. "He's on his way back ███████ now and hates you people more than ever. The thread that could have been used to pull him to our side is completely broken."

"Sadly," I added, recalling how a combination of egos and stupid-ity had ruined a promising and rare opportunity. Even more sadly, it wouldn't be the first time.

Given the billions of dollars we were spending in Afghanistan and the hundreds of billions we had spent since 2001, the way we allocated re-sources often didn't make a lick of sense. ████████████████

████████████████████████████████

████████████████████████████████

Drug runners responded by moving their operations ██████████

██████████████████████. There they operated an open drug bazaar where dealers bartered for *hash hash* (opium seeds), marijuana, hashish, and of course heroin, all while armed to the teeth with automatic weapons. It was the Afghan version of the OK Corral.

Every so often, the US Army's ██████████ rolled out in heavily armored vehicles to patrol the town and attend the local *shura*. The drug dealers, who weren't stupid, would hear they were coming and close up their operations for the day. DOD could say they were deterring illegal drug operations and the Afghan dealers could take the day off.

Thinking that maybe I could recruit someone local to monitor the town, I asked the colonel in charge of ██████████ if the Scorpions and I could accompany them the next time they went. He said, "Sure, but you have to dress in our BDUs." (Battle dress uniform, aka fatigues.)

So Hillbilly, Lolita, and I donned some oversized digital camo and rode with the ▊▊, which was made up largely of clean-shaven eighteen-year-olds from Texas, Arkansas, and Mississippi. They looked at us like we were aliens because the Scorpions had tats running up their arms and neck, and I sported a foot-long beard.

They asked, "Who are you guys? What unit are you attached to?"

"OGA," I answered. (Other Government Agency.)

The soldiers I was talking to got that confused with NGO (Non Government Agency), which they heard more frequently. One of them said, "So you guys are nonprofit."

"Do we look nonprofit?" Lolita growled under his breath.

"I think he just called us a couple of faggots," Hillbilly snarled back.

"How long did it take you to grow that beard?" one of the eighteen-year-olds asked me.

"Mind if I take a look at your ▊▊ sir," another soldier asked.

They were all nice kids who looked at me cross-eyed when I started speaking Pashtu. Afghanistan to them was the dark side of the moon.

The Scorpions and I always brought our own food. But the kids couldn't resist the rice and greasy kebabs served at the *shura*, which inevitably made them sick.

The first time we accompanied ▊▊▊▊▊▊▊▊▊, I found the man in charge of the district *shura*—a reputed drug smuggler—and asked him for the location of the local NDS (National Directorate of Security, Afghanistan's domestic security agency) office.

He pointed to a dilapidated shack two hundred yards away. I walked with the Scorpions past groups of Afghans with AKs and pistols in their belts.

Hillbilly groaned out of the side of his mouth, "This is some shit. We can't protect you when we're surrounded like this, Markhor. Let's go back."

Standing near the shack was a man in an ANA uniform smoking a cigarette. I asked him if he was the NDS officer.

"No," he answered. "I'm his guard."

"Can you tell me where he is?"

"He's not here now."

"Tell him Zmarai stopped by. Here's my number."

A couple of days later I got a call from the NDS officer named Khaliq,[33] who invited me to visit him next time I was ████████.

The twenty-three-year old I met on my next visit was highly intelligent, with an advanced degree ████████████. His office resembled a trashed-out crack den—rusted desk, refuse pushed to the corners, holes in the wall.

"Look at this shit," Khaliq said in Pashtu. "You Americans have spent billions of dollars here, and I'm your counterpart, and look how I live. It's a joke. I have one lousy guard. I also have this AK, Makarov pistol, and a broken-down Corolla all of which I bought myself. How does anyone expect me to collect intel? I'm just trying to stay alive."

I couldn't argue with that. USAID sponsored a program in the province where they handed out free tractors to farmers, but we couldn't supply security to an Afghan government intelligence officer. Furthermore, the local farmers who accepted gifts from us were regularly whacked by the Taliban. How could you hope to run a government or even an aid program without security?

I said, "How about I ████████ get you a better office and some real guards?"

Khaliq responded enthusiastically. In exchange for me fulfilling my offer, he supplied us ████████████████ our first clear understanding of how the Taliban shadow governance worked and enforced their laws.

In early 2011, when the Taliban shot up his office in an attempt to kill him, Khaliq relocated to Kandahar, where we reunited and he worked for me again. Again, the intel he provided was excellent.

In April, his father ████████████████████ was gunned down outside of a mosque.

Suddenly, I stopped hearing from Khaliq. One day, weeks later, I

---

[33] This is a made-up name.

learned that his body had been found in the desert.

It was a tragic loss. Khaliq wanted to improve his country and had the ability to do so. But violence stalked every government official in the South. Assassinations and suicide bombings occurred daily. Kandahar was a teeming mess of dust, fumes, bicycles, raw sewage, rickshaws, jerry-built apartments, blaring police sirens, ISAF convoys, and the sudden whump of a bomb blast. On practically every corner you saw groups of turbaned men who could be Taliban.

The government barely functioned, and corruption was insidious and rampant. A good part of city contracts for lighting, construction, and garbage collection ended up in the pockets of entrepreneurs and government officials, so that the services that did reach the public were woefully inadequate. Power brokers fought for their share of military contracts, building projects, and the opium trade.

This was the environment in which we operated. My thinking was that we had to see it and understand it if we were going to successfully fulfill our mission. While Boss Man and Hooper agreed, their management positions forced them to regard things differently. Because of the always-present danger of Taliban targeting Americans, they didn't want their officers leaving the wire unless they were on a highly important op.

Through Abdul, Haji Jan, and the ███████ other assets I developed, I was getting a constant stream of names and ███████ of enemy combatants living in and around Kandahar, who were then put on the military's tier-one target list. So it made sense that I would get to know the guys who actually went into the city each night to nab them—namely, the men from Ground Branch.

But that's not how things generally worked. Usually, the GBers didn't let anyone within a hundred yards of them. They were cool former special-warfare guys in their later forties and fifties who kept to themselves, didn't talk about their ops, and mistrusted outsiders and regular Agency guys, who in their opinion were low-speed, high-drag.

███

████████████████████████ When I first arrived in Kandahar, I got to know the GB team leader, a former Navy SEAL named Utah. We'd drive around the city together, and I'd point out tips on what was going on in specific areas.

Two months later, Utah left and his successor had no interest in working with me. Then three months later, Utah returned. He said, "If I can help you in any way, say the word." I filled him in on what was going on in the city and ███████████████████████████ █████████████████████████.

Utah introduced me to the guy on his team who ran the logistics and planning of all their ops—a short, stocky former SEAL named Pointer. He said, "Doug's super squared away. He's the guy working on the IED thing."

"Cool," Pointer responded. "What can I do for you, Doug?"

"I want you to share with him what's coming in on our ████████," Utah continued. ████████████████████████████████ ██████████████████████ "Also, I want you to take him around the city to show him what our capabilities are, so he can plan his ops accordingly and we're all on the same page."

Pointer took me into the city and showed me how they tracked someone ██████████████████████████████████ ███ ███. ███ ███ ██████████████████████████ ███ ████████████ ████████████████████████████

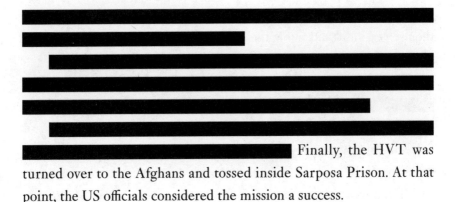 Finally, the HVT was turned over to the Afghans and tossed inside Sarposa Prison. At that point, the US officials considered the mission a success.

But there was a problem. They were discounting the fact that we were in Afghanistan, and nothing operated the way we expected it to. Especially when it came to Sarposa Prison.

14

SARPOSA PRISON[34]

We are not America. We are Afghanistan.

—President Hamid Karzai

Sarposa Prison is a big, old, nasty-looking four-sided compound
right next to the congested Herat Highway on the northern edges of
Kandahar City, surrounded by reinforced cement walls topped with
razor wire. It's the largest state prison in southern Afghanistan, with
a capacity for holding thousands. Its five cell blocks housed all the
Taliban and al-Qaeda insurgents we captured in Kandahar and Helmand provinces, as well as drug traffickers, murderers, rapists, and
thieves.

The Afghans considered it an important high-security facility. But
the security by US standards was a joke. In June 2003, forty-one Taliban and al-Qaeda prisoners in the special political block tunneled to the
outside and escaped. A frantic weeklong search by the ISAF and ANA
yielded only a few escapees.

The June 2008 breach was even worse. Taliban insurgents drove a
truck loaded with two tons of explosives up to the main gate and

[34] Most of the information in this chapter is open-source material found in
various articles, including Luke Mogelson, "The Great Taliban Jail Break," GQ,
June 2012.

detonated. With the gate and main guard tower destroyed, dozens of heavily armed Taliban fighters swarmed into the prison on motorcycles, killing nine guards and releasing over a thousand prisoners, including Taliban military commanders, insurgents, shadow-government officials, and new recruits. It was a total disaster to our efforts to secure the South.

Following the '08 attack, the United States and Canada spent millions on security upgrades—the construction of new guard towers, blast walls with security cameras, and a reinforced underground barrier to obstruct future tunnels. Canadian prison specialists were flown in to train the guards.

All these improvements were in the place when I arrived, in the summer of 2010. An American official had told reporters earlier that year that the only way to bust somebody out now would be to "put a nuke on a motorcycle."

I found the prison to be a dilapidated piece of shit with little security. The facility was run by Afghans and employed so few guards—fifteen at the time of my first visit—that they were used almost exclusively to defend the outside perimeter. Only a handful patrolled the inside of the prison, where prisoners were allowed to move about at will.

The other serious problem was its location, abutting a dense residential neighborhood on two sides and a major highway on the another. I figured that there was little chance the prison would be moved, but went to see Boss Man to tell him how I wanted to help beef up security ██████████████████ ██ ███████████████████ ████████████████████████. ███████████████████ ██ ██████████████ ██████████ ████████ (My employers didn't want me going into the prison, because of what had happened at Abu Ghraib in 2003.)

Like hundreds of thousands of other Americans, I had seen the pictures and read the stories of soldiers of the US 320th Military Police Battalion physically and sexually abusing prisoners in Iraq. I found them sickening and shameful. But Sarposa was different. My concern was keeping dangerous prisoners from escaping, not interrogating them.

I said, "Chief, there are ███ Taliban in there now. If they get out, all the work we've done will go down the drain. The prisoners will disappear into ████████ regroup, and cross back over the border to attack us."

On my second visit, I found prisoners walking around with shovels, and intermingling with unarmed guards. As one of the Scorpions and I rounded a corner, a prisoner came running toward us holding a rock pick. The Scorpion aimed his weapon and ordered the prisoner to drop to the ground. ████████████████████████ ████████████

When the warden ran over to see what was going on I asked him in Pashtu, "What is this prisoner doing with a weapon?"

"It's just a rock pick," the warden explained. "He's helping us build."

"What is this man in here for, petty larceny?"

"No, he's a member of the Taliban."

During that visit I learned that the political block where the Taliban were held was inspected only once a week. And once a week, cell phones (which were not allowed inside the prison) were discovered hidden under rugs and in the walls. That meant that for the six or so days before they were confiscated, their Taliban owners had been able to talk with their colleagues on the outside and plan escapes.

Even more disturbing was the fact that prisoners were allowed to have guests, who were granted admission after a cursory inspection, and could travel around the prison on their own. Within the political block's three contiguous wings, Taliban prisoners were pretty much left to themselves. Leaders resolved disputes, and prisoners knit clothes and blankets. Prayers were held five times a day in a courtyard, led by an imam. Every weekend, visitors arrived with plastic bags filled with food and other supplies, including cushions, rugs, blankets, DVD players, DVDs, electric fans, mirrors, and embroidered tapestries, which prisoners used to trick out their cells.

 I said to the warden, "If you don't have enough guards to monitor visitors when they're in the prison, don't allow visits."

He shook his finger at me and responded, "Oh no, Zmarai, we can't do that."

"Why not? Every week when you scrub the place you find something like thirty cell phones. One day someone's going to smuggle a grenade in here, toss it under your desk, and blow your balls off."

The warden smiled and said, "Well, Zmarai, we are doing our best."

When I returned to the base, I wrote a scathing report to HQ pointing out the dire need to increase security.

The response I got was a slap in the face. It said, "You're not to go back inside that prison under any circumstances. Stand down immediately!"

I fought back, arguing that three guys with RPGs could easily

blast a hole in the perimeter walls, which would allow all of the prisoners to escape. That message was forwarded to the US military,
which decided to assign a small contingent of soldiers to patrol the
perimeter walls.

While I was petitioning HQ for tighter security, an enterprising former resident of Sarposa and Taliban insurgent named Ihasan Ullah
hatched a plan to dig a tunnel from outside the prison, instead of one
from within. First, he rented a dilapidated old house across from the
south corner of the prison, then hired local workers to remodel it and
add a new room. In the evening, after the workers left, Ihasan and three
other insurgents started to dig. Night after night, Ihasan opened the
ground with a pick, while the other three cleared the soil.

The tunnel they dug was too narrow to accommodate a wheelbarrow, so they constructed little lorries of their own using wheels from
children's tricycles. Guided by GPS, they dug for two months before
they added four more insurgents to their crew. The eight men proceeded
at a pace of 4 meters a night. But when they reached 150 meters, they
encountered another problem: Lack of ventilation and oxygen made it
impossible to continue. This was solved with a battery-operated air
pump and pipe. Next, they had to calculate how deep to dig under the
road that carried heavy vehicles to the prison.

More workers were added. A village water line threw them off
course. By the spring of 2011, they reached the middle of the prison
yard. From there they dug two branches—one to a small cell block,
called Tawqif Khana, that segregated important Taliban commanders

from the rest of the population, and another to Cell 7 in the political block.

Roughly six months later, on the night of April 24, the tunnel was completed. Ihasan chose five men to assist him with the extraction. At nine p.m., he alerted two prisoners in Cell 7 and the commander in Tawqif Khana that it was launch time. An hour later, they easily broke through the floor of Tawqif Khana using a car jack and pipes. The concrete floor of Cell 7 was more challenging. Once the holes were cut, pistols, knives, and cell phones were passed through and the prisoners began to enter the tunnel.

By two a.m. all 432 Taliban prisoners inside Sarposa Prison had escaped. When they reached the house across the street, some were herded onto trucks, which merged into the traffic on the Herat Highway. Others hailed taxis or entered the suburbs of Kandahar on foot.

Of the escapees, a man named Muhammed Idris described his experience in the magazine *Al-Somood*. He was the second prisoner to leave from Cell 7.

> The tunnel was wide, but not very much. We could walk kneeling or crawl. . . . Every 15 meters there was a lamp. The mujahedeen had laid six-inch diameter plastic pipe for ventilation. . . . It took us about fifteen minutes to reach the other side. . . . Upon reaching the exit there were fifteen armed mujahedeen. . . . They took everyone's money and divided it up, so each of us had 3,000 rupees. This way everyone had money to reach their destination.

I was awakened at three a.m. by a call from ███████████████ ███████ who informed me that every single member of the Taliban had escaped.

"I guess we should have predicted that," I groaned in response.

"What do you want me to do?" ██████ asked.

"You better alert your superiors and see if they can lock down ██████ ██ the city."

The inspiration for the book cover. Taken in the Gobi Desert shortly before I went to the Farm.

(Photo courtesy of the author)

One of only a handful of photos I have from my time at Wadi Base. A Scorpion took this of me while I was eating a pear for breakfast.

(Photo courtesy of the author)

An Afghan soldier walking among the poppy blossoms, which were actually quite beautiful especially when viewed from overhead.

(DOD photo by Staff Sergeant Kaily Brown, US Army/Released)

"Welcome Back." Somewhere in Afghanistan. Based on my attire, we are heading to a forward operating base.

(Photo courtesy of the author)

Hmm … an American-made weapon… *(Reuters)*

Watching the sunrise over Kandahar City. *(Photo courtesy of the author)*

The outside of Sarposa Prison in Kandahar City where the worst of the worst of Taliban prisoners were housed.   *(Reuters/Ahmad Nadeem)*

The warden of Sarposa Prison pointing at the hole in the ground where all 400-plus Taliban prisoners escaped in the middle of the night under his watch.

(Reuters/Ahmad Nadeem)

Waiting for someone inside a former Taliban-reinforced cave.

(Photo courtesy of the author)

What your typical ISIS badass looks like. He is no more than eighteen years old at best.

(Reuters/Mohamed Abdullah)

Before.

(Photo courtesy of the author)

After.

(Photo courtesy of the author)

What it looks like after an IED blast goes off and the bodies are rounded up by the ANP. This was a near daily occurrence. *(STR/EPA/Newscom)*

Checking comms outside a cave. *(Photo courtesy of the author)*

Another example of why it was so important to me to destroy the Wolverine network: kids like this risking their lives to disarm his dirty work and keep their fellow brothers safe. *(US Army)*

One of my last days in-country, overlooking Kabul. I think that is a child's medium body armor I am wearing. *(Photo courtesy of the author)*

Shaken but not deterred. I fucking love this photo. This is why we fought so hard to take down Wolverine and why it meant so much to me.

(Jeff Bundy/The Omaha World-Herald)

"London Calling." On R&R in London with Kate. I look really happy. Imagine that.

(Photo courtesy of the author)

Heading to work while on the Syrian task force. Parts unknown…

(Photo courtesy of the author)

IED aftermath: what it looks like and the damage it can do.

(Marwan Ibrahim/AFP/Getty Images)

"Catching Mr. Trotsky." The fourteen-kilogram
mahimahi I caught off the coast of Montezuma on
my thirtieth birthday. Eating it that night with the
locals, I finalized my decision that I was going to
leave the Agency. *(Photo courtesy of the author)*

Christmas in Kandahar. Thought it would have made a hell of a Christmas card that year with the phrase "Mele Kalikimaka," since everyone in my life thought I was actually in Hawaii at the time. *(Photo courtesy of the author)*

"Full Native." *(Photo courtesy of the author)*

A young kid burns an image of President Bashar al-Assad.

(Alessio Romenzi/AFP/Getty Images)

A rather ironic shooting gallery I found in the Middle East. Notice the shooter is conspicuously not Arab.

(Photo courtesy of the author)

Paris, France. I asked Kate to take a slew of pictures of me standing in the street so that I could get the license plates of all the vehicles. She had no idea she was helping me conduct an SDR at the time.

(Photo courtesy of the author)

The destroyed blast door of the US embassy in Ankara. This suicide attack took place on February 1, 2013, on my last day of employment at the Agency. I walked through that door, many, many, many times just weeks prior.

(Yavuz Ozden/AFP/Getty Images)

The Afghanistan Campaign Medal was created in 2004 for American service personnel who have served in Afghanistan (or Afghan airspace) for thirty days or more. It is much easier and safer to pick one up in Pakistan.

(Rob Crilly, Afghanistan and Pakistan correspondent of The Daily Telegraph)

For the next forty-eight hours chaos reigned in and around Kandahar as escaped Taliban prisoners set off bombs, attacked police checkpoints, and exacted revenge. Many of them then jumped in taxis and headed for the border. They were able to cross into ███████ easily, because the Afghans had no prison records, fingerprints, or other database that could be checked.

A day later I received a nasty e-mail from headquarters saying that ██████████████████████████████ I should have found out about the breakout ahead of time. Clearly, they wanted to pin the fiasco on me. But I wasn't going to let that happen, not with the three-inch-thick file I had on Sarposa with my recommendations.

I was furious. So were Boss Man and Hooper. When I showed the e-mail to Hooper, he lost his temper and punched a hole in a metal filing cabinet, nearly breaking his hand.

Boss Man said, "You were right, and HQ was wrong. But don't expect them to admit that. Now, it's up to you to recapture those guys."

I felt like shouting, *Fuck that! I've been working seventeen-hour days, seven days a week to capture these guys, and we let the Afghans let them escape.*

Instead, I contacted Abdul, Mahmud, Haji Jan, and my other assets in ████████ and told them to start trying to ID escaped prisoners and get their cell-phone numbers so the GB guys and CTPTs could go through the arduous and dangerous process of picking them up again.

Meanwhile, fingerpointing continued, from Ottawa to Langley to Kabul. One member of the Canadian Parliament asked, "How can we invest in something and it be run so poorly?" President Karzai called it "a disaster." Feeling they needed a scapegoat, his government arrested ███████ (the warden), charged him with treason, and locked him in the prison he had formerly run.

Canada and the United States responded by spending millions more on beefing up security at Sarposa. But the damage had already been done.

I took the whole thing badly. It didn't help that a few days later one of my SF buddies was blown apart by an IED. A day after that some Afghans I knew were killed in a shoot-out and another guy at our base committed suicide. Surrounded by death and daily bomb attacks, and feeling like my efforts were futile, I longed to hear a friendly, sympathetic voice. So I called Kate.

Things had been going relatively well between us. Since meeting in Washington, we'd spent my two R&Rs together, one in Japan and Taiwan and the other in Rio during Carnival. Both had been a great relief, and proof to my mind that we deeply loved one another.

During our last days in Rio, Kate had started to express her resentment of our situation in a backhanded kind of way. First, she complained about the wars in Iraq and Afghanistan and how in her opinion they were a tragic waste of money and life. Then, she told me she knew a woman who worked at the Agency and talked about her in a highly pejorative way.

I still hadn't told Kate the truth about my employment. The only people who knew that I worked for the Agency and was stationed in Afghanistan were my brother and Hannah. I told them I was in Kabul, far away from the violence, writing reports.

To my mind, Kate's frustration was completely understandable. We only got to see each other every three months. In between, she'd e-mail me once every three or four weeks. I cherished every one of the messages, and read them over and over.

Smarting from the Sarposa disaster and recent deaths, I decided to call her. Her first words back to me were, "How's Hawaii?," said in a sarcastic, almost bitter tone of voice.

I started crying, which surprised me because I almost never do that.

"Look," I said, "we both know I'm not in Hawaii. I haven't told you where I am, because I can't and because I don't want you to worry. But I'm having a hard time right now, so please don't bust my balls."

Her tone softened considerably. "I'm sorry, Doug. That's the first time you've been honest with me."

"You know I love you, right? That's not BS."

"I know."

"It's difficult for me, too, okay? I want to explain some things next time I see you. In the meantime, it sure would be nice to have a girlfriend who supports me."

"I do. I love you."

In the Agency we called it "opening the kimono," which meant slowly revealing who you really worked for and what you did for a living. I found it both awkward and weird. Awkward in the sense that if I really did tell Kate everything, she'd probably freak out. At the time, there were daily reports in the US media about the deaths of American soldiers in and around Kandahar.

Also Kate was extremely liberal politically. Even though I believe that most politicians on all sides of the political spectrum are full of shit and she was aware of that, I didn't fancy having my girlfriend question the morality of the larger antiterrorism campaign that I was part of when I wasn't at liberty to share what I knew.

Opening the kimono was weird in the sense that the person I had revealed the most to was my brother Chad. He had responded by entering a strange state of denial, as though he regarded what I was doing as slightly foolish and no big deal. Judging by his attitude, I might as well have been selling Bermuda shorts in Alaska.

The person who seemed to have the best understanding of my situation was my old girlfriend Hannah. She closely followed the news from Afghanistan and would e-mail me weekly, or whenever she read about an attack against Americans. All her messages ended with the coda "Thanks for what you're doing."

Six thousand, eight hundred miles away in the middle of a war zone, those words meant a great deal.

Looking forward to seeing Kate and hoping to further cement the bond between us, I met her in London on my next R&R. Over a meal of chicken marsala and Kingfisher beer, I told her that I was still a military contractor doing some work for the Agency, but had been living in Kabul, not Hawaii. She acted unimpressed and immediately started to bombard me with arguments of why she thought the war in Afghanistan was wrong.

I felt sucker-punched again. All I wanted was to hear her say that she cared. Instead, she harangued me about the immorality of waterboarding and torture and demanded to know if I had participated in them.

"No!" I insisted.

"I'm not sure I believe you, Doug."

"Thanks at lot."

After a few dreary days together in London, we boarded a train to Paris. The City of Light didn't seem to brighten her mood, as I had hoped. Kate remained despondent and distant as we toured the Louvre, dined on the Left Bank, and surveyed the city from the top of the Eiffel Tower.

I kept looking for ways to pull her out of her funk. One beautiful afternoon, as we were walking through the Tuileries observing the garden and the groups of schoolchildren playing among the trees, we passed a woman who gave me a strange look out of the corner of her left eye, as though she knew me. Having been trained in countersurveillance, my antennae immediately went up.

That night Kate and I were sitting in a little bistro off the Champs-Élysées when the same woman walked in. She was in her mid-thirties, medium height, dark brown hair, light skin. Standing at the bar, she did a quick look-around. She spotted me sitting facing the door, registered that I noticed her, and immediately crossed to the back of the bistro, where the bathrooms were located. Fifteen minutes later, she exited the bathroom and the bistro.

Shit! I said to myself. *I might actually be under surveillance!*

I didn't know if the woman worked for French DGSE (General Directorate for Eternal Security), worked for the local police, or was just a common thief. All I knew was that Kate and I were spending several more days in Paris, and now I was going to have to conduct SDRs (surveillance-detection routes) without her knowing.

That night as I lay in bed next to Kate, I quietly planned our movements of the next day. We'd take a bus to Les Halles, walk to the Picasso Museum, take the Number 4 Métro, transfer to the Number 2, get off at the Anvers stop, climb the steps up to Sacré-Coeur Basilica.

As we roamed the city, I saw more evidence of surveillance, including a guy on a Vespa motor scooter whom I spotted twice, once outside the museum and another time near the steps to Sacré-Coeur. I knew it was the same guy because I memorized the license-plate number. We also passed a tall guy in two different parts of the city. The first time he wore a hat. The second time he had no hat and had changed into a different shirt.

When we returned to our hotel near the Champs-Élysées, I noticed a new man behind the front desk. He didn't seem to be doing anything, but every once in a while looked up at me like he knew me.

Kate and I were staying in a corner room next to a large cleaning closet. As we rested, and then showered and changed for dinner, a maid from the hotel kept knocking on the door and bringing us things. Mints the first time, shampoo the next.

I told the maid that we were fine, and didn't want to be disturbed.

The next morning, I left the Do Not Disturb sign on the door and informed the front desk that we wouldn't be back until five p.m. Kate and I ate breakfast at a little café across the street. As we finished our baguettes and coffee, I told Kate I had forgotten my American Express card in the room and had to retrieve it.

I ran back to the hotel, and climbed the stairs to the third floor. As I opened the door to our room and entered, I ran smack into the suspicious-looking desk clerk.

He said, "Monsieur, I was just checking to see if room was up to standards."

"I don't understand," I replied. "I asked you guys not to come in here, and hung the Do Not Disturb placard on the door."

"Yes, I know," the clerk said stiffly in English. "I just wanted to make sure everything is satisfactory. Service is very important to us at this hotel."

As we spoke, I glanced around the room to see if any of our things had been moved. As far as I could tell, they hadn't. I said, "I don't appreciate you being in our room."

He shot me a fuck-you look and left. I thought of reporting the surveillance, but decided that it was probably being carried out by French DGSE and they wanted to make sure I wasn't conducting clandestine operations under their noses.

Besides, it was our last day in Paris. I dispensed with the SDRs. That night as Kate and I walked back to the hotel slightly inebriated on Côtes du Rhône wine, she brought up the subject of our government's right to detain suspected terrorists. I was trying to put my finger on why she continued to be in a sour mood, and not succeeding. Back in our room, we made up and started to make love.

A few seconds after we finished, still sighing and cooing to one another, the phone on the table beside the bed rang abruptly. Kate answered and handed it to me.

"It's for you."

I immediately recognized the voice of the front desk clerk. He said, "Monsieur Laux, this is the front desk. We wanted to make sure that you're having a good time this evening."

"Yes, I am. Thank you."

"Bonsoir."

It was his way of saying, I know you just fucked your girlfriend, and we have it on tape.

Kate left the next morning for DC. I returned to Afghanistan a day later, thinking that it had been a strange trip and wondering where things were going between Kate and me.

Like the Sarposa breakout, maybe the writing was on the wall, and I didn't want to see it. Maybe because of the dangerous nature of my job, I needed to believe she'd be there for me when I needed her. Maybe my expectations were unrealistic. I don't know.

15

WALI DALIR/MULLAH RASHID[35]

Lord, what fools these mortals be.

—WILLIAM SHAKESPEARE

On my return to Kandahar, I picked up where I left off. Mornings I got up at six to jog and work out before the sun grew too intense. The rest of the day and evenings till midnight were spent meeting with assets and writing reports. In addition to weekly meetings with Abdul, Haji Jan, Mahmud, and other guys I was running, I was always on the lookout for new sources.

One of my fellow officers, whom we called Shakespeare ████████ ███ ████████████████ had just returned from his final R&R and was leaving Afghanistan in forty-five days. His replacement wasn't scheduled to arrive before he departed. So Shakespeare, as part of his "checking out" process, was looking to turn over his assets.

Warm turnovers where the departing officer introduced a new officer to the asset were always preferable, but in my experience happened only 10 percent of the time. This was going to be a warm one.

Shakespeare described the young ████████ he had recently met and liked. "He's about twenty," he said. "I learned about him from an-

---

[35] These are made-up names.

other source. He does courier work from Afghanistan to Pakistan for some of the big drug dealers. His job is to run written receipts back and forth across the border to keep track of who owes money to whom. He also likes to take pictures of him and his friends."

As I mentioned before, Pashtu men were in the habit of taking pictures with their male buddies. From my American perspective it made me wonder about their sexuality, because the pictures often depicted them sitting on each other's laps, holding hands, and hugging. Sometimes they would take these photos to computer shops and have them decorated with heart-and-flower-filled borders.

Shakespeare, who was an Ivy League grad and didn't seem comfortable dealing with people from the underbelly, introduced us. He said, "Wali Dalir, this is my colleague Zmarai. I'm going to leave you two to get acquainted." Then he turned on his heels and left.

I stood confronting a confused young man of about twenty, who wore a full beard and a colorful scarf over his *shalwar kameez*. The hand-off couldn't have been more awkward.

I tried to put him at ease, addressing him in Pashtu. "Hi, Wali Dalir, it's a pleasure to meet you. My name is Zmarai. Tell me a little about yourself."

When he got over his shock at hearing an American speak his language, he started to tell me a little about the opium trade and how he ran receipts.

It was mildly interesting. I sat thinking, *The harvest season lasts two weeks, three tops, and happens only once a year. So this guy only has utility three weeks out of the year.*

I asked Wali Dalir if he knew about anything else going on across the border that he thought might interest us.

He seemed to draw a blank and said that Shakespeare had never asked him that before. Wali Dalir struck me as *challak* (clever), but not too smart. As with Mahmud, Abdul, and all the other assets I was running, I didn't have time to help him build access.

After paying him, I said, "Come back in a week with the best information you can find."

A week later, he returned wearing another colorful scarf and a fake Rolex. After drinking tea, and telling me he was a fan of American movies, he related his intel: The opium harvest season was coming up in two months and he would be busy working for certain traffickers.

It wasn't much. I thought to myself, *Nice guy, but this isn't going anywhere.*

I said, "I hear you like to take pictures, Wali Dalir. Let me see your pictures."

He pulled out his cell phone and started to show me photos of himself with various friends. Some were low-level Taliban fighters living in ███████ ███████████. In some of the pictures, they posed with AK-47s and other Russian-made weapons.

He flipped to one where he was cradling a brand-new US-made ████████████ machine gun. I did a double take and asked, "What's this?"

"Those two guys are friends of mine from childhood. Now they're Taliban fighters."

"I don't care about them. But what's going on with the ████████? Where did you get that?"

"We bought it at a bazaar in ███████ [a town in another country]."

██
████████████████████████

"What do you mean, you bought it?" I asked.

"There's a big bazaar in ███████ that sells weapons from the US convoys that travel up from Karachi."

Afghanistan is a landlocked country, so it took a complex, Herculean effort to supply US and ISAF troops in Afghanistan with ammo, food, toothbrushes, fuel, computers, night-vision goggles, concertina wire, etc., at a rate of thousands of tons per day. In 2008, nearly thirty thousand containers were sent to the front. Traffic reportedly doubled in 2009, and doubled a second time in 2010.

The bulk of the cargo was carried by ship to the Indian Ocean port of Karachi, Pakistan, then off-loaded onto trucks. They followed the N-25 highway northwest to Afghanistan—a long, hazardous route that crossed the border in two locations, Chaman in the southern part of the country and through the dangerous Khyber Pass, and on to Kabul. The road from Karachi to Kandahar covered roughly 576 miles, while the northern route was almost twice as long.

What I didn't know until Wali Dalir explained it to me was that the trucks were driven by Pakistanis and traveled with no US military escorts. Like the Wolverine network, this critical supply operation was completely outsourced to Pakistani civilians. It seemed like a critical oversight on our part.[36]

"Everybody knows that gangs rob the caravans," Wali Dalir explained.

"How does that happen?"

"One of the Pakistani drivers talks to one of the local gangsters," he answered. "They negotiate a price and arrange a place where the driver will leave the trailer. The gangsters drive off with it, and the driver reports it as hijacked."

"It's like a scene out of the movie *Goodfellas*," I added.

According to the European Institute—a public-policy study group based in Washington, DC—450 trucks containing US gear had been hijacked in 2009.

I stopped in Boss Man's office and filled him in.

"Yeah, I've heard about it," he confided. "If you can find the people responsible, we'll take a closer look."

I found it hard to believe that the US government knew that this was happening and wasn't doing anything about it. Tons of food, fuel, ammo, and weapons were being stolen and no one seemed to care that a large portion of that was ending up in Taliban hands.

So I directed Wali Dalir to penetrate the stolen-supplies network,

---

[36] All of this is open-source material, including Chris Brummit, "Looted U.S. Army Gear for Sale in Pakistan," NBCNews.com, October 6, 2010.

just as I had tasked Mahmud to enter Wolverine's operation. He started by purchasing ██████ ██ █████████████████████████████████. About a month in, he saw a pair of bomb-sniffing German shepherds for sale at the ████████ bazaar and took a picture.

I carried it with me to the US military canine command on the base and asked them if they had expected a shipment of two bomb-sniffing dogs that had never arrived. They couldn't give me an answer. Instead, they referred me to the procurement people, who were housed in a separate location. Procurement sent me to another office. That office told me to talk to the canine command.

I typed up everything Wali Dalir was finding out about the stolen supplies, including specific items, their prices, and the names of some of the people involved. Each report took about three hours. No one at HQ responded.

It was like telephoning a young woman you're interested in, but she never picks up or returns your call. Despite the fact that Wolverine remained my primary focus, I kept submitting reports on the stolen supplies.

As Wali Dalir became more comfortable with me, I asked him why he was risking his life to work for us. He explained that he was hoping to marry his childhood sweetheart but had to pay her dowry first. According to Pashtun custom, the dowry (*mahar*) is the amount of money the groom has to give to the bride's family for her hand. This tradition is different from that practiced in most of South Asia, where the bride's family has to pay a dowry (*jahez*) to the husband.

██
██
██████████████████████████████████

In addition to the work he did for us, he continued to do seasonal courier duties for opium traffickers and small jobs for the Taliban. But neither yielded very much.

████████████████████████ ██████ ████████████████

During my second R&R, Kate and I had stopped in Santo Domingo on our way to Rio so I could serve as best man in my buddy's wedding. When his fiancée saw me, she found my beard disgusting and insisted that I shave.

My friend said, "If you have a good excuse, Doug, like you're hiding a hideous skin disease, let us know. Otherwise, you look like a homeless man and she doesn't want that in our wedding pictures."

Since I couldn't tell them why I wore the beard, I had to shave. That pissed off Kate, who couldn't understand why I had shaved the beard for my friend's fiancée and not for her.

The real shock came when I returned to Kandahar and the first person I met was Wali Dalir.

Ten minutes into our meeting, he stopped me and asked, "When does Zmarai come back?"

"What are you talking about?" I asked back.

"Zmarai. I spoke with him on the phone and he said he was going to be here. Where is he?"

Wali Dalir liked to joke with me, and laughed out loud when I used the words "shit" and "fuck," which were curse words he had heard in American movies. So I thought for a minute he was pulling my leg.

"This is a joke, right?" I asked.

"No," he replied with a blank stare.

"Wali Dalir," I pleaded. "It's me. Zmarai. How many Americans have you met who speak Pashtu?"

"Only one."

He still wasn't sure it was me, so I called one of the terps, who swore on the Koran that I was Zmarai.

Wali Dalir still looked confused. Never in his life had he seen anyone with a full beard who shaved it off. He actually walked over and touched my face.

"You look even younger than me," he declared.

At the time he was twenty and I was twenty-seven.

"How old did you think I was before?" I asked.

"The same age as my father before he died, forty-four."

He was an honest and open young guy, who thought of me as his boss and brought me little gifts of fruit and nuts. Once, he even gifted me a baby goat.

When it was time for me to leave Afghanistan, Wali Dalir took off one of the colorful *patoos* he wore and handed it to me. "Zmarai, this is my gift to you, my friend."

"Thank you, Wali Dalir."

I still have it and wear it sometimes under my jacket, when the weather's cold.

A much less sympathetic but equally valuable source I developed at Kandahar is someone I'll call Mullah Rashid. He was a Taliban commander with a reputation of being a savage, and high on the US military's objectives list.

During one of my weekly sit-downs with military J2, he said, "We're hearing a lot about this Mullah Rashid guy, who is ███████████ ██ ██ a deadly individual who is targeting us. You have anything on him?"

"I'll ask around."

The next time I saw Mahmud, I asked if he knew anything about Mullah Rashid.

He said, "I know who that is. We call him Akbar. He buys IED components in ██████ and makes his own IEDs. If you want me to, I can get him to buy the components from me. And, I can get his ████████████."

"Thanks, Mahmud," I replied. "You're the man."

When we met again a week later he gave me Mullah Rashid's ██████████████. I passed it on to the J2. ████████████████ ██████████████ ████████████████ ██████████████████████████████

███████████████████████ Two days later, I got an unexpected visit from the team leader of Operation Detachment Alpha (ODA). ODAs were Army Special Forces groups consisting of two officers and ten sergeants with almost unlimited capabilities to operate in hostile or denied areas. They were considered independent and self-sustaining and routinely trained, advised, and assisted other US and allied forces while standing by to perform other special operations. As part of their duties, they did some local intelligence gathering.

The ODA team leader, who was a huge former Navy SEAL named Rusty, asked, "How did you find out about Mullah Rashid?"

I told him.

He nodded and said, "I want to know who Mahmud is."

"Sorry, I can't tell you that. You have Mullah Rashid's ███████ ██████████████ ███."

He said, "No. It's more complicated than that."

"Why?"

"He's one of our sources."

"What? The US military wants to kill this guy because he's blowing up their men, and he's your source?"

"It's complicated," Rusty answered.

Whenever the J2 or other military leaders needed to know something, I'd tell them. But sometimes military intel guys didn't want to share information. This seemed to be one of those cases.

I said, "I need to know what's going on with this guy, because I don't see any reports in the system."

"Mullah Rashid is actually helping us a lot," Rusty answered. "He tells us where IED attacks are likely to take place and we try to stop them."

"That's great, but one of my sources who is a member of the Taliban told me that Mullah Rashid is actually building the IEDs himself."

Rusty frowned at me and said, "You don't know what the fuck you're talking about."

I didn't want to get into an argument with him. So I said, "Next time you meet with him let me sit in so I can ask him some questions."

"Sorry," replied Rusty. "That's not going to happen."

I went to see Boss Man, who had jurisdiction over all intel gathering in the South. He spoke to Rusty and said, "You can either let Doug meet with Mullah Rashid, or we can file a request through the chain of command. How do you want to do this?"

Rusty, being a dick, answered, "If that's what you want to do, put in a formal request."

The approvals were going to take weeks, so next time I saw Mahmud, I said, "I want you to ask Mullah Rashid if he'll meet with me."

Two weeks later, Mahmud came back and said, "He's not willing to meet you yet, but he gave me this picture."

The photo showed a short, bearded Mullah Rashid in front of ██████████████████████████. Standing next to him was one of the members of ODA.

It constituted an almost unthinkable breach of security.

Mahmud said, "If I tried to take a photo of you, you'd probably have me executed, right?"

"That's correct."

"When the Taliban gets hold of this, they'll set up on that ███████████ and wait for the Americans to show up," Mahmud added. "They'll recruit some twelve-year-old to phone them when they roll in, then they'll go in heavy and smoke them."

I showed the photo to Boss Man, who was equally appalled. Then I walked over to ODA with one of my fellow officers to try to get the situation sorted out.

As soon as we entered the trailer, which housed ODA headquarters, the deputy—a guy named Wallace—started to cover the papers on his desk like I was going to look at their reports, which I didn't give a rat's ass about. I informed him that I wanted to see Rusty.

Wallace said, "You can talk to me."

Military-Agency protocol dictated that I was allowed to talk only to the ODA team leader. I pointed this out.

Wallace said, "Let me see if he's here."

He returned twenty minutes later and said, "The chief said you should talk to me."

I didn't have time to waste and wasn't in the mood to play bureaucratic games. "Okay, tell Rusty that the dude we discussed before will now be only talking to me, and it's nonnegotiable."

"Wait here."

Wallace ran back to see his chief again and quickly returned. "Follow me."

My colleague and I followed him to Rusty's office, where we found the ODA leader running on a treadmill with earphones on.

I shouted, "Hey, Rusty, what's going on?"

Rusty didn't stop the treadmill or remove the headphones. He just nodded.

"Can you hear me, Rusty?"

He nodded again but didn't stop.

Trying to keep my cool, I said, "You know the guy we talked about before? Well, I confirmed that he is purchasing, making, and planting IEDs, which is something I have to address with him immediately. If you're willing, I'm going to take that from you, and call him."

Rusty removed the headphones, stopped the treadmill, and got off. Red-faced and dripping with sweat, he said, "No, I don't approve of that. It's not happening."

"Look, I submitted the formal request to Kabul and I've heard that it's going to be approved. So while we wait for the paperwork, and since we're talking about someone who seems to be attacking us while we speak and is also taking money from us, I believe strongly that I should address this now."

"Absolutely not," Rusty growled. "This is exactly why we don't have a working relationship with you people, and everyone here hates you. I don't even want to be talking to you right now."

"You think I'm here to poach your sources, but this isn't what this is about. Your job, and what you're trained to do, is to take down objectives. My job is to provide you with them. I don't tell you how to run your ops, and you should respect the fact that I know how to run sources and develop them. That's why I'm taking this over, not because I don't like you or have a grudge against you. In fact, I want to collaborate. You should want that too."

Rusty got in my face and shouted, "Fuck off, kid!"

Then he put on his headphones and got back on the treadmill. I removed the photo of Mullah Rashid with one of his men from my pocket and held it in front of his face.

"You know who this guy is?"

Rusty's face turned purple. He grabbed the photo away from me and stopped the treadmill. "Where the fuck did you get this, smart-ass?"

"Is he one of your guys?" I asked.

"That's none of your fucking business."

"Okay, Rusty," I replied. "I'll take that as a yes. He is one of your guys and he had his photo taken with a source near your meeting place, which is not smart. So I'm actually doing you a favor by taking Mullah Rashid off your hands. Because he is a Taliban commander, and he is making IEDs that are killing our troops. And the next time you meet him at ███████████████ he might have his men set up on you and take you out."

Rusty threw the photo back at me and stormed out of his own office.

A week later I met Mullah Rashid in person. Since he was afraid that someone in Kandahar might recognize him, he arrived outside our base in the middle of the night. He stood about five foot three, wore a thin mustache, and looked like a classic villain.

He turned out to be fearless and greedy, and therefore willing to do whatever I asked for the right amount of money. A tough, battle-hardened field commander, he didn't have the connections in ████████ that Mahmud did. Nor did he command as many troops.

But he was able to warn us about Taliban operations and ambushes, which saved many American lives. He also brought in a number of different kinds of IEDs, which I then showed to Mahmud, who was able to identify where the parts came from. It helped us understand the entire network from the end users in western Kandahar to the people supplying Wolverine.

Before one night meeting, Mullah Rashid was standing on a designated corner in a suburb of Kandahar waiting ███████ ███████, when he saw someone he knew. Afraid of being discovered, he jumped in an open sewer, swam two miles from the edge of the city to the base, and arrived soaking wet, smelling like shit.

On August 6, 2011, a US CH-47 Chinook military helicopter, call sign Extortion 17, was shot down near a village in the Tangi Valley west of Kabul as it hurried a QRF (quick-reaction force) attempting to reinforce a unit of Army Rangers. The resulting crash killed all thirty-eight people on board, including twenty-two Navy SEALs, five US Navy special warfare support personnel, five United States Army National Guard and Army Reserve crewmen, seven Afghan CTPTs, and one Afghan interpreter—as well as a US military combat dog.

It became the worst single-incident loss of US military life in the Afghan war, surpassing the sixteen QRF soldiers who died in a Chinook crash trying to rescue Marcus Luttrell in June 2005 as part of Operation Redwing—a tragic incident described in Luttrell's bestselling book *Lone Survivor.*

Of the twenty-two Navy SEALs who perished, fifteen were members of the Naval Special Warfare Development group (DEVGRU), also known as SEAL Team Six.[37]

Boss Man came to me the next morning and said, "This was a huge blow. I know you have sources inside the Taliban. It sure would be great if you could talk to them and find out what happened."

Mahmud didn't have access to Taliban insurgents in the Tangi Valley of Wardak Province, where the incident took place, but Mullah Rashid did.

---

[37] This is all open-source material found on Wikipedia and in other publications.

When I asked him about it, he grinned and said, "Yes, there's a lot of talk about that now. All the men in the area are high-fiving one another. We didn't know they were Navy SEALs on the helicopter until we heard it on Al Jazeera."

Despite the fact that he was working with us, he was happy that the SEALs had been killed—a dichotomy he lived with constantly and one that was shared by some of my other assets.

Knowing that he loved money, I said, "If you can find out who did it and how it happened, there's a big payout for you."

A day later he called me back. "I've got the names of the three guys responsible ███████████████████████.

███████████████████████████████████

███████████████████████████████████

███████████████████████████████████

████████ [38]

I wrote up a report with the insurgents' names ██████████████ and Boss Man hurried it over to military headquarters. That's the last I heard about the incident until three weeks later when I was preparing to leave Afghanistan and met with Mullah Rashid for the last time. I introduced him to a colleague and told him that he would be handling him the future.

Mullah Rashid cut me off and asked, "Where's my money?"

"What money?"

"I want my fucking payout, Zmarai. You asked me for the names of the three Taliban who carried out the August sixth attack on the helicopter, and I gave them to you, and you took them out."

"Really?" I asked. "They're dead? I didn't know."

"You killed them within twelve hours of me giving you the information. So pay me, now."

"I need proof."

---

[38] ██████████████████████████████████████

██████████████████████████████████

"Well, Zmarai, didn't you kill them yourself?" he asked.

"No."

Mullah Rashid pointed to one of the Scorpions in the room with us. "Then didn't one of your friends here kill them?"

"No."

I felt like a buffoon because I hadn't been told anything. Mullah Rashid started getting angry. "You're leaving," he growled. "I'll never see you again. And I won't talk to your friend."

I went into my cash box and grabbed everything I had left. It ████████████████████████ which was a fortune to an Afghan. Usually any payment over ███████ had to be approved by Boss Man. But Boss Man had left Afghanistan the week before.

Most people in my position wouldn't have paid Mullah Rashid. But I knew that if I didn't, we would lose him as a source. So I handed him the cash.

When I got back to DC, I found out that the insurgents had been killed in ██████ █████ a day after Mullah Rashid passed me their locations ███████████████. I also got a call from the head of finance, who wanted me to pay back the ████████.

I said, "I just finished serving two tours in a war zone. Each time I was allotted to ██████ buy personal items like body-fitting armor, boots, and winter gear, I only spent ███████ of it. I can also go over my records and expense you for every little nitpicking thing I spent during the last two years."

"That's your prerogative," he offered.

"No, it's your choice. I can either locate my former chief in Kandahar and get him to write a memo explaining what happened, or you can choose the other option, which means you'll see me walking around the building wearing a whole lot of new stuff from Patagonia."

The finance chief asked me to try the first option. I spoke to Boss Man, who wrote a memo that was retro-approved, and the ████████ was taken off the books.

16

WOLVERINE

There are two ways to be fooled. One is to believe what isn't true; the other is to refuse to believe what is true.

—SØREN KIERKEGAARD

In March 2011, Mahmud reported a lot of infighting among Wol-verine's deputies Iceman, Cyclops, and Polaris.[39] Apparently Wolverine had been allowing the three men to skim off the top of IED sales. But Polaris was skimming harder than the others.

During one of our weekly meetings, Mahmud told me that Wolverine had found out about Polaris and was talking about having him killed. The tension between the three lieutenants was building. I warned Mahmud not to take sides.

Because he had all the bona fides of a Taliban commander and was smart, Mahmud was invaluable. He and Mullah Rashid were helping us get a large amount of IEDs off the market and out of the hands of Taliban insurgents. As a result, US and ISAF military commanders were seeing fewer IED attacks against their troops, and consequently a lower number of injuries and casualties.

As welcome and encouraging as this news was, my goal was still to take down the entire network. I also wanted to find out if Wolverine was

---

[39] All these individuals are referred to by made-up names and have since died.

being aided by ▇▇ ▇▇▇▇ (a foreign intelligence service). ▇▇▇▇▇

▇ ▇▇▇▇▇▇▇▇▇▇▇▇▇▇▇▇▇▇▇▇▇▇▇

▇▇▇▇▇▇▇▇▇▇▇▇▇▇▇▇▇▇▇▇▇▇▇▇

▇▇▇▇▇▇▇▇▇▇▇▇▇▇▇▇▇▇▇▇▇▇▇▇

▇▇▇▇▇▇▇▇▇▇▇▇

▇▇▇▇▇▇▇▇▇▇▇▇▇▇▇▇▇▇▇▇▇▇▇▇

▇▇▇▇▇▇▇▇▇▇▇▇▇▇▇▇▇▇▇▇▇▇▇▇

▇▇▇▇▇▇▇▇▇▇▇▇▇▇▇▇

▇▇▇▇▇▇▇▇▇▇▇▇▇▇▇▇▇▇▇▇▇▇▇▇

▇▇▇▇▇▇▇▇▇▇▇▇▇▇▇▇▇▇▇▇▇▇▇▇

▇▇▇▇▇▇▇▇▇▇▇▇▇▇▇▇▇▇▇▇▇▇▇▇

▇▇▇▇▇▇▇▇▇▇▇▇▇▇▇▇▇▇▇▇▇▇▇▇

▇▇▇▇▇▇▇▇▇▇▇▇▇▇▇▇▇▇▇▇▇▇▇▇

▇▇▇▇▇▇▇▇[40]

But HQ didn't want to hear this, ▇▇▇▇▇▇▇▇▇▇▇

▇▇▇▇▇▇▇▇▇▇▇▇▇▇▇▇▇▇▇▇▇▇▇▇

▇▇▇▇▇▇▇▇▇▇▇▇▇▇▇▇ so that the evidence I had gathered never made it into reports read by the White House and other foreign-policy decision makers in DC.

When I complained about this to the chief CMO (Case Management Officer also known as a Reports Officer), he said, "You don't understand. If that information gets out, the eye of Mordor will come down on you."

"I've been hearing it from a number of different people in or associated with the Taliban," I argued. "Why would they lie to me? They're already paid assets. It doesn't make sense."

---

[40] ▇▇▇▇▇▇▇▇▇▇▇▇▇▇▇▇▇▇▇▇▇▇

▇▇▇▇▇▇▇▇▇▇▇▇▇▇▇▇▇▇▇▇▇▇▇▇

▇▇▇▇▇▇▇▇▇▇▇▇▇▇▇▇▇▇▇▇▇▇▇▇

▇▇▇▇▇▇▇▇▇▇▇▇▇▇▇▇▇▇▇▇▇▇▇▇

▇▇▇▇▇▇▇▇▇▇▇▇▇▇▇▇▇▇▇

"Be careful," he warned.

One afternoon in late March, Mahmud texted me on the burner cell phone reserved exclusively for him. "Urgent! 6 pm tomorrow."

██
███████████████████████████ Usually Mahmud and I chatted about his kids (he never talked about his wife) before we got started. This time he barely sat down before he relayed his news. "Zmarai, Iceman and Polaris got into an argument about the extra money Polaris has been skimming. Iceman pulled out a gun and shot Polaris in the head. He's dead."

"Holy shit! What happened to Iceman?" I asked, trying to understand the implications and how this might affect Mahmud.

"Wolverine has put out a contract on him and wants him killed," said Mahmud.

"Where's Iceman now?"

"He's disappeared. He's hiding."

"That leaves Wolverine with only one lieutenant, Cyclops," I observed.

"Yes, Zmarai. Praise God."

"I want you to make friends with Cyclops."

He nodded. "That's not a problem."

"Stay close to Cyclops and Wolverine, and make yourself indispensable. Wolverine is going to need more lieutenants and I want you to become one of them."

"Okay."

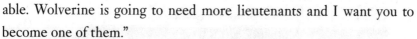

Mahmud was meeting with Wolverine daily, which meant that he had to be even more vigilant than before. One false move on his part and Wolverine would kill Mahmud and his family. He was so busy and closely watched that it was difficult for him to meet with me at our base.

At one of these meetings, he told me that Wolverine had recently sent him to meet an important man in ▮▮▮▮▮▮ I asked him to relate the story in detail. (What follows are the details of that meeting, which were redacted completely due to their extreme sensitivity.)

It seemed obvious that Wolverine had sent Mahmud to be vetted by professionals. The tradecraft used by the clean-cut man and the ████ pointed to a highly trained clandestine service.

I wrote up a report on Mahmud's trip and showed it to Boss Man. "Here's your smoking gun," I offered.

He read it carefully and said, "Maybe Mahmud is bullshitting us."

"Why would he do that? He has nothing to gain. My assessment is that he's telling the truth. And I'm sure the clean-cut guy he described works for ████ [a foreign intelligence service]."

"Why?" Boss Man asked.

"Just do the math. The tradecraft he used was sophisticated, way beyond what I know the Taliban is capable of. Isn't it our job to navigate through this ambiguity and make assessments?"

"Yes."

"Then my assessment is ███████████████████ ██ ██████████████████████."

"That's why this report is never going out," Boss Man concluded.

I understood that he didn't want his ass on the line. But I felt that this information was too critical to ignore. Unable to let it go, I took it up with him again two nights later.

I said, "Think about your college-graduate son, or my brother. My brother's highly intelligent. He's an engineer. Even if he read all the books on the Agency and studied the Jason Bourne movies frame by frame, he still wouldn't have the tradecraft to devise something like what Mahmud was put through. And I can't believe Mahmud made this up after a hundred other things he's told us have proved to be true. He's told us what Wolverine looks like, where he works, his twenty or so cell-phone numbers, and all of it has checked out. Why would he ruin everything by telling us a bogus story?"

Boss Man leaned back in his chair and took a sip of Scotch. "It's a good story. If it's true, you've done amazing work. But nobody in Washington wants to hear this. If I send it out, HQ is going to come after us and ask us dozens of tough questions. You have no proof, so I'm doing you a favor."

"I have lots of proof. I have ███████ separate reports with names and ██████████████. Now I have this. I'm willing to put my name on it and say, This is what I think this proves. That's what I thought I was hired to do."

Boss Man shook his head. "Doug, they simply won't believe you. Nobody is going to put their ass on the line to support someone who has only been in the field two years."

I realized what was happening. I was butting my head against rock-hard political realities. The US government had ████████████████████

██

████, ███████████████████████████████████████. I had evidence that proved that supposition wrong. Even if I did have a smoking gun, Boss Man was telling me it wasn't enough. We needed a cannon to blast through layers of political cement.

I turned to Boss Man and said, "I guess I'll have to keep going after Wolverine and prove I'm right."

"Good idea."

I did, with added vigor, together with my very capable partner, Mahmud. He was moving money and material, which he believed he was getting from ████████. He was recording names and ████████ and secretly snapping pictures of people and locations.

By the summer of ████ we had a complete, detailed understanding of how Wolverine's network worked. We knew the players, suppliers, routes, buyers, end users, and the different kinds of products. With all the pieces of the puzzle neatly in place, it was time to get Wolverine and dismantle his network.

I wanted to understand our options, and protect Mahmud. Developing a cover story for him was imperative. I also needed to hide our hand. ████████████████████████████████ ████████████████████████████

Complicating the situation ████████████████ was the fact that US-Pakistan relations were at an all-time low due to two major incidents that had happened earlier that year. One was the Ray Davis fiasco, and the second was the raid against Osama bin Laden.

On January 27, 2011, a US contractor named Ray Davis, who was doing protective security for us in Lahore, Pakistan, was driving through the city checking routes ███████████████████████ ███████████████████████. Davis was a former Special Forces soldier and the task he was performing that day was routine.

At some point during his protective security assignment, Davis stopped at a bank machine and withdrew money. As he got back into his white Honda Civic and drove in the Mozang Chungi area of the city, he sensed that he was being followed by two men on a motorcycle. When he stopped at a traffic light, the motorcycle pulled up beside him and one of the men brandished a pistol.

Fearing that he was about to be robbed, Davis opened fire with his 9mm Glock, killing the two men on the spot. Davis got out of his car and took pictures of the men with his cell phone. As a crowd gathered, he radioed for backup.

Minutes later, a four-man quick-reaction force left the Lahore Consulate in a Toyota Land Cruiser. When they got stuck in traffic on Jail Road, the driver of the Cruiser jumped the divider and hit a motorcycle head-on, resulting in the motorcyclist's death. The QRF fled the scene. Davis took off, also, but was later stopped by police and arrested.

News of the murders became headline news across Pakistan. Davis's appearance before a Pakistani judicial officer (PJO) was broadcast on live television and went like this:

> Davis: I'm not answering any questions. I have diplomatic immunity.
> PJO: But your passport is not diplomatic.
> Davis: You have my passport? Can I see it?
> PJO: Yes, it's here.
> Davis: I am a diplomat and have immunity.

The problem was that Davis wasn't a diplomat; nor were diplomats, Agency officers, or Agency contractors permitted to carry weapons. Furthermore, the three murders fueled the paranoia of US-hating Pakistanis. It proved to them that CIA officers operated openly in their country and killed with impunity.[41]

The Pakistani media ran the story of the investigation nonstop. Police learned that the Toyota Land Cruiser used by the QRF carried

---

[41] All this material regarding Ray Davis and his activities in Pakistan can be found in open sources.

fake registration plates. An unnamed ▮▮ official claimed that Davis had met with people in the western tribal areas without approval.

Angry protesters took to the streets of Lahore and Peshawar demanding that Davis be hanged for murder. President Barack Obama argued that Davis was protected by the Vienna Convention on Diplomatic Relations and asked Pakistan to release him immediately. Pakistani officials disputed the claim of immunity and questioned the scope of Davis's activities in Pakistan.

A tense diplomatic standoff dragged on for weeks. After much back-and-forth, charges were dropped and Davis was released on March 16 under the principle of Sharia in Islamic law, which allowed that murder charges could be dismissed if a *diyya* was paid to the deceased's families. The US was rumored to have paid between $1.4 million and $3 million to the dead men's families.

From January through March, while the Davis case was a daily topic of discussion in Pakistan, I noticed a change in my assets, ▮▮▮▮▮▮▮▮▮▮▮▮▮▮▮▮▮▮▮▮▮▮▮. They seemed edgier with me and asked me pointed questions about our activities in their country. These were guys who watched James Bond and Jason Bourne movies and thought they were real. They didn't want spies in their homeland, and they didn't want Americans violating their sovereignty and killing their people.

Pakistan was still recovering from the Ray Davis incident when, on the night of May 1, two dozen heavily armed Navy SEALs entered Pakistan and raided a compound in Abbottabad, sixty miles from the capital of Islamabad, killing al-Qaeda founder Osama bin Laden, his adult son, his courier, and the courier's brother and wife.

At 11:35 p.m. EST, President Obama appeared on major television networks to announce the terrorist leader's death. "To those families who have lost loved ones to al-Qaeda's terror," he said, "justice has been done." US officials later announced that they chose not to share information about the raid with the government of Pakistan until it was over.

I found out about it at seven the next morning as I walked into the base cafeteria and saw the news on CNN. Shocked, I ran back to the

Agency compound, where everyone was celebrating. I was glad we got bin Laden, but ███████████████████████████████████████.

I knew the Pakistanis were going to be pissed and they were. Thousands of angry protesters took to the streets demanding retaliation for the US raid. In an address to the Pakistani parliament, Pakistan's prime minister Yousaf Raza Gillani said, "Our people are rightly incensed on the issue of violation of sovereignty as typified by the covert US air and ground assault on the Osama hideout in Abbottabad."

███████████████████████████████████████

███████████████████████████████████████

███████████████████████

The president and his advisors had deliberately kept the circle extremely small for reasons of security. Part of me was thrilled that we had eighty-sixed bin Laden. I had dreamed for years of killing him myself. But another part of me was annoyed. It would have been nice if the organization we worked for had given us a heads-up. The raid had the potential to jeopardize everything my colleagues and I had been working on for months.

I spent the next three days working the phones nonstop, talking to my assets, telling them to stand down until the dust settled, and trying to convince them that I didn't know about the raid ahead of time.

None of them believed me. They wanted me to know that the raid had put their lives and the lives of their families in peril.

As I tried to patch things up, I started to wonder if the juice was worth the squeeze in terms of the raid. Once we knew where bin Laden was, where was he going to go? If we were going to risk sending SEALs into Pakistan, why didn't we grab him, interrogate him, and throw him in jail?

The intel we could have extracted from him and the public-relations coup could have been enormous. What we learned about bin Laden from materials seized from his house was that he was a cranky, isolated old man who felt disrespected by young jihadists who were using the al-Qaeda name. He had been living quietly with several of his wives, children, and grandchildren in Abbottabad among other refugees from the Swat Valley without the knowledge of the Pakistani government since 2005.

What most Americans didn't understand was that before his trusted courier Arshad Khan (aka Abu Ahmed al-Kuwaiti) was observed entering the Abbottabad compound, bin Laden was not a major concern within the US government. ███████████████████████████ ███, because he was almost completely silent, had lost credibility among young jihadists, had no following on jihadist websites, and didn't appear to be actively playing a role in planning future operations. The attitude in the Agency was: One day he'll pop his head up and we'll terminate him—which is exactly what happened.

As spring 2011 turned into summer, I struggled to steady the ops I was running and keep them on course. Wolverine kept appearing bigger and bigger in our sights. I wanted to believe that the resentment caused by Ray Davis and the bin Laden raid had waned. I also wanted to believe that when my tour ended in August and I returned to Washington Kate and I would pick up where we left off.

I was wrong on both fronts.

17

TERMINATION

When you betray somebody else, you also betray yourself.

—Isaac Bashevis Singer

Without question Abdul had been the key to my success. Starting with our meeting back at Wadi, he helped me piece together a spy network link by link. He was so good that from the first day he approached me at the ▮▮▮▮▮ *shura* (Wadi Base), I wondered if maybe he was ▮▮▮▮ plant. But the intel he had brought me in the intervening eighteen months consistently checked out, and the men he recruited had yielded results.

I learned to trust him and came to realize that he was a greedy dude with huge ambitions. Every time we met, he complained that he was running the whole network and not getting paid enough. I took it all in stride, because he was getting a fortune by Afghan standards.

I usually found him jovial and eager to please—an Afghan version of Jerry Maguire. But starting in late May 2011, I started to notice a change in his attitude. Instead of joking around and trying to act like an American, he'd smoke incessantly and stared at me sullenly. I didn't know if the change in his demeanor was a result of the Ray Davis incident, OBL's death, or something else.

Concurrent with the change in Abdul's attitude, Haji Jan and others seemed to be acting fidgety around him. So I called Abdul in individually and asked him, "What's up? You seem different the last couple of weeks."

He answered, "No. Everything's fine, Zmarai. I'm just a little stressed out about this land dispute I'm involved in. I was wondering if you could set up a meeting for me with Ahmed Wali Karzai."

AWK, whom I've mentioned before, was President Karzai's brother and the most powerful man in southern Afghanistan.

I said, "No, Abdul, I can't do that, and I doubt that Ahmed Wali Karzai is going to be interested in your land dispute."

"Well, how about you give me money so that I can pay him a bribe?"

"No, Abdul. I can't do that."

His sullen attitude continued into June. So did Haji Jan's discomfort in his presence. During a meeting with the two of them at the beginning of the month, I asked Haji Jan if everything was okay. He glanced furtively at Abdul and immediately tensed up.

Sensing that something was going on between them, I spoke to Haji Jan's ███████ Mahmud and asked him to talk to his uncle and find out what was going on.

That night I got a text message from Haji Jan that said, "Zmarai, in the future, I only want to meet with you alone. It's Abdul's fault. I don't trust him and you shouldn't, either. Can I come in and see you tomorrow?"

I'd seen Haji Jan only a few days prior, but I texted back, "Yes, absolutely. Come in tomorrow."

He arrived at our base in a taxi. Soon after dispensing pleasantries in the meeting room, he said, "Zmarai, this is what has been going on. Abdul has been complaining from the beginning that you don't respect him enough, and you're not giving him enough ███."

"What?" I exclaimed. "He makes more than everyone else. Every time he brings someone in, I give him ████████."

"I know. But he complains that it's not enough."

██

██

██

████████████████████████████████

But like I said before, Abdul was a greedy bastard.

██

████████████████████████

"What?" I was shocked. "Why didn't anyone tell me before?"

"Abdul told us that you knew," replied Haji Jan. "We thought you were okay with it, and we wanted to continue to work with you, so we took what we got."

What Haji Jan and the others didn't know and Abdul had failed to tell them was that Abdul was getting his own salary. They were under the mistaken impression that he was only earning ████████ I handed out each time when we met with them.

It was an oversight on my part, and I was pissed.

"Mahmud told Abdul that he wasn't going to give him half anymore," Haji Jan explained. "Abdul said, If you do that I'll tell Zmarai and have you fired. Mahmud didn't care. He knew he was important. He told Abdul to leave him alone or he'd cut his throat."

Aware that I had a major problem on my hands, I said, "Haji Jan, thanks for sharing this with me. I'll tell Abdul that I learned this from Mahmud, and ask him if he's doing it to everyone."

Next, I confirmed Haji Jan's story with Mahmud.

Mahmud said, "I told Abdul to fuck off, I wasn't going to give him

██████████████. And if he didn't leave me alone, I'd send my men to kill him and his family."

It was time to call Abdul in. After we shared a meal of pizza and Diet Pepsi, I spoke. "Abdul, we need to have an honest conversation. I asked you to be my right-hand man. I trusted you, but now I'm starting to wonder if my trust was misplaced."

"Why do you say that?" he asked, surprised.

"Because Mahmud told me about the conversation he had with you several months ago when you were asking for ██ ████████ and he told you that he was going to stop."

Abdul dropped his cigarette on the floor and waved his hand. "No, Zmarai. It didn't happen the way. I only asked him ██████████ ███, because I have a big family with lots of responsibilities."

"Abdul, did I ever give you permission ████████████████? No, I didn't, and I'm the boss. I'm ██████████ men for a service that they do for me. You have no right to interfere."

He shook his head. "No. No, it's not like that, Zmarai. It was just a couple of times when I was ████████████."

"I'm not sure I believe you. Everybody has been acting strange. If I call Haji Jan tonight, what is he going to say?"

"Nothing, Zmarai. By the grace of God, he'll say nothing."

"You better be telling me the truth, because if you're lying I'll find out, and I'll be mad."

"It's the truth, Zmarai."

I warned, "Stay away from Mahmud, and don't piss off his ████. You fuck with these guys, and you'll put yourself in danger."

He left looking frightened, and I thought the matter was resolved.

One night in early August I got a call from Haji Jan ██████████ which was a violation of security protocol. He said, "Zmarai, we need to talk."

██
████████████████████████████

"I need to tell you what's going on, and I can't talk about this in front of Abdul."

"Okay, when you arrive for your scheduled meeting with Abdul on Friday, I'll announce to you both that we've instituted a new protocol and have the Scorpions separate you and put you in different rooms."

"Zmarai, this is important. It's something you need to know."

"Okay. We'll talk Friday."

Friday when he arrived with Abdul, I had the Scorpions escort Abdul to a separate meeting room. Then I turned to Haji Jan and asked, "What's up? Tell me your news."

"Abdul confronted me three days ago and asked me why I told you I was giving him a cut. Screaming, he said, 'Don't you know Zmarai and I are brothers, and now he's mad at you?'"

Damn, I said to myself. *This is worse than I thought.*

"He asked, 'Why are you loyal to Zmarai, anyway? He's a foreigner. I can't believe that you would squeal on me to a foreigner,'" Haji Jan continued. "I asked him, 'Why are you talking about Zmarai like this?' He said, 'I have been thinking about this situation. What we are doing is wrong according to the Koran and the code of *Pashtunwali.* We are betraying our own people.'"

"Abdul said that?" I asked.

"Yes. Then he said, 'I have a way for us to ███████████ trick the foreigners. ████████████████████████████████ ████████████████ ██████.'"

████████████████████████████████ ████████
██

I felt my blood pressure shoot up.

"I said to him, I don't even know how to approach them," Haji Jan said. "And why would I? I'm ████████████████ ex-Taliban, so it's not a good idea for me. ████████████████████ ██ ██████
██████.'"

"What did Abdul say to that?"

"We got into a big argument. He said, 'If you don't work with ████████████, the next time we ██████████████, you'll be arrested.'"

Holy shit. Now I had an even bigger problem and one that had to be addressed immediately.

"Do you know who Abdul is meeting with?" I asked.

"No," answered Haji Jan.

"Be careful what you tell Abdul from now on, and I'll figure out another way to get you ████████ ████████."

I walked to a nearby room, where I found Abdul smoking like a chimney. I asked, "What's going on with Haji Jan? Do you think he's still worth working with?"

"I don't know if we can trust him," Abdul answered. "I'll keep an eye on him."

Motherfucker.

Then I summoned Haji Jan and the three of us met together. Haji Jan related the information he had brought with him, and Abdul went into his usual routine about how he really deserved the credit. Each one thought that the joke was on the other. The truth was that I believed Haji Jan was telling the truth and wanted to slap Abdul silly.

As soon as the meeting ended, I texted instructions to Mahmud to rendezvous with me at ██████████████████.

The subject of our confab was Abdul. Mahmud said, "I think Abdul is meeting with someone ██████████, which is dangerous for me. If he tells them about me, and I'm arrested, I'm fucked."

Undoubtedly.

Not wanting to jeopardize all the work we had done in terms of Wolverine, I did some quick checking of my own. I found out that the day after I confronted Abdul in June, he drove directly to ████████ ██████████ (a friendly intelligence service). ███████████████████ ██

This posed a huge risk for us, and wasn't smart on his part. ██████████ ██

███████████████████████████████████████

███████████████████████████████████████

████████████████

Most of what I was learning from Abdul, Mahmud, and the others concerned Taliban activities ██████████. But if I received news of a pending attack in Afghanistan, I'd pass it on to Boss Man, ████████████████ ████████████████████████.

At this point, Mahmud and Haji Jan were more important to me than Abdul. Eager to find out how much damage he had done, and wanting to gather as much evidence against him as I could, I pulled all the reports ██.

███████████████████████████████████████

███████████████████████████████████████

██████████████████████████████

███████████████████████████████████████

███████████████████████████████████████

███████████████████████████████████████

███████████████████████████████████████

████████████████████████

When I went through the ████████████████████████████████, I found nothing about Mahmud and Wolverine, which was a big relief. But I did discover about a dozen items that came from sources high up ████████████████████ that Abdul knew about. Two of the dozen were particularly valuable.

Looking back at reports earlier than May (when Abdul first ████████████████), I didn't find mention of these topics.

When I discussed my findings with HQ, Boss Man, and Deputy Hooper, they all agreed that there was only a very slight chance that ██████ had learned this information from someone other than Abdul.

Boss Man said, "Combined with what Haji Jan told you, I'd say it's pretty clear that Abdul has flipped. That means you're going to have to terminate him."

██████████████████████████ I asked.

"There's no need for us to address this with them," Boss Man answered. "But you need to talk to Abdul."

"Will do."

"It's your job to manage the fallout."

Great.

I'd been taught that the best way to terminate a source was using the three Fs—firm, fair, final. Finality was the most important, followed by firmness, and evenhandedness. We didn't want him coming back two months later knocking on our door.

The situation I faced was tricky, because I couldn't tell Abdul about what we had received ▮▮▮▮▮▮▮▮, nor could I reveal what I had heard from Haji Jan. And I didn't have hard evidence like a photo to stick in his face as a way of saying, I caught you red-handed.

My big fear was that he would dime out Mahmud and Haji Jan ▮▮▮▮▮▮▮▮▮▮▮▮▮▮▮▮▮▮▮▮. Knowing the termination was going to be challenging, I went through my arguments with Hooper, then told Abdul to meet me at the base.

The morning of the meeting, I warned the Scorpions about what I was about to do, in case Abdul freaked out.

They were both shocked. Hillbilly asked, "What the fuck happened? He's been your main guy for a year and a half."

I explained that I wanted him and Lolita to stand outside the door of the meeting room even though it was a hundred degrees outside. I would have a radio on me. If Abdul became violent, I figured I could take him down. But I didn't want him hurting the terp, who had been briefed as well.

The room was deliberately staged with no food, no cashews, no cigarettes, no tea, nothing.

Abdul looked around, perplexed. He asked, "Am I allowed to smoke cigarettes at this meeting?"

"Yes," I answered. "But you'll have to smoke your own."

I walked to the door, asked Hillbilly, who was holding Abdul's personal possessions, to hand me his cigarettes, then tossed them to Abdul.

He said, "Zmarai, my brother, you're usually the cigarette king. What's going on?"

In the past, I had always put a couple of packs of his favorite brand on the table. I said, "You notice that something is different today, don't you?"

"Yes," answered Abdul, lighting up.

"Well, I've been noticing something different for some time now. You've been acting differently, so I'm acting differently."

"What are you talking about?" he asked.

"The reality is, Abdul, that I've trusted you. And I told you from the beginning that our relationship would be built on trust. Trusting you the way I did, I kept you at the center of everything. You were my eyes and ears in the places I couldn't go. You understand that, right?"

Abdul's hands started to tremble. He crushed out his cigarette and quickly lit another. "Yes, Zmarai, and I've been doing that. Why are you talking to me like this?"

"Abdul, the truth is that you used to do that for me. Now you do that for other people as well."

"W-what?" he stammered.

I remained firm, looking him in the eye. "I told you at the beginning that I didn't want you to ever meet with ███████████ [another intelligence service]. Didn't I tell you that?"

He waved his arms and shouted, "Are you accusing me of working ████████. Never, Zmarai! NEVER!!!!"

"*Hamush.*" (Be quiet.) "*Aram shah.*" (Calm down.)

His hands shaking, he lit another cigarette and started chewing his lip.

"I told you also, I didn't want you working with anyone else. I said, Don't work with ███████████████████████████████ ███████████████. Didn't I say that?"

"I never worked with ██ ████████!" he screamed at the top of his lungs. "You're crazy, Zmarai! You are crazy!"

I could tell from his expression that he knew where this was going.

Trying to remain calm, I continued. "I never said that you were working with the ███████. I mentioned a number of different groups. But I know why *you* mentioned them. I know everything. Because of the actions you've taken over the last several months, we will no longer be working together, Abdul."

The blood drained out of his face.

"You are no longer my employee, and you are no longer to contact me or any other American in this country."

He jumped to his feet and shouted, "What are you talking about now? This is crazy! Crazy! Crazy!"

"You're not supposed to talk to Mahmud, and you're not supposed to talk to Haji Jan. Sit down!"

He sat, but continued yelling. "No! No!"

I picked up a document from the table beside me and handed it to him. "I've written everything here in Pashtu for you to review. After you read it, ██████████████████."

He threw it on the table and shouted, "You're crazy! Crazy! I'm not ██████████."

I picked the document up and handed it to the terp. "Read this out loud to him," I said in English. "Then let him ███ ██."

The terp read the document aloud in Pashtu with Abdul protesting the whole time.

At the end, Abdul screamed, "This is a lie, Zmarai! Who is accusing me of these things?"

I looked him in the eye and said, "Abdul, nothing you say is going to change our minds. You knew that we were capable of finding things out and verifying them. I've used every resource available to me, and they've proved without a shadow of a doubt that you've been working for someone else."

He stopped and grasped his shaking hands. All Afghans thought we had satellites and secret listening devices watching and recording everything they did or said.

Looking up at me, he sputtered, "S-show me this evidence. Show me this evidence!"

"Abdul, how about I show you this evidence? Then what? I have it right here. What are you going to do if I show you a video, picture, and voice recordings of you meeting with someone else? Because I have them. What are you going to do?"

He seemed stunned. He reached for another cigarette and started to light it. His hands shook so much that the flame went out. He flicked the lighter again.

"How are you going to feel?" I asked, playing out the bluff. "Because you're lying right now. Lying to my face. I'd rather that you just ▉▉▉▉▉▉▉▉▉▉ and adhere to the agreement. Because if I show you the evidence, you'll never have your honor again. And we both know that."

Abdul started to cry. Sobbing and smoking, he picked up the document and read it to himself.

He looked up at me with tears in his eyes and asked, "Why did it come to this, Zmarai? Why, my brother?"

"Abdul, it happened as a result of your actions. If you want to explain why you did what you did, I'll sit here and listen. If not, I suggest that you ▉▉▉▉▉▉▉▉▉ and leave, and we'll call it the end of the relationship."

Tears dripped down his face onto the floor. "I just don't know what to say," he said. "What can I do?"

"You can't do anything, Abdul. Just adhere to what is said on the paper, because I can assure you that I'll know what you're doing. If you try to sell information to another American ▉▉▉▉▉, I'm going to hear about it, and the consequences for you are going to be very bad."

He sat looking devastated. It was clear that he had never thought of the consequences. ▉▉▉▉▉▉▉▉▉▉▉▉▉▉▉▉▉▉ For that measly ▉▉▉, he had risked ▉▉▉▉▉▉▉▉▉▉▉▉▉▉, and lost.

The risk he had taken was high and offered little gain, which was fascinating. The people who did what he did for a living were gamblers and sociopaths who often became divorced from reality. Once they'd gotten away with selling information for a period of time without being discovered, they often took unreasonable chances. CIA snitch Aldrich Ames had meticulous op sec (operational security) when he started selling intel to the Soviets, but at the end was throwing documents to his KGB handler across a table in Chadwicks bar in Georgetown.

Abdul had overplayed his hand. He now sat sobbing and staring at the document. I said, "I need you to ██ ██."

Tears dripped onto the paper ████████. I used the radio to call the Scorpions.

They burst through the door with guns ready. Abdul cowered and trembled.

I said, "It's okay, guys. Stay calm. Everything went well. Escort Abdul back to his vehicle. He's never to be allowed back on this base again."

The four of us—the two Scorpions, the terp, and myself—walked Abdul to his Corolla. As he got in he muttered, "Well, good-bye, Zmarai."

"Good-bye, Abdul," I said back.

As he drove off, I thought, *There goes eighteen months of hard work.* I felt sorry for him, but having gotten to know Abdul as well as I had, knew that it was probably inevitable that he would overplay his hand.

A few weeks later and two days before I was scheduled to depart, Abdul called on the phone ███████████ and asked to come in for a meeting. The terp who answered told him never to call the number again.

The next morning I took the phone with me to the shooting range and put a 5.56 round through the center. Our relationship with Abdul was over.

It was time to wrap up what he had helped initiate and move on.

18

KATE

We can recognize the dawn and decline of love by the uneasiness we feel when alone together.

—Jean de La Bruyère

Late in August 2011, as I prepared to leave Afghanistan, it was time to plan the endgame with Wolverine. We faced two problems. One, Wolverine never traveled outside his country ███████████████, which meant our options were limited. And, two, we needed a cover for Mahmud so he wouldn't be exposed ██████████████ ██████.

Even though Mahmud offered to deliver the coup de grâce to Wolverine himself, regulations prevented us from hiring someone to commit murder. ████████████████████████████████ ██ ██

In consultation with Boss Man, Hooper, and HQ, I came up with a plan to make the takedown of Wolverine look like ██████████. ██ ████████████████████████████████████

We had all his ████████████ and could therefore track his movements. ███

███████████████████████████████████

███████████████████████████████████

████████████████████████████

With the plan in place, I proceeded to hand over my assets to my colleague Jimmy and pack my gear.

The first week of September, I left Kandahar with a sense of accomplishment, hope, and expectation. After a year and a half working in a war zone, I was looking forward to seeing Kate, getting some TLC, and putting my personal life in order.

The next three days, waiting in Kabul for a flight to DC, were the longest of my life. I felt like I was running the last mile of a long race. Instead of being elated as I approached the finish line, I was miserable and agitated and didn't understand why.

As I sat in Kabul Airport waiting to board my eighteen-hour flight to DC, I received an e-mail from Kate. "Do you need a ride from the airport? Where are you living?"

I hadn't given either much thought, because my mind had been totally occupied with Wolverine and Afghanistan. I looked at everything else as A-type problems—meaning, money would solve them. And I just happened to be flush with cash for the first time in my life.

I e-mailed back, "Will take a cab. Probably a hotel."

With hours to kill, I decided to e-mail my buddy Matt and ask him to pick me up at Dulles, and searched Craigslist for the biggest apartment in DC available for rent month-to-month.

Then I e-mailed my ex-roommate Austin. "Austin, go over to this rental agency and put down a deposit to hold the apartment listed below. It has three bedrooms, so if you do this, I will let you live with me for as long as you like."

Austin responded immediately. "Fuck yeah! Done and done."

Having taken care of that, I collected my Agency-owned items and handed them into the armorer—███████████████████████

███████████████████████████████████

███████████████████████████████████

████████████████████████████.

He let me keep the flashlight.

"Much appreciated."

"Have a nice life."

As I boarded the Boeing 777, I stopped and looked out at Kabul. On my first day in-country, the logs guy had told me that I would get used to the stench. He was right. It smelled like Afghanistan now.

I felt some regret for leaving Mahmud in the middle of the operation and feared it would lose momentum. But what really worried me was my ability to adjust to life outside the war zone.

Six a.m. the next day I was back at Dulles, collecting my bags, and looking for Matt. Finding him nowhere, I called him on the burner phone I used for personal calls in the US. He didn't pick up. I phoned another three times. No answer.

Welcome home.

He showed up an hour later at the wheel of his mother's minivan.

"Am I going to have to move a baby seat to get into this thing?" I joked.

"Good to see you, too, Doug."

Matt was a senior at West Point doing a semester internship at the Pentagon. I had met him at the Rhino bar in DC on a previous R&R. While I never told him what I did or where I was, he had quickly figured it out. In fact, he sent me an electronic thank-you card the day after bin Laden's death.

"So how was Hawaii?" he asked sarcastically.

"Gnarly. How's it feel to be wearing the white cotton women's panties that come standard with this minivan?"

"Pretty goddamn comfy. The real question is where do you wanna go?"

Flying on adrenaline, I knew exactly—the only place in Georgetown that would be serving Budweiser at this hour. "Take me to the Daily Grill on Wisconsin Avenue."

Matt yapped on and on about his shitty job at the Pentagon (coffee boy), his girlfriend and how she was hot but he was still banging chicks on the side, and oh, he had even banged Kate's best friend Ariana. Speaking of Kate, did I want to see Kate? Was I still talking to her? My head started to hurt.

At the Daily Grill, we ordered Buds. We had the bar to ourselves except for some dude in a Dallas Cowboys jersey. After our first round, he moved a barstool away from us, which was strange. I gave the guy a fuck-off look because I didn't want him listening to our conversation.

He noticed. "You got a problem, homeboy?"

I raised my bottle of beer and smiled. "Nope, no problem."

Matt and I returned to our conversation. Homeboy started burning lasers into both of us with his stare. I could tell he was going to be a problem. *Jesus Christ, I'm home five minutes and some wannabe gangster has to pick a fight with me? Can this be happening?*

Matt was a big dude with a high and tight haircut, a state champion wrestler, and in excellent shape. I sported a shaved head and a foot-long beard, and had been pressing 305 on the bench in Kandahar and practicing Brazilian jujitsu for the past decade. Bottom line, we weren't the first two guys you'd pick a fight with in a bar at eight a.m. But then again, we were the *only* other men in the bar, so something had to give.

The dude in the Cowboys jersey called to the bartender, "Look at these white-power motherfuckers. Can you believe this shit? Coming into my bar like this?"

The bartender was terrified but still managed, "It's not only your bar. Relax."

"I'm not going to relax with these skinheads in my bar. They got to go and they got to go now."

I stood up and smiled at him. Five days prior I was sparring in the gym with the Scorpions. Six days prior I was cutting up bricks of C-4 to destroy a cache of IEDs I bought from a Taliban commander. I considered this guy a layup.

Truth be told, we should have walked. I should have adhered to the

Pashtun saying that goes: "He who gets angry first, loses." I had followed it religiously during my time in Afghanistan. But now I was on my home turf, where we were all on the same side and stupid shit like this wasn't supposed to happen.

Or was it?

Loudmouth was midstream in another round of slurs about our shaved heads when Matt turned to face him. "Yo, dude," he said, "we're in the military, so shut the fuck up."

"Y'all are in the military?" Cowboys Jersey shot back. "Fuck that shit. Y'all fightin' some wars we never should have gotten in to begin with. Jokes on y'all."

Matt growled, "Yeah, thanks for your service, too, brother."

"You wanna sass me boy you're gonna get dealt with. I can guarantee ya that."

Matt looked at me and responded, "You and what army?" He was on the verge of asking the guy to step outside to fight.

"I don't need no army, son. Keep up the tough talk and I'm gonna serve your ass with a Smith and Wesson."

"Pull it out," I said without thinking. "Don't brag about it unless you're willing to use it. Now pull it out and see what happens."

I had shifted back into my war-zone mentality, figuring that the chances of him actually packing a pistol were slim. I also knew that if he moved his hand to his waistline, I could close on him and snap his wrist before he could remove any sort of weapon and actually use it.

Now that he'd been called out, Troublemaker tried to cover his bluff by screaming about how he was going to shoot up the place. The bartender ran from behind the bar to the kitchen to call the police.

"Can't do any shooting with it tucked in your draws, tough guy," I said.

I could tell from the look on his face that he didn't have a weapon. I stepped in between him and Matt and said, "Now's your chance."

He pushed me backward and then took a swing at Matt, which he easily blocked. Before Matt could retaliate, I grabbed the guy with my right hand, picked up a stool with my left, and smashed it into his face.

He wasn't knocked unconscious but was seriously stunned, lying on his back looking up at us in shock.

Matt grabbed me and pushed me toward the door. I pulled a hundred-dollar bill out of my pocket, threw it on the bar and said, "The fight was self-defense. Not paying for the beers will get us arrested. Overpaying for the beers will ensure the bartender defends us to the police."

Matt couldn't help laughing. "That's some pretty good situational awareness, Doug. You learn that in Hawaii?"

Welcome home.

Austin, who was still living at our old row house a few blocks up the street, had taken the day off. We plopped in his living room and told him what had happened at Daily Grill. "Jesus, Doug. Try not to get us all killed before noon, huh?"

We fired up the grill in the backyard while Matt and Austin filled me in on everything I had missed in the last six months. Not surprisingly, the conversation turned to my status with Kate and how I expected things to turn out with her. I told them what I really thought: It all depended on how soon I had to return to Hawaii.

"Do you have to go back to Hawaii? Couldn't you just get a job here at your DC office like you had before?"

The truth was that I was waiting for a visa to go to my next assignment in ███████ (another Middle Eastern country) not Hawaii. ███████ ██ ████████████████████████████████████, I'd been warned that my visa could take up to six months to get approved, if it was granted at all. Since I couldn't tell anyone about that, I had to start lying again.

We sat around and drank beers for the rest of the afternoon while my old buddies trickled in to welcome me back. Since I hadn't touched a drop of booze since Paris, it didn't take long for me to get drunk, which gave me the courage to text Kate.

I told her that we would be celebrating at my favorite Georgetown bar, Rhino Bar and Grill, and that she should stop by later if she didn't have other plans.

Not surprisingly, by eleven p.m., when Kate arrived at Rhino with her friend Ariana, I was smashed. Seeing me like that, she turned on her heels and left.

I woke the next morning at the Four Seasons Hotel with a box of Domino's pizza in my bed and several hate texts from Kate on my phone. Austin lay in a heap of clothes on the floor. Matt was asleep in the shower.

I spent the next two weeks at the Four Seasons throwing monumental parties while I waited for my new apartment and Kate to forgive me. One night I entered my suite after a night of partying to find Austin drinking champagne and eating chicken fingers with three naked young women.

Wildly depressed that Kate had refused to meet me since seeing me drunk at Rhino, I warned Austin not to get ketchup on the sheets and left for a walk along the C&O Canal to think things over.

Once again, like it had for the past seven years, the Agency seemed to be dictating every aspect of my life. Was it time to regain control? I had gotten so wrapped up in the Wolverine network and destroying the IED trade that an assignment ██████████ (to another Middle Eastern country) seemed like the only logical next step in my career. Yet here I was walking along an abandoned canal at five in the morning feeling heartbroken, alone, and lost.

I pulled the cell phone out of my pocket and called Kate. I wasn't sure what I was going to say, and was pretty sure the call would go straight to voice mail.

She picked up.

"What are you doing, Doug? It's five a.m."

"Kate, uh, hey. I know you're probably asleep right now and I apologize for waking you, but I need to get this off my chest and if you want to hang up you can. I'm standing here right now in the middle of Georgetown and I'm the only one on the street. I'm just... I'm pretty lost with-

out you and just entirely exhausted by everything going on right now. I
don't know...I just...I just miss holding you, Kate. I really miss that
most."

"Come over," she said.

An electric shock shot through my body. "Uhhhh, when?"

"Now."

"Yeah, okay," I stammered. "I'm coming."

I wind-sprinted back to the Four Seasons and jumped in a cab. My
heart was racing so fast I could barely breathe.

Twenty minutes later, I arrived at her apartment building in Chinatown. I buzzed through the front door and informed the female security guard that I was there to visit Kate.

"Daniel, right?"

"No, Doug."

*Daniel, Doug...close enough. Kate must have phoned down to let the guard
know I was coming and she screwed up the name. No big deal.*

I stood in front of her door for a solid ten minutes composing myself before I summoned the courage to knock. She answered immediately and let me in. Her eyes were red and it looked like she'd been
crying.

"Come to bed," she said.

I followed her into the bedroom and slid under the covers with all
my clothes on, which felt immensely strange. Kate pulled my arm over
her and backed into my body.

"Hold me," she whispered.

Those two words aroused an intense response. I grabbed Kate and
pulled her close with all of my might. She spun around to kiss me and
within seconds we were making love.

It was incredibly thrilling for all kinds of reasons, but most of all
because it signaled to me that she still had affection for me and we were
back together.

I awoke around nine a.m. alone. Since it was a Sunday, she didn't
have to work and I knew she wasn't at church. I discovered her in the

bathroom with the door locked. I went back to sleep and woke again a few hours later.

The bathroom door was still closed and I could hear the shower running. I knocked on the bathroom door and then tried the handle. It was locked.

"Kate. Hey, is everything okay in there? Can you hear me?"

No response.

Shortly before I started to panic, I heard the water shut off.

"Kate, are you okay?"

Still no response. When she finally came out, it was obvious that she had been crying. I tried to console her, but she didn't want to be touched.

A voice in my head said, *This is bad. Real bad.*

I had learned from experience that it was best to keep your mouth shut when a woman was upset with you and you weren't sure what you'd done wrong. Kate and I watched television in silence for most of the afternoon. At four p.m. she went to her room to answer a phone call and shut the door. When she returned, a flurry of text messages to her cell followed.

"Is everything okay?" I asked.

She nodded, but didn't speak.

"You wanna tell me who you were talking to?"

No response.

I informed Kate that I was going to go to the local deli to pick up something to eat. I figured this would give her time to call whoever she was texting with and sort things out. My brain told me that something was very wrong, but my heart didn't want to hear it.

Returning to the apartment, I found Kate in her room with the door shut speaking on the telephone. When she reappeared an hour later, I told her we needed to talk.

She asked, "What time are you planning to leave?"

It was like a slap to the head. Confused, hurt, and stunned, I said, "Well, if you want me to leave, I guess I'll take off right now."

I returned to the Four Seasons, where I found Austin lying on the bed in a bathrobe and slippers. As we shipped champagne left over from the night before, I filled him in on my last twelve hours with Kate.

He said, "Take it easy, dude. Just wait her out. She'll come around. She always does."

I texted her the following day and offered to go to her place and cook dinner, so it would be ready when she came back from work.

"Yes!" she texted back.

I spent the day shopping and let myself into her apartment with the key she had given me months before.

When she came home from work, she found her entire living room filled with over two hundred flowers and me waiting in my best suit. I kissed her and presented her with a series of gifts including a pair of Louboutin heels. I figured if they didn't cheer her up, there was very little hope.

The gifts, flowers, and dinner appeared to work. She said she was willing to talk about the future of our relationship.

I told her I wanted a simple yes or no answer. "Are we going to stay together or move on?"

"That depends. Are you leaving again, and for how long?"

"Truthfully, I don't know."

"Then I don't know, either."

Stalemate.

The mysterious texts and phone calls started again. She let the first five go to voice mail, but answered the sixth in her bedroom with the door closed. I was getting annoyed.

When she came out of her room, I broached the subject we had both been avoiding.

"Do you want to tell me about him or should I just keep playing dumb until you make up your mind on who you want to be with?"

"I don't know what you're talking about, Doug."

"Should I just assume that you've been dating someone while I was gone?"

"I'm not dating someone," she began. "I went on a date with this guy like one time. I'm sorry he actually likes me."

"Like one time, or exactly once?"

She sighed heavily and said, "Why do you insist on doing this, Doug?"

"You're avoiding the question. You also won't look me in the eyes and your hand is covering your mouth when you speak. You don't even realize you're doing it but that's because you *do realize* you're lying right now and your body is attempting to cover for you."

"You're unbelievable."

I walked over to the window and stared at the moon. A year ago a receipt had fallen out of her car that proved that she was lying about seeing another guy. I had hoped that was behind us. I was wrong.

Her phone kept pinging with incoming messages. The night was turning into my worst fucking nightmare.

"Would you at least mind silencing your phone and stop answering his calls in front of me?"

We stared at each other in silence. I knew I should leave, but didn't want to go back to the Four Seasons and be cheered up by Austin.

I said, "I'm not hungry anymore. I need to sleep because my mind is exhausted."

"You can sleep here and walk me to work in the morning."

It was only seven p.m., but I fell asleep immediately. I was awakened at two a.m. by Kate's phone. She sat up and silenced it. Then I heard three knocks on her front door.

KNOCK. KNOCK. KNOCK.

I froze.

KNOCK. KNOCK. KNOCK.

I sat up in bed and glanced over at Kate, who was pale as a ghost and had a panicked look on her face. My heart was racing so hard and fast I could feel my carotid artery beating through my throat.

Switching into combat mode, I slowly got out of bed, crept to the door, and listened from two feet away. The next series of knocks would help me zero in on the guy's exact location. I would then rip open the door and destroy who or whatever was on the other side. I waited. No knocks came.

I was just about to look out the peephole when a hand grabbed my right arm from behind. Without thinking I spun around, grabbed both shoulders, and started to push them against the wall. I was in such a state that I didn't even realize it was Kate.

"Doug!" she screamed. "What the fuck are you doing!?"

She scared the shit out of me. The person on the other side of the door took off running. I locked eyes with Kate and we both immediately knew what was about to happen.

I ripped open the door, looked left and right down the hallway, and saw nothing. Hearing the elevator open around the corner, I took off in a sprint. The doors had just closed, so I started for the stairway so I could cut him off in the lobby.

Kate grabbed me from behind.

"Doug, what are you doing? Stop it! What's wrong with you?"

I was standing in my boxers at 2:30 in the morning about to chase someone I didn't know through Chinatown. I didn't even know what he looked like!

I couldn't speak. Kate started shaking uncontrollably. I walked back to her apartment, flipped on the lights, and got dressed. Kate stood in the kitchen trembling.

I said, "I'm going to go out of town for a while. Take that time to sort out whatever it is you need to with whoever the fuck that was. When I get back, have your mind made up on whether you want to stay together or be with that guy. If you want to work it out, I'll back out of my next assignment to stay here in DC with you for at least a year. If not, I'll accelerate everything and be gone by the end of the month."

With that I returned to the Four Seasons, where I went online and started searching for flights out of DC. It was late September, so I figured Oktoberfest in Munich was a logical choice.

I booked a flight for the following afternoon, then e-mailed my buddy Joe living in Berlin and asked him to join me. Two days later, I was balancing beer steins on my head in the Löwenbräu Tent while Joe told German ladies that I was a former stunt double for a young Jake Gyllenhaal.

We partied hard for five days straight. After the festivities closed down, I took a taxi to the airport and bought the first ticket home. While I waited for my flight, I wandered into the beer garden located inside Munich's international terminal, which had Wi-Fi, and checked my e-mail for the first time in a week.

Two very sweet e-mails from Kate awaited me. In them she said she was sorry that she had upset me, was looking forward to me coming back home, and was hopeful we could work things out and stay together.

Elated, I called Kate as soon as I landed at Dulles and she invited me over for dinner. I brought with me a teddy bear wearing lederhosen and the gigantic heart-shaped cookie I had bought in Germany that read "Ich Liebe Dich." As I was signing in at the front desk the same guard lady from before noticed my gifts and asked me if I was related to Kate. When I told her I wasn't, she gave a slight shake of her head and looked back down at her paperwork.

Kate appeared genuinely happy to see me. I handed her the teddy bear and cookie and let her know the cookie read "I Love You."

"Well, I love you, too, Doug. Here let me cut this up and let's have some."

"No, no," I stopped her. "I'll cut it up. You have a seat and give your new bear a hug."

As I stood in her kitchen, I realized there was a gigantic elephant that needed to be addressed. For the moment I wanted to pretend that the last night we had been together had never happened.

Opening Kate's trash can to throw away the cellophane, I found it completely full. Two bottles of wine took up most of the space, so I removed them and placed them in the sink. Staring at me from the top of the remaining trash was an envelope addressed to Kate from a gentleman named Daniel. It had been delivered that day, opened, and its contents removed.

I carried it numbly into the living room and handed it to Kate. She said nothing. As we stared into each other's eyes, I knew that our relationship was over.

But I didn't want to accept it, so I asked: "How long have you guys been together?" My voice sounded guttural and dark.

"Since June."

"Before or after we met in Paris?"

"After."

I had a lump in my throat that I couldn't choke down. I didn't feel like crying; I was far too upset for that. My mouth was so dry I could barely speak.

"Did you two have sex while I was in Germany?"

"I'm sorry, Doug. Yes."

Welcome home.

19

SUCKER-PUNCHED

One seeks to make the loved one entirely happy, or, if that cannot
be, entirely wretched.

—Jean de La Bruyère

Kate sat on her sofa, clutching the envelope, crying. "What did you
expect me to do?" she implored. "You're gone ten months out of the year
and I'm left here alone, crying to myself every night wondering what
the hell I'm doing in a relationship like this. Which isn't even a relationship by the way. This is chaos!"

I was so upset, I had trouble speaking. "Kate, I apologize for my lack
of empathy. If you hate my guts, break up with me. Don't let me come
home to find out the hard way that you're fucking some other guy!"

"Fuck you, Doug!" Kate shouted as she ran to her bedroom, slammed
the door, and locked it.

I sat in silence. I wanted to leave, but couldn't—not just her apartment, but the entire relationship. Not yet.

Kate emerged a few minutes later. She'd pulled her hair up, removed
her makeup, and was staring right through me like she was ready to
speak the truth.

"You know something, buddy," she started. "Whether you want to believe it or not, I did everything I could to try and make this work. And I get
it, you're so tough and badass that nothing ever bothers you. Well, I'm not.

I tried to be, but I'm not. I went to a psychiatrist to try and learn to cope, but it didn't work. She told me to keep a diary, which I did, but it only made me angry that the only thing I had to write about was you. Everything in my entire life revolved around you. My daily routine, my weekend plans, my work schedule, my vacation time, everything. I was so obsessed with just being able to talk to you most days that I couldn't focus at work because I was afraid you would suddenly call me and I would be busy and miss you. Which happened several times by the way. Do you know how bad that crushed me? I felt like I was letting you down by not being there for you when you reached out. Which was rare, but I accepted it by telling myself that you would eventually come home to me and everything would work itself out. But you know, after a while, I realized that I had become a miserable person and I hated myself. So yes, I started going out again and I did meet Daniel and he reminded me what it was like to have someone care about you, and not just on their terms. And it felt amazing."

I had to stop her before she went any further. "Kate, I really don't want to hear about how great this guy is. He's a fucking Jodie. He knew I was gone and he manipulated your sadness into his bed. Fuck that guy. I'll probably end up breaking his neck."

"You just don't get it, do you, Doug? I never slept with Daniel because I thought he was better than you. He's far from it. I did it to *hurt* you. I knew that sleeping with him would be unforgivable in your eyes and it would force you to leave me because I would never be strong enough to leave you on my own."

There! She hit the jugular.

She'd stated the reality that we both knew to be true. I wasn't sure if I wanted to cry or vomit. My chest felt like it was about to collapse into itself. I couldn't stop my knees from bouncing, nor could I speak.

Too upset to even move, I reclined on the sofa and lay there with my eyes open until the sun came up and Kate slipped quietly out the door.

As I put on my coat, I remembered that she had mentioned a diary. I needed to see it, to fully understand her side of the story. Our relationship was over, but I wanted to know why.

I found the three-ring notebook in her closet inside of a Tory Burch shoe box. A pen stuck in the middle marked her last entry. Like all the other entries, this one was addressed to me. It's paraphrased below:

04 July 2011

I don't think I can do this anymore. I can't live like this! It's the Fourth of July, my parents are here and I'm in my room crying like a baby. WTF?! I just got in a huge fight with your friend Matt at a house party and then abandoned my parents and took a cab home. I'm such a mess!

I overheard Matt and John talking about you outside in the backyard. I asked them what was up and they changed the subject. I told Matt I heard him mention your name and asked what he was talking about. He said he wished you would email him back because this time next year he will be in Afghanistan after he graduates West Point. Why didn't you tell me that you told Matt you were in Afghanistan?!

I told him I had no idea what he was talking about and reminded him that you were in Hawaii. John and Matt both started laughing in my face and Matt said "Hey Kate whatever you got to tell yourself." I said "No Matt, that's not what I tell myself. That's what Doug tells me and that's what he tells you as well. I don't think he would like you spreading rumors like that."

I got so mad after thinking about it though that I went up to Matt a few minutes later in the middle of the party and yelled at him. I said "If Doug is in Afghanistan it's obviously not something he wants to talk about with your dumb ass! And if he is there then maybe you should be a little more respectful considering it's the Fourth of July and and you're in DC with a beer in your hand. You're not over there so why don't you fuck off Matt!"

My mom and dad heard all of this and tried consoling me which made me even more furious because they don't know what you do or where you are and I know that they suspect something as well. I couldn't take it so I stormed out and got a cab and came back here. I am now sitting on my bedroom floor, ignoring my parents, and bawling in a Chanel dress! I'm not doing this anymore, Doug! I'm tired of looking stupid every time I have to defend you. I'm sending you an email right now!

I remembered that e-mail. She sounded upset, but didn't explain why. I had no idea my buddy Matt had been turning her screws.

02 May 2011

Yaaaaaaay! Congratulations boo! You finally got him!! I am so proud of you!! <3<3<3

It had been written the night after the OBL raid. Nice.

28 April 2011

You are ignoring me this week. I don't know why you do this. We had such a nice time in Rio and now you're being a jackass again. What is it with you? Why can't you just love me with some consistency?

For the first time in three years, her perspective was starting to sink into my thick skull.

12 October 2010

You called me for the first time today from Hawaii which was the highlight of my life. You have NO IDEA how much that meant to me. I know you are busy baby, and I love you for all that you do to keep us safe, but I really hope I get to hear your voice more often. I feel like I could dance right now! I'M SO HAPPY!!

She'd written that a year ago almost to the day. Tears started to well up in my eyes. I skipped to the first entry.

03 September 2010

> *You left me two weeks ago and I am struggling like a muthaaaaaaa*
> *fucckkkkaaaaa.*

I laughed out loud and wiped away the tears. Smiling, I placed the diary back in the closet. I removed her key from my key ring, placed it on the kitchen counter, and exited her apartment thinking, *It has to end this way. Once again, it's the only thing that makes sense.*

The following Monday my mandatory leave ended and I returned to Langley. ██
██

The branch chief—a fellow case officer named Morris—welcomed me when I stuck my head in his office.

"Hey, Doug" he said, "we're happy to have you in the branch until you get your visa. Feel free to stop in anytime and chat. We'll keep you apprised of your visa status as it moves along."

"Thanks, Chief, but that could be a while. What should I be doing in the meantime?"

COs between assignments weren't required to do anything but check in and read the newspaper until they left for their next assignment. A couple of days I could handle. But because I suspected my visa could take months and I wanted to occupy my mind with something other than my breakup with Kate, I needed something to do.

Morris said, "Doug I'm not going to ask you to do desk work, but we could always use some help. If you want an account, I can facilitate."

"To tell you the truth, Chief, it would be excellent if you could get me access to the Kandahar account so I can assist my buddy who is currently handling the Wolverine case. I am already intimately aware of all the details so it shouldn't be too big of a deal to officially read me in."

██
██
██
███████████████████████████████

████████████████████████████████████

████████████████████████████████████

████████████████████████████████████

████████████████████████████████████

██████████

It took Chief Morris two weeks to convince the legal department to give me a waiver to be read in on the Wolverine case. Previously, there had been only ████████████████ in HQ taking care of all of Kandahar and Wadi, which comprised a gigantic account with hundreds of requests coming in a week. So, no matter how important Mahmud had become, there were still other things that needed to be handled that could slow down momentum. When I got in touch with Jimmy and let him know that he had another hand at the desk, he welcomed the news. Now he had a CO at headquarters covering one single asset, which was unheard of.

I knew how frustrating it was when you were in the field and HQ dragged its feet. So I personally walked approvals to other offices that needed to sign off on issues regarding Wolverine and Mahmud and sat there until they took action. This raised some eyebrows in Legal, but soon everyone involved with Wolverine knew it was my account and understood that if they didn't handle my requests quickly, I'd sit by their desks until they did.

Jimmy, of course, was thrilled. The bureaucratic tentacles that had been holding up the Wolverine case the past year had been severed. ██

████████████████████████████████████

████████████████████████████████

In November, senior management approved of Wolverine's capture should he enter Afghanistan. This was academic, because Wolverine was too smart to enter Afghanistan.

I spent the next month lobbying for his capture in ██████ (his home country) arguing that Wolverine was also too clever to enter the tribal regions ████████████████████████████████

████████████████████████████████████.

My reasoning to the seventh floor went like this: If Wolverine is

which will result in another OBL-type raid ███████████
██████. If he's not working ████████████████████████
██
██████.

   With Chief Morris's help, the powers that be agreed to petition
███ as soon as we had Wolverine in a fixed location outside of ██████████.
That was easy, because Mahmud continued to report Wolverine's
daily whereabouts and travel schedule. The decision was reached just
before Christmas 2011.

   Like other federal agencies, the CIA shuts most of its offices from
the twenty-third of December until the Monday after New Year's. So I
decided to return home to Indiana.

   Some members of my extended family hadn't seen me in four years.
Moments after I greeted my aunt Elizabeth, she asked me if I was in
the military. My aunt Tracey wanted to know if I worked for the FBI.
My uncle Nate joked that I was probably in the Taliban because of my
long beard.

   I repeated the same lie I told everyone: I've been living in Hawaii
doing contract work for the ██████████.

   Uncle Nate wasn't buying it. Pointing at what he called my "Taliban beard," he asked where I had "learned the Taliban language." Nate
was a guy who had never left the Midwest.

   I said, "Nate, I presume my father told you I speak Arabic. While
that's true, it's not the language of the Taliban. They speak Pashtu. Next
time, you should accuse me of speaking the language of al-Qaeda and
you'll be right on point."

   I left on the twenty-sixth to visit my brother in Chicago and his
two children, whom I had never met. They were three and two and broke
into tears every time I entered the room.

   Shortly before midnight New Year's Eve, Kate texted me to say
hello. I replied, and we texted back and forth. As hope started to rise

again she dashed it by asking when I would be back in DC so she could return the stuff I had been storing in her apartment.

I got back to DC on the third and immediately started ramping up for Wolverine's capture. A week of twelve-hour workdays followed.

The next weekend she arrived at my apartment with a box of belongings. "How ya been?" I asked, upon letting her in.

"I've been good, Doug. Really good."

I felt like I was stuck in a bad romantic comedy, acting like everything was cool, but really dying inside. I poured her a glass of Chardonnay, which she declined.

"Well it's a good thing we always liked the same type of wine then, isn't it?"

She smiled and started to cry.

I was searching for something that would make me look stoic. All I could come up with was "It's going to take a long time to get over this."

Kate smiled again, turned, and silently walked out of my apartment. I didn't want this to be my last image of her, so I went up to the rooftop balcony and watched her exit the building and head down the street. Instead of walking to the Metro, she took a left at the corner, and then another left, where she buzzed into the apartment building two blocks west of me.

I hadn't really noticed the street address on the envelope I had found in her trash can. Now I found out that her new beau Daniel and I were neighbors.

How about that?

Trying not to wallow in self-pity, I started spending every waking hour at work. If the Wolverines of the world were going to cost me so much in terms of happiness, then I was going to make sure they paid the price.

In the midst of a frigid spell in the middle of January I caught the flu. When I returned to HQ on Tuesday, the seventeenth of January, I got a ping from Jimmy letting me know that he would be off the grid for the next couple of days while visiting a FOB ████████.

"No worries, buddy. I'm just playing catch-up anyhow. We will fillet this fish when you get back. Be safe."

I still wasn't feeling a hundred percent so I went home early the next two days. Friday, January 20, 2012, I woke up feeling better. It was also my twenty-ninth birthday. Determined to make it a special day, I stopped at my favorite café in Georgetown for breakfast.

When I reached HQ, booted up my computer, and entered my passwords, I saw a message from Jimmy on our internal service.

"FUCK MAN! WHERE THE FUCK YOU BEEN?!? WE GOT HIM DUDE! WE FUCKING FINALLY GOT HIM!!!!!!!!!!"

It was the best birthday present I could imagine! Unable to move anything except my index finger, I pushed the spacebar key and then the return key to signify that I was speechless.

Jimmy went on to explain that while he was at the FOB, he got a text from Mahmud informing him that Wolverine was on the move. Jimmy immediately flew back to Kandahar to try to reach me to get the ball rolling. That happened at ten a.m. in Afghanistan which meant it was just past midnight in DC and I was fast asleep.

██

██
██████████████████████████████████
██
██
██
██
██
██████████
██
██
██
████████████████████████████████████ They confirmed Wolverine's identity, then notified us.

Jimmy was alerted at seven p.m. Kandahar time. Chief Morris got the news at headquarters, just as I was finishing breakfast.

He hadn't seen me enter the office. Now I leaned back in my chair and shouted "MOTHERFUCKER!!!!" at the top of my lungs.

Chief Morris ran over to my desk and said, "Get your ass in my office now!"

He shut the door behind me as I jumped up and down shouting celebratory obscenities.

"All right, all right, Doug. Calm down!! The rest of the office is going to think I'm fucking your girlfriend or something and this is a throw-down. Go take a run outside to burn off that energy and then let's game-plan what to do next."

I ran in my suit around the Agency campus from one parking lot to the other until I felt like my chest was going to explode. Then I re-entered the lobby, crossing over the seal and pumping my fist. I high-fived the security guard as I passed through the turnstiles. This was by far the greatest accomplishment of my life!

Chief Morris wasn't in his office when I returned. I wasn't sure if he went home from exhaustion, or had been summoned to the seventh floor. It didn't matter either way. I chatted with Jimmy for another hour or so before he told me he had to go do some serious celebrating. I agreed to do my part from seven thousand miles away.

I had planned to spend a low-key birthday. As I left work, I texted all my DC friends and told them I had changed my mind. "It's going to be a blowout at Lima Lounge on K Street. Your presence is required!"

We partied hard, finishing three magnums of champagne and turning the place inside out. By three a.m., when someone put me in a cab, I was feeling no pain.

I woke up the next morning in agony. My ankle had swollen to the size of a football. I figured that I must have slipped on ice somewhere between the club and my apartment.

My buddies arrived at noon to inform me that some girls we had met the night before wanted to keep the party going. I hobbled around on my sore ankle until the pain became unbearable and I had to return home. The next morning when I awoke, my entire foot had turned black.

Emergency-room X-rays revealed that I had separated my foot from both my tibia and fibula. I had also severed all of the connecting tendons. The doctor instructed me to keep the leg elevated for the next five days to reduce the swelling and then return to determine if I needed surgery.

Five days later, the orthopedic surgeon inserted a plate in my ankle and told me to keep my foot elevated for two more weeks. A week later, in mid-February, I couldn't stand sitting in my apartment any longer and hobbled back into work on crutches.

Even with the pain, cast, and crutches, I was still elated about Wolverine's capture. Minutes after returning to my desk, I learned ███████ ██.

I was furious. ██. But they were making it clear that ███████████████████████ ████████████ they were going to handle it their way without our interference.

Okay, fine, I thought. *Handle him any way you want.* ███████████ ██████████████████████████████████████ *but Wolverine is in jail and his network is fucked, which is what's important.*

One warm afternoon a week and a half later, Chief Morris called me into his office.

"Doug," he said. "I've got bad news. Wolverine has been released. ████████████ said they didn't have enough evidence to charge him and our information is not admissible in a court of law."

I felt completely deflated. It was by far the biggest sucker punch of my career.

"Is... Is there anything we can do?" I managed to get out.

"Probably not."

My greatest success had become my greatest failure. If I had been responding via our instant-messenger service, I would have simply pressed spacebar and then return again. Instead, I grabbed my crutches and hobbled to the door.

"Chief," I said, "I'm going to be taking some time off."

20

DOWNWARD SPIRAL

A drug is neither moral nor immoral—it's a chemical compound. The compound itself is not a menace to society until a human being treats it as if consumption bestowed a temporary license to act like an asshole.

—Frank Zappa

I opened my eyes but couldn't make out anything in the dark. I was cold, naked, and lying on my stomach. As I rolled onto my back, something sharp pierced my abdomen, producing intense pain. I put my hands down to push myself up, and they were cut with something, too.

Slowly, I realized that I was on my kitchen floor surrounded by shattered glass. My head felt swollen and heavy, and my stomach was clenched in agony. Reaching up, I grabbed on to the countertop and slowly pulled myself up. In the mottled light, I saw cuts and gashes across my belly, the most serious of which had a one-inch piece of glass still stuck in it. I pulled the long shard out and watched blood drip from the wound down my legs to the floor.

The pain produced some mental clarity. Crawling to the bathroom, I grabbed a towel, and wrapped it tightly around my stomach. I remembered that there are no main arteries running through the area, which meant I wasn't going to bleed out. Nor had the glass penetrated deeply enough to pierce an organ. The wounds to my hands were superficial. I lay on my back on the bathroom floor trying to figure out what day it was and wondering what to do next.

I passed out, awoke some minutes later, crawled to the bedroom, and pulled myself into bed.

"What are you doing?" a woman's voice asked.

Not knowing who it was, I reached out in the dark in the direction of the voice and grabbed some flesh.

"Doug, what are you doing?! Stop it!"

I shimmied closer until I recognized the cute blonde who worked in the bar across the street.

"Emma?"

What is she doing here?

"Doug, what's wrong with you? Where have you been? Why do you have that towel on?"

"Just…just go back to sleep. I'm fine."

When I woke up again hours later, light shone through the gaps in the blinds. It took me a few minutes to remember why my stomach hurt like hell. The white towel lay on the floor caked with dried blood. I heard a television on in the living room. The clock beside my bed read 2:30 p.m.

On my phone, I found eleven missed calls from Austin and a series of text messages. He was checking in to see if I was okay. Apparently, Emma had called him in tears early in the morning to tell him that I was bleeding and unconscious and she didn't know why.

I found her sitting on the couch in my living room watching the Kardashians with empty food containers and coffee cups scattered around her. I had no memory of being with her the night before.

"Hey," I grunted.

She sat with her knees clutched in front of her staring at the screen.

I tried again. "So what's up with the Kardashian girls?"

Emma used the remote to turn off the TV. "I picked up all the glass in the kitchen but left the blood as a reminder," she said, looking up at me with a hurt, worried expression.

Entering the kitchen, I found a deep red smear across the floor that extended down the hallway to the bathroom, and ended with bloody handprints on the toilet and sink. "Wow, looks pretty scary in here."

"No," Emma responded, "what's scary is you climbing into bed last night soaked in blood and then passing out with your eyes rolled back in your head."

When I nodded, my head felt like it weighed a hundred pounds. "Yeah, I saw you called Austin. Not cool. Don't call my friends like that and air my dirty laundry."

"Your dirty laundry?! Doug, I thought you were going to die!"

She was upset and my head was throbbing. I pulled a bloodstained glass out of the sink, washed it, and started to fix myself a White Russian.

"What the hell are you doing?" Emma exclaimed. "Are you drinking again? Are you insane? You blacked out last night and fell on the glass you were holding because you were so fucked up, and now you want to drink more?"

"Well, I'm sober now, so yes, that's the plan."

"I can't believe this! I took care of you all night! I haven't slept and have been checking on your breathing and your pulse since five a.m.!"

"Well, thank you, Emma. I'm completely embarrassed. What else do you want me to do?"

"How about having the decency to not drink in front of me right now? How about wanting to be with me for once when you're not drunk? Is that too much to ask?!"

She had a point. All I could do was raise my eyebrows and stare at her in silence.

"Fuck you, Doug. I hate you."

"Don't worry, Emma, no one hates me more than I hate myself."

She collected her things, stuffed them in her overnight bag, and stormed out. I stepped around the blood on the kitchen floor, opened the drawer where I kept my pills, shook out two 750mg OxyContins, and washed them down with the White Russian.

Returning to the bedroom, I made sure to avoid my reflection in the mirror on the wall. I lay down and waited for the Oxys to knock me out, aware that I was caught in a downward spiral that seemed to be picking up speed. What had started out as a way to kill the pain from my shattered ankle had morphed into a cure for boredom and depression.

Since I was still waiting for my visa, this was the first time since elementary school that I had time off with absolutely nothing to do and no obligations. I wasn't a big TV fan and couldn't read because the meds blurred my vision. I was pissed at my employer for letting Wolverine slip through our fingers, and I was alternately mad at myself and Kate.

Aimless, hurt, and frustrated, I woke around ten a.m. from the searing pain in my ankle and began the routine I'd followed for the last month: First, four OxyContin 7.5/750s, followed by two ondansetron tablets to control the nausea from the overload of acetaminophen in my body. Then I showered, dressed, and hobbled into Georgetown on my crutches for lunch. Craving human interaction, I hung at the Daily Grill drinking beers until five p.m., when my favorite bars—Old Glory, Tony & Joe's, and Rhino—opened for business.

The ondansetron allowed me to consume as many as twenty beers without puking, and the alcohol in my system amplified the effect of the OxyContin. By closing time, I was passed out at the end of the bar. Since I was too drunk to use my crutches, some compassionate individual like Emma helped me home.

By the time my cast came off, in mid-March, I considered detoxing, and returning to work. HQ knew I was recovering from a broken ankle and had expressed no concern about my condition or my whereabouts. They assumed I'd report when I was medically cleared.

Since it was impossible to communicate with anyone about ongoing operations without entering the building, I had no idea what was going on in Afghanistan. Nor was I aware that my good friend Jimmy was scheduled to return to DC on R&R. His phone call woke me the morning of Saint Patrick's Day 2011.

Emma, being the angel she was, drove me to an Irish pub in Alexandria, where Jimmy greeted me. As soon as we sat at a table he started updating me on news on the front. Wolverine had disappeared and couldn't be found. Mahmud and Haji Jan had ███████████. Mullah Rashid had been blown apart by an IED; and Wali Dalir's fiancée had died ███████████.

It was too much bad news for my mind to process all at once. I took a deep breath and said, "Jesus Christ, man. How in the fuck did shit get so sideways?"

"Listen, brother," Jimmy continued, "I tried to respond to the trauma as best I could, but an entire team of 18-Deltas couldn't have stopped the hemorrhage. It's getting a whole lot worse. Just be thankful you stayed left-of-boom and got out when you did. We don't even leave the wire anymore after what happened to Spartan."[42]

Spartan was my replacement in Kandahar. ███████████ ███████████ I felt like I was on the verge of having a panic attack. I managed to ask, "What are you talking about? What happened to Spartan?"

"You didn't hear?"

I shook my head. "No."

Jimmy sat his beer on the table and turned away to look at the TV. In the corner of his left eye, I saw tears.

Fuck!

Jimmy was a former SF hard-ass who I didn't think was capable of crying. My whole body started to tremble.

While continuing to stare at the TV, Jimmy reached out and grabbed my hand in a vise grip and shook it a couple times. I squeezed back.

He said, "Spartan was killed two weeks ago in an IED attack at ███████████."

I felt something collapse inside me. The ███████████

---

[42] Spartan is a made-up name.

████████████ was one that I had visited frequently. When Jimmy described the exact location ████████████ I remembered that I had stood there many times.

Trying not to fall apart in front of Jimmy, I told him that my foot was killing me, exited, and took a cab back to my apartment. Upon entering, I crossed directly to the pill drawer in the kitchen, pushed aside the weak stuff, and grabbed the most potent OxyContin I could find. The 10mgs were five times stronger than the 750s. I popped two in my mouth and crawled into bed.

I slept through the next few days without eating. When I ran out of 10mgs, I switched back to a diet of 750s and alcohol. I had around fifty Oxy 750s left and about eighty Oxy 5/325s, and had stopped going out of my apartment altogether. At the rate I was taking the Oxys, I estimated it would take about a month before I'd run out.

Life without OxyContin wasn't a prospect I thought I could face. So, I planned to take the last fifteen 325s all at once with a fifth of whiskey and end my life. In the miserably desperate state of mind I was in, it made perfect sense.

Then, as often happens in life, something unexpected happened. Following the night I had cut myself on the kitchen floor, Emma had made it a habit of coming over to my apartment after work at seven p.m. She'd usually find me passed out on the couch with a drink either in my hand or spilled on myself. She'd sleep over because she cared for me rather than the sex—which was rare and mediocre at best—and leave around seven a.m. for work.

One morning several weeks after the meeting with Jimmy, I woke up at ten a.m. to find her lying next to me reading a book.

"Babe, it's a Wednesday," I said, glancing at the clock. "Don't you have work?"

"I do, but I'm staying with you."

"Okay. Well, that's cool. But won't you get fired?"

She sat up and looked me straight in the eye. "Doug, I've decided that if you're not leaving this apartment, neither am I until you get your shit together."

"Wait, what?"

"You heard me. When you go to work again, I'll start going to work again. If you never go back, I guess I'll just get fired."

I paused for a second. "Emma, this is crazy talk. I don't want you screwing up your life on account of me."

Emma blinked a few times and closed her book. She walked out of the bedroom and came back a minute later with a photograph in her hand. Straddling me and holding the photo up to my face, she asked, "Do you know who they are?"

Judging from the faded tone of the snapshot and the clothes the couple in it were wearing, I figured it had been taken in the eighties. I shook my head.

"Those are my parents," Emma said. "Have you ever wondered why you haven't met them?"

"I mean, no, not really. I just figured they lived out of town."

"Nope, because if they were alive they would still be living a few miles from here where I was born and I can assure you I would have forced you to meet them by now."

"Okay."

"What I'm getting at, Doug, is that I don't have anyone else. I had my parents and they are gone. I had my friends from high school, but I lost them when I moved away for college. I had my friends at college, but I lost them when I moved back to DC. I had a boyfriend here in DC, but he left me for another girl and moved to Boston. Now I'm here, completely alone, wondering what I'm doing with my life and I meet this wonderful guy on crutches one night in the bar. He's the sweetest guy I've ever met even though he's usually pretty drunk when I see him. But when I do see him, I see a lot more in him than the other drunken idiots who come into the bar. From talking to him, I can tell he is highly intelligent, which makes me wonder why he drinks so much. He's too smart for that. So, out of curiosity, I start to go on dates with him and pretty soon I learn that there's a lot more to this iceberg than meets the eye. Turns out, he's lived in Afghanistan since 2010 and speaks an obscure language from that country. I know this, because he drunkenly navigated our Afghan cabdriver home one night in that language.

"I figured he was in the military but he says he's not, which makes me think he works for the government. I assume he drinks because of his job, which is why he refuses to talk about it because it makes him depressed. On the other hand, I know that nothing makes him happier than looking at the pictures of his brother's kids he keeps on his phone and will readily show to any stranger. His brother is the only person he trusts and is the only person I have ever heard him talk to on the phone besides his parents. He has a troubled relationship with his parents, because like me, they care about him and suspect he's hiding something. I think this weighs on him a lot, and combined with his job and everything else, I understand why he's upset and does what he does. That's why I support him. What I need though, is for him to be around so that I can love him. Because I do love him, and he's all I got. Which is more than enough."

The nicest, sweetest speech I'd ever heard passed through my drug-and-alcohol-addled mind and hit me in the heart.

Choking back the tears, I said, "Just to be clear, you're talking about your obsession with George Clooney, right?"

She laughed, and I laughed. Then Emma kissed me and said she meant every word she'd just said.

A cynical voice in my head said, *Here we go again.* Since my breakup with Kate I'd vowed never to put another woman through the hell of dating me.

I took a deep breath and said, "I'll make you a deal, Emma. If you drive, we'll both go into work tomorrow. I need to figure out exactly what's going on with my job, because I may very likely be quitting soon. Which means I'll be home a lot more than I already am until I find a new one. The problem with that is, I don't actually like being home. I'm sure that sounds awful, but I actually like being away and I really like what I've been doing. I just hate what it does to me. Does that make sense?"

"Perfect."

It was a crazy promise, because I'd learned from detoxing after my trip to Spain that going cold turkey after a long binge was not the best solution. But like everything else with me it was all in or nothing.

Emma and I made love and spent the entire day together, which started out great until I started experiencing withdrawal symptoms and knew they would only get worse. When seated, I couldn't stop my knees from bouncing, and while walking I felt like I was about to faint. After one bite of lunch, I got nauseous and experienced an almost crippling anxiety. I was sure my chest was about to collapse.

That night I couldn't sleep. Instead I shook in Emma's arms until morning, when I felt like a total wreck. Still, I was determined to meet the commitment I'd made to both Emma and myself and return to work.

Not wanting her to know the name of my employer, I had her drop me off at Tyson's Corner. From there it was a three-mile cab ride to Langley. I swiped my badge and hobbled into HQ for the first time in two months.

Hoping to avoid being seen, I logged in from a terminal in the library. My plan was to inquire about my visa and leave. If the visa still wasn't ready I was going to ask for another assignment. As I started to draft an e-mail to the personnel manager of my division, I realized I couldn't keep my hands steady enough to type the way I normally do. Instead, I pecked with two fingers. By the time I finished, my vision was completely blurry and I felt like I had shards of glass embedded in my hands and feet.

I tried not to panic and took a couple of deep breaths, which brought on cottonmouth and nausea. Feeling like I was about to vomit, I crawled backward down the stairs to the gymnasium bathroom. My entire left arm was immobile and my cheeks were starting to twitch. I tore off my suit, stood in a shower, and drenched myself with cold water.

My cheeks fluttering uncontrollably and a strange paralysis spreading through my body, I kneeled on the tile and leaned on the wall with my right hand, thinking, *Is this how I'm going to check out? Soaking wet and naked in the Agency showers, dead from alcohol withdrawal at the age of twenty-nine?*

It was too pathetic to accept. So I held on for dear life and waited fifteen minutes until some movement returned to my arms and feet. Since they still felt as if they were filled with needles and shards of glass, I decided I would close down my terminal, take a cab to Georgetown Hospital, and check myself in. But I had to get back to the library first.

I didn't have a towel, so I put my clothes on over my wet body and slowly climbed the stairs. Safely back in the library, I unlocked the computer and saw a response waiting for me from personnel.

It read, "I have been trying to reach you for the past month. Come to my office as soon as you read this.—Chief PERS"

Just my luck. Chief PERS was a GS-15, former COS, and gigantic asshole who would burn me at the stake if I bailed on him. I took a deep breath and made my way to the Near East Division Front Office, where all the big shots were located. Being summoned there usually meant either a death sentence or a promotion. As I hobbled toward it on my crutches, I understood how my sources had felt when called to meet at Mullah Omar's house.

My hands were shaking uncontrollably as I walked in the door. I informed the secretary that I was there to see C/PERS and no, I didn't have an appointment, but he had asked me to come to his office immediately.

I waited ten minutes before I heard him shout, "Sanchez. Get in here."

Sanchez was the pseudonym that I used in cable traffic and official Agency correspondence. It's common practice for COs to call each other by their pseudos because we type more cables than anyone else in the Agency and therefore memorize each other's pseudos so we know who was responsible for the content we read. Some of my buddies still call me Sanchez to this day.

I walked into the chief's office and knew to remain standing until he asked me to have a seat.

"Shut the door. Sit down."

I prayed not to have another meltdown in front of him.

"Sanchez, I'd really like some explanations about what's going on with you. I have been hearing a lot of rumors about what you've been up to since you returned and I'm less than impressed. So now I'd like you to tell me what's really going on."

C/PERS was using one of the oldest tricks in the book, one that I had used with Abdul during his termination meeting. He was trying to get me to incriminate myself by making me think he already knew everything. Since I had been sitting on the other side of interrogations a thousand times, I knew just how to play it.

"Chief, well, not sure if you heard, but I broke my ankle badly and the doctors had to put a plate and some screws in me—"

He cut me off. "I've had a broken ankle before, Sanchez. It doesn't take two months for you to get on some crutches and return to work. You're going to have to do better than that."

"Correct, that's why I was out the first month. But then something really awful happened to my fiancée and I've been taking care of her and helping her recuperate. I know I probably should have come in and let you guys know, but it's been a pretty horrible start to 2011, sir, and really, it's not something I'm really comfortable talking about."

C/PERS nodded a couple of times and remained silent as he considered what to say next. I knew it was against Agency regulations to discipline an employee who is taking time off for "personal matters at home." I didn't have a fiancée, but C/PERS didn't know that. And I was pretty sure he wasn't going to ask me what had happened to her.

"Well, I'm sorry to hear that, Sanchez. Let us know if you need anything. In the meantime, your visa still hasn't come in, so I am going to assign you to a desk job here at headquarters while you continue to wait. Go speak with Chief Lee on Monday and she'll fill you in. That's all I got."

It was a mixed bag for sure. Yes, I was off the hook in terms of being disciplined, but Emily Lee had the reputation of being a total bitch. She felt every female case officer was discriminated against and played that card every day of her career. It had worked to get her promoted to a chief's position in the ███████ branch, but everyone who worked for her—both men and women—hated her guts.

I had until next Monday to figure out how to deal with Emily. In the meantime, I needed to get out of C/PERS's office before I passed out on his floor or puked on his shoes. I stood up slowly and was starting to cross the thirty feet out of the front office when I heard someone call my name.

"Markhor."

What?

Markhor was my radio call sign in Afghanistan. I spun around to find Boss Man leaning out of an office.

"I thought that was you," he said. "Step into my office for a minute."

If there was one person in the entire building I didn't want to see me in my current condition, it was Boss Man. I admired his intelligence and candor and knew he wouldn't hold anything back.

As I hobbled into his office, I almost ran into the chief of the Near East Division, C/NE, who was collecting some folders and about to exit. As the chief of two active war zones and an unknown number of covert actions, he answered only to the director of CIA or the president himself. This dude was all balls.

What the hell is C/NE doing in Boss Man's office?

"Doug, you know John Henderson, right?"

Holy fuck, Boss Man just called C/NE by his true first and last name. I didn't even know what it was until then.

"Hello, Chief."

We shook hands.

"Henderson, Doug's the guy I was telling you about who served under me in Kandahar. Fluent in Pashtu. Had this giant beard and would dress in the local clothes. You should have seen it. It was like when we were in Dushanbe back in '82. Guy went totally native."

C/NE smiled and said, "Excellent. That's what we should all be doing. Keep that up, young man. Blake, you let me know if you need anything to get this thing up and running. Anything at all."

What the hell? Chief Henderson just called Boss Man by his *first name!* I couldn't believe what was going on.

As soon as Chief Henderson left, Boss Man turned to me and said, "Well, you look like shit."

It never took him long to get to the point.

"Shut the door," he continued. "Tell me what's wrong with you. You look like you're in need of medical attention. Did you eat some bad tuna or something?"

I shut the door and sat down. "I don't know, Boss. I feel sick as hell today. I don't know what it is. Maybe the flu."

"That's bullshit and we both know it. You haven't been in for two months and you decide to come in on the one day you feel like shit? What's the issue? Do you have a serious condition right now we need to talk about?"

He had me dead to rights. I told him about my broken ankle and how the medicine had made me sick. I could tell he wasn't buying it. My left cheek started to twitch. I needed to exit his office immediately.

"Boss, look, I know I'm not making any sense right now, but just let me get my shit together and I'll be back on Monday good as new."

Boss Man got up from his desk and stood directly in front of me.

"We got enough drunks in this organization fucking things up as it is. Meet me at Nathan Hale nine a.m. Monday."

"Thanks, Boss. See you Monday."

The life-size Nathan Hale statue stood outside between the auditorium and the old headquarters building. I knew that Boss Man wanted to meet me there because he didn't want anyone to eavesdrop on our conversation. After all, we were working in a den of spies.

What's he want? I asked myself as I waited by the gate for the taxi I had called to pick me up. Even though it was a cool spring day, I sweated profusely.

When the driver arrived I instructed him to take me to George-town Hospital. The doctors there informed me that I had survived a mild heart attack and had developed a condition called "alcoholic car-diomyopathy," which meant the toxins from the alcohol had weakened my heart muscle to the point where it was no longer pumping blood ef-ficiently. The only cure was to lay off the booze.

At twenty-nine years old. *Nice.*

21

SYRIA

It's when the "international community" expresses "concern" about your "situation" that your situation is well and truly fucked.

—MICHAEL D. WEISS

Monday morning at nine a.m. I entered the gate at Langley and limped over to Boss Man standing near the statue of Nathan Hale. He looked me over as he took a drag of his cigarette, and asked, "When are you getting rid of those crutches?"

"Soon."

"Man up, Markhor, and get a cane, because I'd like you to be my man in Syria. But I've got to make sure you're committed first."

The fighting in Syria had been front-page news for more than a year. What had started out as protests against the repressive Assad government in March 2011 escalated into an armed insurgency. *So that's what he was talking to C/NE about.*

Immediately intrigued, I said, "I am."

"You got your shit squared away?" Boss Man asked. "Because I'm going to be sending you into the eye of the storm."

"Yes, I do."

"You sure? You still fucked up?"

"No, sir."

"You better be sure, because you'll be up to your neck in shit."

"I'm in."

I returned to my apartment, threw all the OxyContin and other pain medication in the trash, and tore up the prescription. Then I stopped drinking, bought myself a cool cane with a cowboy boot on the top, rode a bike at the gym daily, and read up on Syria.

I learned that the situation on the ground was extremely complex and reflected the ethnic and religious diversity of Syria itself. A country of twenty-two million, it's composed of Alawites, Sunnis, Christian Arabs, Armenians, Assurians, Druze, Kurds, and Turks. President Bashar al-Assad ruled over a single-party state established by his father Hafez al-Assad, who seized power in 1971. The Assad family came from the minority Alawite religious group, an offshoot of Shiite Islam, which controlled much of the country's political and economic resources.

Sunni Muslims, who make up 60 percent of the population, Sunni Kurds, and others had for many years complained about discrimination, government repression, and inequity.

When the Arab Spring mass antigovernment protests that began in Tunisia started to spread east, Sunnis and others took to the streets of Syria in early 2011 protesting Assad government corruption and human-rights abuses. The government responded with large-scale arrests, police brutality, and some concessions. By late April, as antigovernment protests continued to grow, Assad launched military operations against rebellious towns and cities, resulting in a large number of civilian deaths.

Thousands of Syrian soldiers shed their uniforms and joined the protesters. Other protesters began to take up arms. In late July, a group of defected officers announced the formation of the Free Syrian Army (FSA), which sought to remove President Assad and his government from power. By December the FSA had swelled to an estimated twenty thousand fighters. It had almost doubled in size since then.

The establishment of the FSA marked the beginning of the Syrian civil war. Since then and up to April 2012 when I was reading about it, the FSA had wrested control of swaths of territory in the north, west, and south, and were clashing with Syrian Army troops around the sub-urbs of Damascus. The Syrian Army counterattacked with vicious ar-tillery barrages and bombings that resulted in wide-scale destruction and an estimated forty thousand civilian deaths. Hundreds of thousands of other Syrians had fled the country altogether and were clogging make-shift refugee camps in Turkey, Jordan, and Lebanon.

As the war spread, other foreign fighters joined the opposition to Assad. These included the al-Qaeda–linked Ahrar ash-Sham, the Suqour al-Sham Brigade, the Al-Nusra Front, and the Islamic State of Iraq (ISI). Their stated goal was to impose a government based on Sharia law. They opposed the Syrian National Council, which was a coalition of antigovernment groups based in Turkey that sought to end Assad rule and establish a modern, civil, democratic state.

All sides in the conflict were getting strong and active support from other countries. The Assad government was receiving military and lo-gistical support from Hezbollah, Iran, and Russia, while the opposition groups were getting money, arms, and political backing from major Sunni states in the Middle East, including Turkey, Qatar, and Saudi Arabia.

The United States, the United Kingdom, and France had voiced their opposition to the brutal military tactics Assad used against his own people and were looking for ways to further a civil and more democratic outcome in Syria. Their sympathies aligned with the ███████████. ████████████████████████████ Boss Man decided that would be my first stop.

I submitted my paperwork for a diplomatic visa and then took the mandatory in-house medical examination. I didn't tell the doctors about my heart attack or the related drinking and drug abuse, which would have constituted career suicide. Interestingly, they declared me to be in top physical condition, aside from the ankle, which was healing well.

Worried that they might have missed something, I consulted a car-diologist at Georgetown Hospital, who told me that my heart appeared sound, but recommended that I see a psychiatrist for my "dependency issues." As someone who had been highly trained to manipulate others, I was very wary.

Dr. Horton entered the waiting room flanked by a student wearing a white lab coat that was four sizes too big.

"Hello, Doug. I'm Dr. Horton and this is my student-in-training, Jeremy. Do you mind if he's part of our initial evaluation?"

"Nope. Just don't tweet about what I tell you today."

"Oh, I can assure you that we would never do that."

"It was a joke, Doc. How do we start?"

"Why don't you go ahead and tell us about your chemical-dependency issues and how you got to where you are now? When did you start drinking heavily and at what point did you incorporate the pain medication? And most importantly, why?"

"Okay, I can do that, but... you legally can't report what I'm about to tell you outside of this room, right?"

"The only thing I would have to report is if you were planning to physically hurt yourself or someone else. We are here to help you, Doug. If we can."

Still, the only people who knew what I did for a living were my brother and Hannah. Choosing to be candid with the doctor in hope that he could help me, I took a deep breath and plunged in.

"So you're a spy?" he asked.

"No. A spy would be someone who works for me. We call them agents."

"But you're a CIA agent, correct?"

"No, I don't work for the CIA. I work for the government. I just... I like... I kinda do some of that same kind of work."

I was starting to sound stupid. I still didn't trust him.

Dr. Horton frowned and said, "Look, Doug, I think I understand where you're coming from and I can tell you're trying to be as honest with me as you can, so let me put it to you like this. I once had a patient many years ago who was an undercover officer for the FBI. He had been working a particular criminal case for over a year pretending to be someone else. He lived with these criminals on a day-to-day basis and for the most part, had to act like these really unsavory guys in order to convince them that he was one of them. Well, after a year of this, it was starting to take a pretty huge toll on him because he was starting to believe he was more of the criminal than he was the federal agent. Essentially, he had 'faked' it for so long that it eventually didn't require 'faking' any longer. It's who he had become."

Fascinated, I asked, "So what was your recommendation?"

"Well, he was a hard one to convince. As a physician specializing in neuropsychiatry, I could tell that he was suffering from severe depression as well as depersonalization disorder, which is to say he no longer felt in control of his feelings, emotions, or behaviors. He was aware of his actions, but felt he was watching them from a third-person perspective. I recommended he take corrective action to reduce the depression and anxiety he was experiencing. This of course, meant he would have to pull himself out of his deep-cover assignment and thereby ruin the case. He made it clear this was not something he was willing to do until his efforts led to an arrest. Otherwise, all the suffering he had endured previously would have been in vain."

"Interesting."

"Very. His occupation was the cause of immense mental-health issues, but he still justified his presence in a toxic environment as sacrificing himself for the greater good. Certainly admirable on paper, but I knew that continuing in his current mental state would have resulted in severe health issues and possible death."

"So did he quit?" I asked.

"I don't know. He never came back after his initial evaluation."

With that, Dr. Horton took off his glasses and began to clean them with a tissue. He was waiting for me to say something. I knew there wasn't a chance in hell that I was was going to quit and disappoint Boss Man.

So I said, "Thanks for sharing that story, Doc. I really appreciate it.

I can definitely relate to that FBI agent and, honestly, would have chosen to remain in place as well."

"Does this mean that this will be the last time I'll see you as well?"

"No, but I think that's all for today. You've given me a lot to think about."

I nodded and made my way to the door. Dr. Horton stopped me and asked his student to leave the room.

"Doug, I can only help you if you let me. I shared that story with you because you remind me of that gentleman. Do you recognize parallels between yourself and him?"

I thought about that for a moment, then responded, "Doc, I currently have three passports under three separate names. I go by a pseudonym at my real job, but have business cards and a badge for a company I haven't worked for a day in my life. I tell my friends I work for myself, and my family something entirely different. I have eight cell phones in my apartment that I answer under different names and languages. If anything, you could say I have somewhat of an identity crisis."

Dr. Horton handed me his card and said, "Well this is my *real* business card and that is my *real* cell-phone number. Call me anytime day or night. Please."

A few days later I left for ██████ (a Middle Eastern country) on a tourist visa. Under normal circumstances, a CO like myself would never travel on Agency business without a diplomatic passport to ensure immunity. But Boss Man didn't want to wait for my diplomatic visa to be approved. He personally called the directors of the intelligence agencies of the countries I was visiting so that I wouldn't have a problem getting through customs. Agents from ████████████████ ████████████████ met me at the airport and drove me to my hotel.

████████████████████████████████
████████████████████████████████
████████████████████████

While I can't talk about the details of what I did or the names of people I met, I can say that suspicion of US motives was a major obstacle. Many of the Syrians I met with were ███████████████

██

███ so in most cases I was the first representative of the USG they had ever met. ██

These men were not going to return to their positions ██████

██████████████████, so what I was doing was strictly debriefing. ██████

██

████████████████████████████

██

██

██

██

████████████████████████████████████

I often met these gentlemen for tea ███████████████████

████████████████████. One of the most important ████████ was a man known as MARATHON/1 (M/1), whom I spent weeks trying to get to cooperate. At the conclusion of one meeting, as we were descending the stairwell of ████████ he pressed a piece of paper into my hand.

████████████████████████████

As a known intel officer, I presumed I was under 24/7 surveillance. So I got in my car, drove to a small restaurant, and sat down for dinner. After a cup of tea, I went to the bathroom to read M/1's note, then ripped it up and flushed the pieces down the toilet. It read: "Skype—Muhammed123."

I got it. He wanted to pass me information ████████████████████. *Done and done.*

(The following redaction describes a conversation about security for a meeting.) ██████████████████████████

██

██

██

I drove back to my hotel, parked the car, and then went on an SDR to determine the level ▮▮▮▮▮ surveillance. Surprisingly, I didn't notice any, which was fairly easy to determine since there were very few people on the street. That meant the ▮▮▮▮▮▮▮▮▮▮▮▮▮▮▮▮▮ ▮▮▮, or had left me alone for the day because they knew who I was and weren't worried about me.

The ▮▮▮▮▮ Hotel stood six stories tall and only had street parking and no valet. That worked to my advantage, because it eliminated individuals entering the hotel from an underground parking garage without being seen. They would have to walk in either the front entrance, the back entrance, or the employee entrance located on the side of the building. I entered through the back entrance and proceeded up the stairwell to the second floor. ████████████████████████

████████████████████

I didn't see anyone on any of the floors, so I took the elevator down to the lobby and did a quick walk-through. Again, no one ████████████ ████████████████████████████ reentering the lobby one minute before I was scheduled to meet Rami (M/1's son). It was empty except for the concierge and a bellboy. I sat in the lobby and waited.

Approximately fifteen minutes later a man came out from the elevator and proceeded out the front door. Five minutes after that, two men and a woman passed through the lobby. Several more people entered and saw me waiting.

Not cool, I thought to myself. *Rami knows I'm CIA and I don't even know what he looks like.*

Aware that any of the people around me could have been sent to do me harm, I rose to my feet and started walking toward the rear exit. As I passed the elevator a short man of about ████████ stepped out wearing a Ralph Lauren Polo shirt and designer jeans.

His skin was lighter than mine and he had ████████████ which led me to believe he might even be European.

"Ana asim Ismael?" he asked. (Are you Ismael?)

Ismael was the name I was using with M/1.

"Es usted hijo de Señor M?" I responded in Spanish. (Are you the son of Mr. M?)

He didn't understand.

"Lo siento, no hablo Árabe. Inglés?" (I'm sorry, I don't speak Arabic. English?) I was pretending not to know Arabic.

"Yes," he responded back in English.

"What is your name?"

"My name is Rami."

"I think you know my friend on Skype, ████████████. Yes?"

His eyes lit up. "Yes, I know ▮▮▮▮▮▮▮. And you know my father. He is upstairs. Come with me, Ismael."

Rami called the elevator, stepped inside, and pushed the sixth-floor button.

As the antiquated mechanism creaked and slowly started to lift us up, I asked in Arabic, *"Keyf al hal, Abu Rami?"* (How are you, Rami?)

He didn't respond. Instead, he reached into his pants pocket, removed something in his closed hand, and held it close to his leg. Alarm bells went off in my head.

When the elevator opened, Rami motioned for me to exit. I pointed to his closed hand, too scared to talk.

"Go. You go," Rami said, holding the door open and waving at me to exit in front of him.

I didn't want to hit him before I found out what was in his hand. I figured it was either a gun or a knife.

Rami let the door close and flipped the lever on the control panel from RUN to STOP. Now we stood in the six-by-six-foot car glaring at one another. Even though he stood about five-five and weighed no more than 120 pounds and I was confident I could kick his ass, I didn't want to engage the guy unless I had to.

With a look of intense hatred in his eyes, he slowly opened his palm to reveal a three-inch folding knife, which was still closed. A million thoughts raced through my mind. The solution was to talk him out of doing something stupid. If he opened the blade, I'd slam him in the neck and drive the blade into his chest.

Don't open that fucking blade.

"You have gun?" he mumbled in English.

"What?"

"You have gun, give me."

"I don't have a gun, Rami."

Is he serious? If I had a gun you'd be dead right now, kid.

I lifted up my shirt. "No gun. No knife."

Rami wiped sweat from his forehead and slipped the knife back in his pocket. Then he flipped the switch back to RUN, which immediately sent the elevator hurtling down to the lobby. A man and his son entered, pushed three, and got off on the third floor. We then proceeded back to the sixth.

As soon as the doors opened I dashed out into the hallway and Rami followed. I was out of my mind on adrenaline and fucking pissed.

"This way," he grunted.

"Fuck you, motherfucker. You pulled a knife on me. *Eiree feek, sharmuta!*" (Fuck you, bitch!)

Rami appeared shocked. I decided that if his hand so much as flinched toward his pocket, I was going to shatter his orbital socket and quickly leave the hotel.

Rami, looking unsure of himself, turned his back to me, started walking down the hallway, and waved to me to follow. I proceeded at a distance until he stopped in front of a door.

"Do you understand my English, Rami?"

"Yes."

"Good. Who is in this room?"

"My father."

"Anyone else? Your mother? Your uncles? Your cousins? ████ ██?"

"No, just my father. This is a secret."

"Okay, then here's what you're going to do. Open the door and hold it open for me. Then take the knife out of your pocket and place it on the floor inside. Do you understand?"

"Yes."

Rami did exactly as I told him. I peered in the room and saw that the bedroom and bathroom doors were both closed. *Not a good sign.*

Standing in the hallway, I instructed Rami to open both doors. He refused and asked me to step inside first and close the door behind me.

I called out loudly to M/1 and said, "This is Ismael. Show yourself!"

M/1 emerged from the bedroom. "What is going on, Ismael? Shut the door! Someone might see me."

There was no one in the bedroom behind him, but the bathroom door was still shut. I stepped into the room, but kept my foot in the door to prevent it from fully closing.

"Open the bathroom now. This is not a joke. Open the bathroom door now!"

M/1 looked at me like I was crazy, then opened the bathroom door to reveal that it, too, was empty. With that I shut the door behind me and in the same movement kicked Rami's knife on the floor into the living room.

Keyed up the way I was, my Arabic came out worse than usual.

I said, "What is wrong, M/1? That is a knife. Why? Your son's knife. Why with me? What are you doing?"

Rami started to explain what had just occurred. M/1 waved his hands slightly as though it was no big deal and mentioned something about "security."

What the fuck did he think I was going to do? Come in and shoot him?

I found out later that that's exactly what he thought. He and other Syrians I met had been brainwashed into believing that ▮▮▮▮▮ had been actively trying to destroy Syria for the last forty years.

I was so angry and keyed up that I had no patience. "Rami, you translate. M/1, what do you want? Why am I here? I have ten minutes. Go."

M/1 frowned at Rami's translation.

Rami translated back, "He wants to know why you offend him."

"Tell him this isn't a game for children. I'm risking my life being here. So is he. Now tell me what this is about before I leave."

M/1 laughed.

"He says you should calm yourself. We are safe. He wants you have sit."

"M/1, I don't know what ▮▮▮▮▮ have been telling you but your personal safety, believe me, has a shelf life. Do you really think the regime won't come after you ████████████████████ ██.

That's going to require my help ███████████████. If you try doing it on your own, they will find you, and they will kill you. So you need to start taking this seriously and stop wasting my time arguing about money and other chickenshit nonsense."

"What means 'chickenshit'?"

"For fuck's sake, Rami. It means 'unimportant.' Now tell him what I just said."

M/1's face started to contort into a deeper frown as Rami translated.

"Ismael, you don't understand the Arab culture. We negotiate first before we provide the service. Not the other way around."

"M/1, do you have anything to talk about today besides money? Do you have any information for me at all? ██████████████████ ████████████████."

"Na'am." (Yes.)

I pulled the pen and piece of paper from my back pocket. "Begin."

M/1 and Rami looked at each other in amazement. Then the two started arguing about whether Rami had translated properly. M/1 demanded that Rami repeat the part about Arab negotiations.

"Okay, so he says, again, that you have to give us money first and then—"

"Fuck this."

I returned the pen and paper to my pocket. I had no control over this guy. If he wasn't going to budge on the money issue, then this was a waste of my time. Even if I did offer to pay him, it wouldn't be enough and he would still have the upper hand.

I walked out of the room and drove back to my hotel, unsure of how ████████ M/1 would react. Two days later he and his son slipped out ████████████ were never heard from again.

███████████████████████████████████

████████████████

In the following weeks and months, I saw this pattern repeated by a number of ████████████████████. A precious few cared about the future of Syria, the rest were cynical bastards looking for a way of cashing out while their country burned to the ground.

Shame on them.

22

ENDGAME

The greatest enemy of a good plan is the dream of a perfect plan.

—CARL VON CLAUSEWITZ

After spending a couple months talking with ▬▬▬▬▬ **members** of the Syrian opposition (which I'm not at liberty to write about), Boss Man summoned me back to Washington to try to drum up support for a possible covert-action campaign. My mission was to establish exactly what the USG was willing to do given the realities of the situation on the ground in Syria.

In late June 2012, I briefed my superiors at HQ, then met with DOD, where we discussed what elements they could possibly contribute. Meanwhile, Boss Man was summoned to Capitol Hill to brief members of Congress.

Even with our program in its infancy, Boss Man warned, "This is going to be an onslaught."

It became clear right away that everyone involved in the Syrian issue, from the White House on down, regarded it as a political hot potato. They wanted to aid the Syrian rebels, but were wary of being drawn into a war that could spread throughout the region, and make them look bad politically.

Roughly two months of fourteen-hour workdays at DOD, HQ, and Capitol Hill followed. Because I had literally no time or energy to spare, work took a huge bite out of my personal life and my relationship with Emma.

Here we go again, I said to myself.

I wasn't pleased, but had no choice. Emma had been my angel, and I cared for her deeply. At the same time, I didn't want to repeat the heartache of my previous relationships.

With no time to spend with her while I was in town, I lied and told her that I was traveling overseas. And to avoid the embarrassment of running into her in the event she walked in front of my apartment, I entered through the loading dock at the side of the building.

In August, with the rough outlines of a Syrian plan in hand, I flew to Europe to meet with our European allies. This was the start of an elaborate diplomatic feeling-out process.

Day after day in different European capitals, I presented carefully prescribed briefs describing what we could do to help the Syrian rebels, and the Europeans responded with limited briefs of their own. It quickly became clear that they wanted to support the program, but expected us to do everything.

It was the equivalent of inviting people out for a steak dinner, paying for the meal, and listening to them criticize it as you walked out the door. Massively annoying and frustrating.

Meanwhile, the human-rights situation in Syria went from bad to worse as the Assad government unleashed aerial bombardments on rebel-held areas. Large sections of Syria's second-largest city, Aleppo, had been turned into rubble. While some rebel units battled government troops for control of the city's highways and other rebels attacked prisons to free the thousands of political prisoners, reporters who had managed to enter the desolation described a fetid stench of death, refuse, and raw sewage.

They found rotting bodies, destroyed buildings, and burned-out city buses, but very few residents. Most of them had joined the stream of two hundred thousand Syrians who had fled to refugee camps in Turkey, Jordan, Lebanon, and Iraq.

While I was in a European capital briefing officials there, Secretary of State Hillary Clinton traveled to Turkey. On August 10, after conferring with Turkish foreign minister Ahmet Davutoglu, she announced that the US was considering enforcing a no-fly zone over Syria. This signaled that the US and its allies were moving closer to the kind of military intervention they undertook in Libya the year before, when they actively supported rebels opposing Muammar Gaddafi.[43]

Completely surprised by the announcement, I immediately traveled to ▮▮▮▮▮▮ meet with Syrian rebel leaders. They were elated by Clinton's statement. Finally, the US and its allies would be delivering the kind of decisive action they had been clamoring for.

For the next few days, rebel leaders who had been suspicious of US motives before happily shared everything with me—the state of their forces, where they were deployed, the names of important leaders, etc. It yielded an intel bonanza.

But after a week, they started to ask me when the US jets were coming. After two weeks, as the Assad government stepped up their air attacks, the rebels demanded to know when the no-fly zone was going into effect. After three weeks, they were so angry that they refused to even meet with me.

The no-fly-zone pledge turned out to be a bluff to try to get Assad's allies to put more pressure on him to resign. I wasn't told that, either. What it accomplished was to flush the slim credibility we had in Syria down the drain.

Appearing to have hit a dead end with the rebels and our European allies, I returned to DC in September. Surprisingly, I found that the program I helped put together had gained traction in Washington while I was gone. Specifically, ▮▮▮▮▮▮▮ (a top government intelligence official) ▮▮▮▮▮▮▮▮▮▮▮▮▮▮▮▮▮▮▮▮▮▮▮▮,

---

[43] This is open-source material available from various news outlets, including "Hillary Clinton Floats a Syria No-Fly Zone," the *Christian Science Monitor,* August 13, 2012.

had taken a strong interest in the Syrian crisis and was determined to get the Agency involved.

Boss Man and I started meeting with him on a weekly basis. One of the problems we discussed was the fact that most of the Arab states—including Qatar, Jordan, Saudi Arabia, and Kuwait—were ██████████████████ to specific Syrian rebel groups. Hoping to get the Arabs to work together and support the rebel umbrella group FSA, I traveled to ███████████████████ confer with the various Arab intel services. One by one they nodded their heads in agreement, then went out and proceeded the same way they had before.

It was immensely frustrating. Our friends in Europe and the Middle East were refusing to cooperate, the FSA had lost faith in us, and the political leadership in Washington wasn't taking decisive action.

Meanwhile, Russia, China, and Iran stepped up their support of the Assad military, resulting in even more civilian deaths and refugees.

I called Boss Man from ██████ one night and said, "None of our allies are listening. Everybody wants to be part of our task force in case it's a success, but they don't want to do anything."

"I'm in complete agreement, Sanchez. This is turning into a clusterfuck with Syria in the middle."

"Nobody's going to come up with a plan unless we just give it to them on a silver platter."

"That's why we pay you the big bucks."

I started drafting an ops plan that could be deployed immediately and hopefully adopted by our allies. Halfway through I realized that it was sounding more like a policy white paper, since its implementation depended heavily on political contingencies in Washington. At the time President Obama and Secretary of State Clinton were on the defensive in the aftermath of the Benghazi disaster.

Realizing that given the current political climate, the administration would be extremely reticent about putting more US personnel ██████████████████ in harm's way, I concluded my plan with the following caveat.

These recommendations must be implemented in their entirety as they are universally intertwined and depend on each other to succeed. They cannot be selectively initiated on the grounds of liking one specific option but disliking another. This is the absolute minimum of what must be enacted to achieve the desired result of removing President Bashar al-Assad from power.

I was sticking my neck out further than I should have. As a case officer, my job was to remain entirely apolitical and support any mission regardless of how sound I thought it might be. Whatever action was taken in Syria or elsewhere, I was prepared to do anything in my power to mitigate the risks to my country.

Escalation or deescalation in Syria, didn't matter. As long as I knew the end goal, I was good to go.

Leadership on the seventh floor and the White House had made it clear from the beginning that the goal of our task force was to find ways to remove President Assad from office. We had come up with fifty good options to facilitate that. My ops plan laid them out in black and white. But political leadership ▮▮▮▮▮▮▮▮▮▮ hadn't given us the go-ahead to implement a single one.

In the midst of this "stagmire," my ops plan made the rounds at HQ. The general feedback I got was positive, but nothing happened.

After a month of continued stasis, I wrote a memo suggesting that we change our end goal from removing Assad to backing away from the conflict. I avoided the question of whether or not it was morally right or wrong to forcibly remove Assad from power. I simply argued that since we had tried but failed to get our allies to embrace a unified plan and now appeared feckless and weak in the eyes of people all over the globe, we should pull out of the Syria crisis completely.

Even though I was stating what Boss Man and other people in upper management had expressed privately, my memo didn't go over well.

Boss Man said firmly, "Not smart, Sanchez. ▮▮ ▮▮▮ wants us to remove Assad from power. So stick to the narrative and don't tell the emperor he's not wearing any clothes."

"Yes, sir."

It was the week before Halloween. Boss Man ordered me to go to ▮▮▮▮▮▮ to meet with their intelligence service, ▮▮▮▮▮ ▮▮▮▮▮▮▮▮▮▮ again. I knew that my talking to them would accomplish nothing.

"Sure, Boss," I responded. "I'll be wearing my Halloween mask, so if they ▮▮▮▮▮ laugh at me I won't be insulted."

"All right, smart-ass. Very funny. I'm going to be out there next week with ▮▮▮▮▮ so don't cause any drama until *after* we leave."

Back in Kandahar, he had told me that if I kept shoving the point of the spear into the chest of the enemy, he would back me up no matter what. Now he was telling me to play nice and keep my nose clean. Sadly, I was watching the bureaucracy eat Boss Man alive.

Frustrated, bored, and starting to question what I was doing with my life, I visited Dr. Horton again the morning before I left. After an hour of conversation, we came to the conclusion that if I wasn't ready to quit, I should at least take an extended break to clear my head and regain my health. The Agency Leave Without Pay (LWOP) program offered an officer the option of pursuing an advanced degree or other life goal while remaining in the system as an unpaid employee. With money saved up from my previous deployments, it sounded like a reasonable plan.

Dr. Horton suggested, "Take six months off and do absolutely nothing that causes you stress. Pick up a hobby or two and take it easy for a while. Then, when you are nice and relaxed, try your hand at another occupation. You might find that you like it more than what you are currently doing and decide not return to your current job."

It sounded good, but I had reservations. "I'm not sure there's much else out there that I would be good at, Doc," I answered. "My whole skill set, my whole career... hell, my whole life has been this for the past seven years nonstop."

Smiling wryly, he said, "Would you believe I was a stockbroker and then an attorney before becoming a psychiatrist? Neither one of those had any relevance in medical school, yet I was unhappy in those positions and realized I needed to enjoy what I was doing every day or it would make for a miserable life."

"And now you're happy?" I asked.

"Very."

Sold. I left his office determined to submit my LWOP paperwork as soon as I returned from ███████.

A few hours later, at Dulles Airport, I ran into an old high-school buddy who was on his way back to Indiana. He told me I looked worn-out and as though I were in my late fifties instead of twenty-nine.

Thanks, asshole, for the affirmation.

My first week in ███████ (a friendly Middle Eastern country) went entirely as I had predicted, making the LWOP sound sweeter by the minute.

I said to myself, *No more bashing my head against the wall.*

Feeling as though I was halfway out the door, I relaxed. When ████ officials gave me the runaround, I cracked a joke. My old self would have gone nuclear.

As promised, Boss Man showed up the following week with ████████████ (a top US intelligence official). They met in private with ██████████. I knew that as the lead task-force representative in the country, I would eventually be summoned or blamed if shit went sideways.

███████████ (The intelligence official) convened a private confab with me, Boss Man, and his executive staff on the morning of November 5. ██████████, who had been intense and all business in the past, seemed jovial and relaxed. Instead of his usual black suit and tie, he wore a polo shirt and khakis.

Usually, I'd sit next to Boss Man and remain silent until he asked me to impart specific details, which I would report to Boss Man, who would then repeat them to ███████. I had never addressed ███████ directly; nor had he spoken directly to me.

But this time he turned to me and asked, "What's your take on all of this, CO?"

I almost fell out of my chair. "Ummm...Well...could you be more specific, sir?"

"I mean on this whole damn thing."

As outlined above, I had written numerous ops plans and memos over the past year suggesting various courses of action based on what I had seen on the ground. As none of them had been implemented, I knew they weren't worth bringing up again.

Before I had a chance to say something, Boss Man cut in.

"Sir, Doug is the guy who was meeting with all of the initial ███████. He's been doing a hell of a job for us."

███████ (the US intelligence official) smiled. "Ahhh...so that means you were meeting with Marathon Man before he ███████ ███████?"

What?

"Actually, ummm, no sir...I mean, yes, sir, I did meet with MAR-ATHON/1, but we never ███████."

███████ (the US intelligence official) turned his full attention to me and said, "I see. How did we manage to let him ███████ without knowing he ███████. Aren't we supposed to ███████?"

Boss Man shifted uncomfortably in his seat. According to bureaucratic protocol I was supposed to say that we were looking into the problem and would report back on what we found. But since I already knew what had happened, wasn't about to accept any blame, and was planning to go on LWOP, I said, "Sir, I can give you the honest answer if you like."

"I expect nothing less."

Boss Man shot me a warning look.

I took a deep breath and let loose. "Well, okay…ummm…sir, the reality is that we're looking at a situation where we have absolutely no control because we ███████████████ in Syria. So, you know, when I hear everyone comparing this to the Libyan situation that actually couldn't be further from the truth ████████████████ ████████. This situation is more relatable to North Korea or Iran, which are entirely isolated. So everything we are doing has to happen from the outside or with a liaison partner that has access. Either way, both options allow for little to no validation since we can't see it for ourselves. And everyone knows that, which is why everyone is taking advantage of us. They know we are blind, sir."

███████████ (the US intelligence official) nodded. I continued, "So to answer your question about ████████, I believe it was facilitated by █████████████████ that we consider an ally but we have no idea that they're stabbing us in the back every chance they get. Actually, let me correct myself, we *do* know that they're stabbing us in the back, but just don't care. Or we do care, but are incapable of stopping them because our hands are tied. I'm sure you know better than I why we allow this to happen. But I kinda feel like Winston Smith going through the motions."

"Winston Smith?" one of ██████████ (his) staff asked.

"Oh…yeah," I answered. "It's from the book *1984.* 'I understand the how, I do not understand the why.'"

Boss Man said, "The why and the how are the same, in this case. Politics."

███████████ sat up in his chair and turned serious. "That's unacceptable," he asserted. "If our partners are screwing us over, I need to step in and address it. We may be limited by what our government is willing to do, but we for damn sure aren't going to put up with nonsense from ████████████████████████████."

"Yes, sir," I responded.

"All right, that's it then. I have a meeting with the ▮▮▮▮▮▮▮ ▮▮▮▮▮▮ this evening. I plan to address this with them. Thank you, gentlemen. Please note that you have my full support."

With that, we ended the meeting and I returned to my hotel room. That night, as I considered what ▮▮▮▮▮▮ had said, two thoughts came to the fore. The first: *I think I like* ▮▮▮▮▮▮▮▮▮. *He's not in the dark about realities, nor is he ignoring the problems.*

And secondly: *I wonder what he's saying* ▮▮▮▮▮▮▮▮ *right now?*

I got the answer an hour later, when a colleague called and requested that I meet him for a brief encounter (BE) at a predetermined location. He didn't waste time getting to the point.

"▮▮▮▮▮▮ just told the ▮▮ ▮▮▮▮▮ collectively to get their heads out of their asses and start cooperating."

"Good. Fucking good. How did they respond?"

"There was some kickback. ▮▮▮."

"This is excellent news," I said.

My colleague looked at me like I was crazy. "Are you fucking high?" he exclaimed. "This is a disaster! No one is going to work with us now. We're going to be completely shut out! We're through!"

"Fuck 'em," I responded. "We were never going to do anything anyway. At least now we don't look weak."

▮▮▮▮▮▮▮▮▮▮▮▮▮▮▮▮▮▮▮▮▮▮▮▮▮▮▮▮▮▮▮▮▮▮▮▮
▮▮▮▮▮▮▮▮▮▮▮▮▮▮▮▮▮▮▮▮▮▮▮▮▮▮▮▮▮▮▮▮▮▮▮▮
▮▮▮▮▮▮▮▮▮▮▮▮▮▮▮▮▮▮▮▮▮▮▮▮▮▮▮▮▮▮▮▮▮▮▮▮
▮▮▮▮▮▮▮▮▮▮▮▮▮▮▮▮▮▮▮▮▮▮▮▮▮▮▮▮▮▮▮▮▮▮▮▮
▮▮▮▮▮▮▮▮▮▮▮▮▮▮▮▮▮▮▮▮▮▮▮▮▮▮▮▮▮▮▮▮▮▮▮▮
▮▮▮▮▮▮▮▮▮▮▮▮▮▮▮▮▮▮▮▮▮▮▮▮▮▮▮▮▮▮▮▮
▮▮▮▮▮▮▮▮▮▮▮▮▮▮▮▮▮▮▮▮▮▮▮▮▮▮▮▮▮▮▮▮▮▮▮▮
▮▮▮▮▮▮▮▮▮▮▮▮▮▮▮▮▮▮▮▮▮▮▮▮▮▮▮▮▮▮▮▮▮▮▮▮
▮▮▮▮▮▮▮▮▮▮▮▮▮▮▮▮▮▮▮▮▮▮▮▮▮▮▮▮▮▮▮▮▮▮▮▮

██

██

██

██

██

████████████████████████████████

██

██

██

████████████████████████████████████

██

Now I was stuck in the Middle East even more marginalized than before, and the White House tucked its tail even tighter between its legs.

For the next month, I spent most of my time in ████ helping DOD assist the ████████████ manage the massive number of refugees flooding across the border—rewarding work, without a doubt, but in no way advancing a cooperative plan toward aiding the Syrian opposition.

My colleagues on the task force who were with me ████ noticed that I stopped meeting with ████ on a regular basis. I still showed up at their offices when summoned, but didn't bother meeting with them otherwise for the sake of keeping up appearances. What was the point?

Too afraid to confront me individually, they waited until Thanksgiving dinner held at ████ restaurant to hit me with their concerns together. It felt as if I were part of a bad intervention from the reality show *Jersey Shore*.

The scene was so absurd I didn't know whether to scream, laugh, or cry. I had worked my ass off for almost a year, risked my life, and compromised my health and personal life because I was seriously trying to come up with a plan to help the Syrian opposition that would meet the approval of the administration, Congress, and our Arab and

European allies, only to see it subverted by ███████████████,
████████████████, and I was being taken to task for not meeting with
one of the ███████████ that had screwed us and pretending that everything was hunky-dory?

Fuck that! I got up, walked away from the table in silence, paid the
waiter for the meal, and hailed a taxi back to my hotel. Then I sent an
e-mail to Boss Man informing him that I was done and wanted to return home.

He replied back immediately, telling me that he understood and
asking me to stay in ████████ until the twentieth of December, when some
of my task-force colleagues would be returning.

Not wanting to leave all bridges on fire for Boss Man, I visited each
of the countries we were working with one last time and played nice.
For my final act, I sat down and typed everything I had learned over
the past year and saved it as a Word document, because I knew management would never have allowed it into official cable traffic. I e-mailed
the document back to my account at HQ and figured I would hand a
hard copy to my replacement.

I was never given the chance.

23

RESIGNATION

I always made an awkward bow.

—JOHN KEATS

I returned from ███████ **(the Middle East) three days before** Christmas and called Emma to let her know that I was home. On Christmas Eve the two of us dined at Café Milano in Georgetown. The last time I had spoken to her was in October. After my recent frustrations overseas, it was a relief to sit with a beautiful woman and not have to talk about work.

She said, "I get that you can't tell me about your job and I'm okay with that, but there's no way in hell I'm going to date you if I can't speak to you daily and see you regularly. I'm smoking hot, remember?"

I laughed out loud at her candor. The truth was I wasn't ready to commit to anything until I got my shit together.

I said, "All right, well, since neither one of us has any family in this city, how about we at least spend Christmas together?"

"I may not have family but I do now have friends, so it looks like you're going to just have to watch *A Christmas Carol* alone, buster," Emma answered with a smile. "I know you expect everything to freeze in place when you leave, but we all have lives, too, ya know?"

I nodded. "Yes." Experience told me that truer words had never been spoken.

"Buuut," Emma continued, "I do have a dog now that I will have to let out. So I'll have to go home early. If you want, you could come over around seven p.m. and meet him."

"Absolutely."

Christmas morning, I got up early and went for a long run to find DC completely dead for the holidays. I did find a macaroon store that was open, and stopped to buy Emma a Christmas gift. I paced around my apartment the rest of the day and made calls to my brother and parents. Both were surprised I was home and asked how Paris had been.

"*Bon*, always."

At 7:00:01 p.m. I knocked on Emma's door, and heard her dog barking and some movement in the living room. A few minutes later, when no one answered, I knocked again.

"Just a second!" The barking stopped. I said to myself, *Please don't let this end badly.*

Just as my mind started imagining a terrible outcome, Emma opened the door in a velvet Santa Claus outfit with a low-cut top, a miniskirt, and a Santa hat. "Merry Christmas, Doug. Do you like your present?"

"Dear Lord..."

We spent an amazing week together. Then Emma left with her girl-friends to celebrate New Year's Eve in New York City, while I went with some of my friends to Philly for the Mummers Parade. During the train ride there one of my buddies started waxing on about a recent surfing trip he'd been on. When it became obvious that I was the only one who had never surfed, I logged on to Amtrak Wi-Fi on my iPhone and booked a one-way ticket to Costa Rica leaving the next week. I figured work wouldn't care, since I was going on LWOP anyway.

The Monday after New Year's, I returned to HQ and entered the Syrian Branch for the first time in four months.

"Where's Boss Man?" I asked the branch secretary as I looked around and noticed that all the people there were new.

"Oh, I'm not really sure. I think he's gone for the next two weeks overseas."

Perfect. Now all I have to do is check my e-mails and lay low all week and I'll be on my way to Costa Rica. But when I signed on to the system I saw a message on our internal service from C/PERS. "See me, asap."

C/PERS sat with his deputy, Harrison, who was known to do the majority of his dirty work and was therefore hated as much as the chief himself. Harrison instructed me to have a seat and then shut the door behind me.

"So nice of you to join us, Sanchez," Harrison began.

I watched C/PERS smirk and clasp his hands together under his nose in what is commonly referred to as the "power pyramid." They seemed to have rehearsed. Harrison was going to play bad cop, while Chief would try to catch me on something I said.

"Thank you. What can I do for you today, Chief?" I asked C/PERS.

Harrison said, "Sanchez, Sanchez, Sanchez. Always the thorn in management's side. You do know you have that reputation around here, right?"

"I wasn't aware of that, sir. I have always just tried to be the thorn in the side of our enemies."

"Ha! You think you're so fucking special, don't you? What is it with your generation? You guys think you go to the war zone and it makes you a hero just because you met a guy with a Kalishnikov. You have no idea what this organization is about, do you?"

I kept my cool, confident that I was going on LWOP for a year regardless of what they had to say to me.

"Sir," I said, "I've been told every day since I started that it is solely about the 'needs of the mission.'"

"That's exactly right. Yet you, and many of your little buddies, tend to think it's all about you instead!"

I could have told him that our ultimate boss, the president of the United States, had defined our primary mission as Afghanistan, and that's precisely where I'd served until the president's focus shifted to Syria, when I followed suit. Instead, I let him rant a while longer.

When Harrison finished, I cracked my knuckles—a habit when I grow impatient.

Harrison broke the silence, growling, "Sanchez, it seems to me you need to spend some time in the penalty box. I don't give a shit about what you accomplished in Afghanistan. I think you need a year behind a desk again to cool your jets."

"I'm a field officer, sir, and like every field officer I know, I don't like being back here at headquarters a minute longer than I have to. As far as riding the pine for a year, I think a better way for me to cool off would be to go on LWOP and then come back for a 2014 assignment."

"LWOP! LWOP!??" Harrison sputtered. "Are you kidding me? LWOP is for officers who are going away to improve themselves to enhance their career here, not for personal gain or to go Alpine skiing for a year. So unless you're enrolled at Harvard, LWOP is not, I repeat not an option for you. Actually, no matter what it's not an option for you. Can you fucking believe he just asked that, Chief?"

C/PERS finally spoke. "Are you in fact attempting to go to graduate school?"

"No, sir."

"Then what exactly is your plan for LWOP?"

"To be honest, sir, I planned to just relax and get my life back in order."

"Are you saying that you are suffering from post-traumatic stress disorder?"

I knew what he was doing. If I played the PTSD card, I would be off the hook and could likely take LWOP. But I would also have to see the Agency psychiatrist, which would go into my file and effectively terminate my career overseas. Upon my return from LWOP, I would have to meet with the psychiatrist on a continual basis until I was cleared for a new assignment, which would take about a year. During that time I'd be assigned to a desk just like the Chief wanted.

The cunning bastards had backed me into a corner.

"No, Chief," I answered, "I don't have PTSD. I'm just really burnt out from three consecutive war-zone assignments and would like to take an extended break. I haven't taken an R-and-R for eighteen months."

That caught him by surprise. Although I had been home for an extended period between my tour in Afghanistan and my tour in the Middle East, I had not been given an Agency-sanctioned R&R since June 2011. While it surprised C/PERS, it didn't seem to change his mind.

Leaning back in his leather chair, he said, "Sanchez, when Icarus flew too close to the sun I think it's safe to say he learned his lesson. When I spoke to you a year ago, you were having problems with your fiancée and I suggested you stay out of the field and work the desk to get your affairs in order. Instead, you jumped right back into a war zone on your own accord. Now you're trying to tell us that it's our fault that you spent the past three years in war zones, and we're supposed to drop everything and lose an officer for a year while he thinks about what he wants to do next. Oh, but we should hold a slot open for him for 2014 so he can just waltz right back in without missing a beat. That doesn't sound like needs of the mission to me. That sounds like the needs of Sanchez."

I took a deep breath and said, "Sir, you're absolutely right. The fault lies entirely with me because I didn't anticipate my last assignment to turn out the way it did. Truth be told, none of my assignments turned out the way I expected. I went into each assignment with far too much optimism, which fueled my narcissism that I could actually break through the bureaucracy when others had failed. I was wrong. I admit that. And, honestly, now that I know that, taking a year off isn't going to change a thing. I'm not going to come back a better officer. If anything, I'll probably lose a step, which I hadn't really thought about until now. So, Chief, I think I'd actually like the paperwork to resign."

What the fuck had I just done? The Agency wasn't a place where you talked about quitting unless you meant it. This was the biggest decision of my life up until that point and I made it in less than sixty seconds. I wasn't just burning a bridge, I was going full-on Viking burial.

Harrison looked like he had just been shot but couldn't find the entry wound. Chief, who I expected to be pleased by what I had just said, remained stoic. I despised the man but couldn't deny that he was extremely intelligent and a bureaucratic genius who had spent thirty years navigating one storm after the other.

He said, "Sanchez, it's not an easy job. Believe me, I understand you're upset and I have been there many times in my career as well. I've been so angry with this place at times I could have set fire to it. But as you know, it's more than just the struggle it is to work here, it controls your personal life as well. Personally, it's strained my relationship with my wife to the point where we have almost divorced on several occasions. We don't have children as a result of my chosen profession. I made the decision I wouldn't raise a child in an environment in which I wasn't around. I've missed the birthdays, the holidays, the funerals, and the weddings for going on three decades. Do I regret the decisions I've made to get to where I am now? Maybe some, but I've made them and I can't worry about the past. You have your entire future in front of you, Sanchez. For a young man like yourself, the question isn't about whether you need a year off or a vacation to clear your mind. The real question is, do you want to end up like me?"

Wow. C/PERS had opened up to me in a way I never would have believed possible. By having lived through three decades of what I had experienced, he was able to relate to me and humanize himself.

The question he had asked that stuck in my mind was: Do you want to end up like me?

I didn't have to take long to consider it. "No, sir," I answered. "I don't."

C/PERS smirked, shook his head, and said, "I haven't had a case officer quit on me in quite a while, Sanchez. Give me some time to draw up the paperwork and I'll send you a message when it's complete."

With that, he stood up and shook my hand. "Sorry to see you go. You're an outstanding officer."

Deputy Harrison looked like he had shit himself. It was evident that he'd never heard the chief open up like that before, especially to some punk kid like me.

"So what's next, Sanchez?"

"I think I'm going surfing. The Alps are too cold this time of year."

I spent the next two weeks driving along the west coast of Costa Rica from surf town to surf town trying to learn how to hang ten. On the morning of my thirtieth birthday, I caught a fourteen-kilo mahimahi off the coast of Montezuma. That night I invited the entire town to celebrate with me. After dinner, as I sat on the beach looking out at the Pacific Ocean, I remembered the question C/PERS had posed to me. And I felt something completely unexpected—gratitude!

Nasty, coldhearted C/PERS had actually helped me find my way out the door. I was thirty years old and soon to be unemployed, but completely at peace. A wise man named Oscar Wilde had once said, "We can have in life but one great experience at best, and the secret of life is to reproduce that experience as often as possible."

Would I? I'd see.

I returned to HQ two weeks later, picked up my resignation paperwork, and walked the packet to twenty different offices so they could grant me permission to roll back my cover. That would give me the ability to publicly announce that I was a former Agency employee.

With nineteen signatures affixed, I only needed one, Boss Man's. I wasn't looking forward to confronting him, so I figured I'd wait until after the weekend, which would give me time to inform my closest friends in the Agency first.

We met at my favorite spot, the Rhino bar in Georgetown, which was the bar we had all gone to as trainees before being sent to different posts around the globe. Luckily several of my friends happened to be rotating through HQ, in from their previous assignments, so we had a good crowd.

No one seemed shocked by my announcement, but everyone was curious about what I planned to do next. Intel officers tend to be fastidious types, so my friends were amazed that I had quit with no plan for the future. I explained that I had saved a good chunk of money, so I'd be able to live comfortably while I figured out what I wanted to do next.

Someone shouted, "Cheers to that!" Drinks were served and war stories were told. As I sat listening, I wondered how long it would be before I missed being Zmarai Khan and craved the excitement.

As I pondered that question, my friend Carla asked to speak with me privately. Carla was a fantastic case officer on a steep career trajectory. I imagined her running a small station within ten years and moving on to the seventh floor.

"Doug Laux. Mr. Sanchez. I'm really proud of you. If anybody had the balls to do it, though, it was you."

"Thanks, Carla."

She'd had a few cocktails and I was afraid she was about to say something she would regret in the morning.

"So, Sanchez, tell me something."

"Shoot, Carla."

"We all know you're Mr. War Zone and went to all the cool places and are so fucking tough. But in all seriousness, I want to know something, have you ever lost an asset?"

Wo-ah! Carla had gotten heavy on me. Among COs it was considered bad form to talk about the death of an asset, because it was hands-down the hardest thing to handle. It wouldn't damage your career, unless the loss could be attributed to your personal negligence, which was rare, but to lose an asset via capture or death was always a tremendous blow to your psyche. Even if it wasn't your fault, you felt like you'd failed.

"Carla, hey...uh...not something we should be talking about in a bar, you know what I mean? Let's go back over to our friends and get another beer."

Carla grabbed my arm and started weeping uncontrollably.

"I already know the answer, Doug. I know you've lost several. What I really need to know is how you stay so fucking calm about it. Because my asset was killed over a month ago and I still can't think about anything else. I go over and over what happened in my head all day long and am incapable of getting over it. Everyone keeps telling me there was nothing I could do, but that's bullshit. He was my asset! And no matter how much I rationalize it and second-guess myself, and blame myself, and hate myself, he's dead and it's entirely my fault."

I pulled Carla in and hugged her as tight as I could. I knew exactly what she was going through. Many of my sources had been killed. Whether it was by an IED or car accident, I always felt it was my fault for not protecting them better. It was a sense of responsibility that stemmed from having so much control over someone and having convinced them to participate in the world's deadliest game for what the average American earned stacking shelves at Walmart.

Even worse was the fact that COs who had gone through it were afraid to seek psychiatric help because it was a security violation to talk about operations to an external doctor and talking to the internal psychiatrists resulted in serious red marks on your personal file. Also, being alpha COs we all figured: Who needs to talk to a shrink?

Carla had graduated from an Ivy League university, like the vast majority of case officers. She came from a distinguished family, had earned exceptional grades, and had kept her nose clean and never broken the law. How could you expect someone with her background to manipulate another human into taking life-threatening risks and then not have a meltdown if he ended up getting killed? From Carla's perspective, she had committed a form of homicide.

I whispered in her ear that even though I was leaving, I was always available to talk and would always be there to support her. She grabbed me tighter and shook with deep sobs. Knowing that more liquor wouldn't help her, I walked her outside and helped her into a cab.

"Hey, you're a fucking hero, Carla. Don't let me down, all right?"

I figured that was enough drama for the night, so I told my friends that I was going to take off and not to worry about Carla, who was just upset that I was leaving. No big deal.

But it was a big deal. So I called her the next morning and told her that I had sought outside counsel from a Dr. Horton, who had been in-strumental in helping me deal with my guilt.

When Monday rolled around, I waited until just before five p.m. to head to Boss Man's office, because I knew he would have to leave soon to give a briefing on the current state of affairs in Syria. As I approached his office, I started to feel nauseous. He was *the* guy in the entire Agency that I admired the most and I knew I would be letting him down.

When I got to his office, I found his door shut. His secretary in-formed me that he was out of town. I took three steps to the left and poked my head into Boss Man's deputy's office.

"Hey, Bob," I said, "I was hoping you could sign this paperwork for me."

Boss Man's deputy took a look at the packet and signed it without hesitation.

"Blake mentioned to me that you were resigning. He was wonder-ing when you were going to bring the paperwork by."

Fuck! Boss already knows I'm quitting! Of course he did; he heard everything. As I left, the secretary said that she supposed he'd be back Thursday, Friday at the latest. Part of me was relieved. Another part knew that I couldn't sneak out without saying good-bye, face-to-face.

The next few days were relatively carefree as I turned in my be-longings and was debriefed, or "read out," of all of my clearances. On my last day of work, Friday, February 1, 2013, I walked through the ground floor and noticed a group of people crowded around the tele-vision in the cafeteria with shocked looks on their faces. CNN was broadcasting a breaking story about a bombing at the embassy in An-kara, Turkey. ███████████████████

████████████

I sprinted back to my office and logged in to read the situation re-ports that were coming in from the field. A suicide bomber had deto-nated explosives at the side entrance to the embassy shortly after one that afternoon. No Americans were killed. One Turkish security guard

died and three Turkish citizens were wounded. ███████████
███████████

I presumed the attacker was armed with very low-grade explosives, but as the facts came in I learned that he was strapped with six kilos of trinitrotoluene (TNT) and a hand grenade. The heroics of the Turkish security guard, Mustafa Akarsu, had prevented further loss of life.

On the dozens of flat-screen television sets inside our office, experts on the major networks speculated that this was an attack by al-Qaeda. Turns out, it was a lone attacker from the Revolutionary People's Liberation Party-Front, a Marxist-Leninist party. The bomber was thirty-year-old Ecevit Sanli, who had previously been imprisoned in Turkey for attacking a military establishment with a flamethrower. Connections to al-Qaeda? Zero. In fact, the exact opposite was true. Sanli had launched the attack to protest Turkish support for the Syrian opposition, which was chock-full of al-Qaeda under the banner ISI.

As often happened, the bomber's true motives were never picked up by the media, leaving many Americans, including my ███████████
███████████, to believe that the attack was perpetrated by AQ.

This would probably be the last time in my life that I would hear the true facts of an incident like this ahead of time. I didn't know whether that was good or bad, since the knowledge I had in the past was secret and, therefore, couldn't be shared and used to correct false assertions made in the media.

Security had asked me to vacate the building at five p.m. As I walked back to my desk for the last time at 4:30 holding a cup of coffee, I found Boss Man sitting in my seat.

"There he is," he said with a wry smile. "I saw you were still logged on so I figured you would have to return sooner or later."

"Hey, Boss. Thought you were out of town. Welcome back."

"Yeah, thanks. How was Costa Rica?"

I hadn't told Boss Man or anyone in the office where I went on my vacation, but he knew. Damn, he was good!

"Uhhhh...yeah, Boss, it was really cool. I learned how to surf which was pretty sweet and I didn't drown in the process so I feel good about that."

"That's excellent. I was talking to my wife about your trip down there and my young daughter overheard us. She now keeps talking about a place called 'rosta kita.'"

"Ha, ha. That's really cute."

Boss Man stood and shook my hand.

"Well, I'll let you get back to it then."

He looked me straight in the eye and gave my hand an extra squeeze at the end, which said all he needed to say.

"Thanks, Boss."

With that, he turned the corner and left.

I signed out of my terminal at 4:50 and made my way down to the ground floor to turn in my badge and depart through the main entry. I wanted to walk across the Agency seal one last time and pay my respects to the stars on the Memorial Wall. As I exited and looked left, I saw Boss Man standing next to the Nathan Hale statute having a smoke. He saw me and I saw him, but neither one of us said a word.

I heard later that he deployed overseas to a new assignment that summer and took his family. I thought of calling him to congratulate him, but preferred to leave things as they were when we parted. He knew what kind of CO I was, what I had accomplished and why I had left, and he knew that I knew. That's all that really mattered.

I returned the rental car provided by the Agency for use between assignments, and boarded the Metro to make my way home. This was the first time I'd been on the Orange Line since I was a trainee dating Hannah. As the train made its way to DC, I remembered a conversation the two of us had one Saturday afternoon.

"Do you ever sit here and wonder what each one of these people do and who they are?" I asked.

"I don't know, I guess sometimes. Why?" asked Hannah.

"Well, I mean like, do you ever look at their faces and try to determine what they do for a living and what they like doing in their spare time? If they're a good person or bad?"

"Doug, I'm from New York," Hannah answered. "I think everyone on the train is a serial killer."

I laughed. "Yeah, I guess you've got a point. But we never really do know, do we?"

"Nope. Things are seldom what they seem."

It made me smile.

I received this handwritten letter while I was at Camp Gecko in the summer of 2011.

Hello. My name is ▓▓▓ Rose ▓▓▓ I am 11 years old and I live in ▓▓▓ ▓▓▓ I know it is silly to get a letter from somebody you don't know but I wanted to write to you. In the town we live in my daddy and I went shopping in downtown on main street by the downtown park. There were a bunch of people at the park having a protest about something and they kept saying things about the CIA being bad for our contry and terrible people in the CIA are. Daddy said they are stupid and don't know what they are talking about. I agree with my dad because people who help keep us safe are the good guys right? I think so any way. When I was little I used to get scared of things on the news about people trying to hurt americans. Now that I am older I know that there are people like you who are doing everything that you can do to keep all of us safe. Even the people who say stupid stuff about you. Thats why I wanted to write to you. To let you know that even though I am nobody special I think you are doing a great job. I have also sent you some thank you cards and pictures. I hope you like them. Maybe you can send me some pictures to? Any way please don't laugh at my letter and cards. They are the only things I could do to tell you all you are awsome.

▓▓▓ Rose